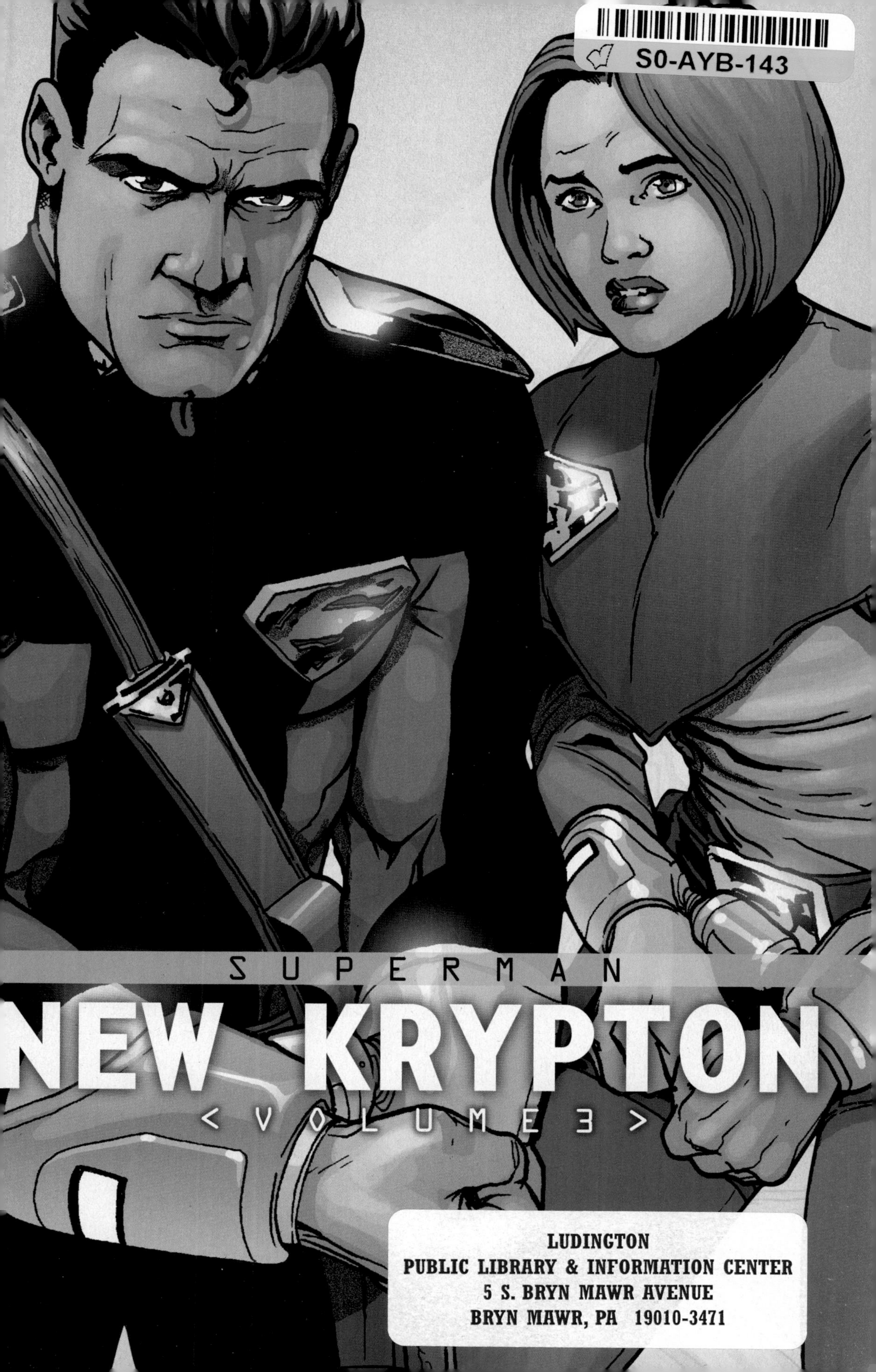
SUPERMAN
NEW KRYPTON
<VOLUME 3>

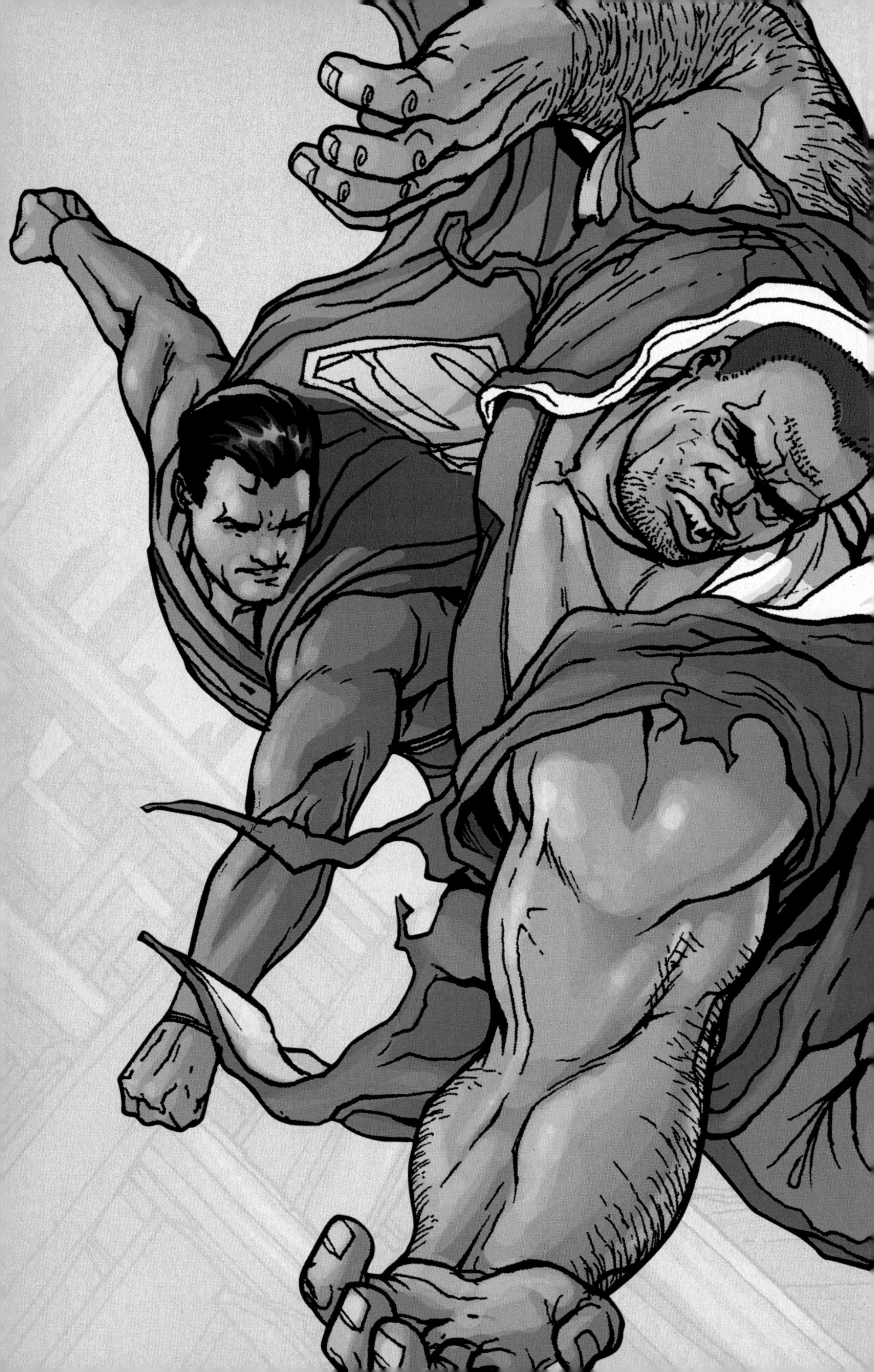

S U P E R M A N

NEW KRYPTON

VOLUME **THREE**

//WORLD OF NEW KRYPTON

JAMES ROBINSON & GREG RUCKA <WRITERS>
PETE WOODS <ARTIST>
BRAD ANDERSON <COLORIST>
STEVE WANDS <LETTERER>

//THE CRIMINALS OF KRYPTON

GEOFF JOHNS WITH RICHARD DONNER <WRITERS>
RAGS MORALES <PENCILLER>
MARK FARMER <INKER>
EDGAR DELGADO <COLORIST>
TRAVIS LANHAM <LETTERER>

<SUPERMAN> **CREATED BY JERRY SIEGEL AND JOE SHUSTER**

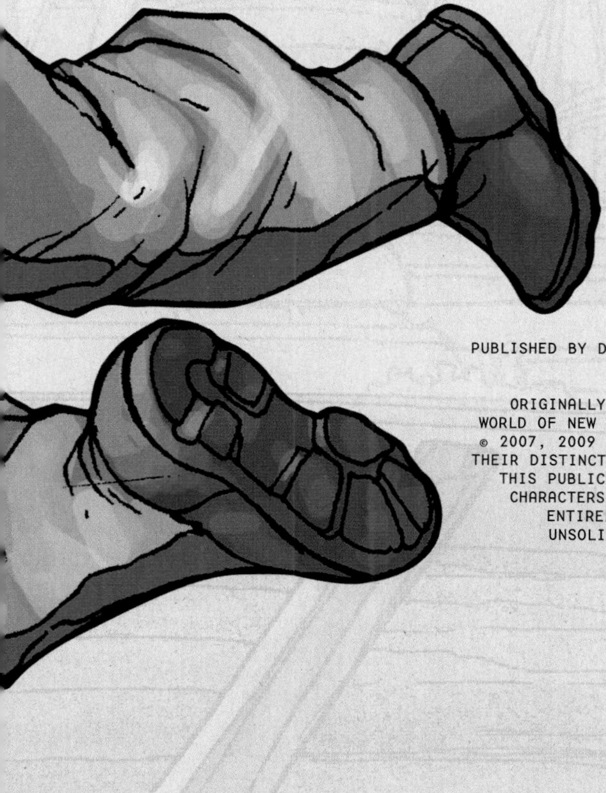

//
DAN DIDIO <SVP-EXECUTIVE EDITOR>
MATT IDELSON <EDITOR-ORIGINAL SERIES>
NACHIE CASTRO <ASSOCIATE EDITOR-ORIGINAL SERIES>
WIL MOSS <ASSISTANT EDITOR-ORIGINAL SERIES>
GEORG BREWER <VP-DESIGN & DC DIRECT CREATIVE>
BOB HARRAS <GROUP EDITOR-COLLECTED EDITIONS>
ROBBIN BROSTERMAN <DESIGN DIRECTOR-BOOKS>

DC COMICS
PAUL LEVITZ <PRESIDENT & PUBLISHER>
RICHARD BRUNING <SVP-CREATIVE DIRECTOR>
PATRICK CALDON <EVP-FINANCE & OPERATIONS>
AMY GENKINS <SVP-BUSINESS & LEGAL AFFAIRS>
JIM LEE <EDITORIAL DIRECTOR-WILDSTORM>
GREGORY NOVECK <SVP-CREATIVE AFFAIRS>
STEVE ROTTERDAM <SVP-SALES & MARKETING>
CHERYL RUBIN <SVP-BRAND MANAGEMENT>

//
Cover by EDDY BARROWS
Publication design by ROBBIE BIEDERMAN

DC Comics, 1700 Broadway, New York, NY 10019
A Warner Bros. Entertainment Company
Printed by RR Donnelley, Salem, VA, USA
2/16/11. First Printing.
SC ISBN: 978-1-4012-2637-4

SUSTAINABLE FORESTRY INITIATIVE
Certified Chain of Custody
Promoting Sustainable Forest Management
www.sfiprogram.org

Fiber used in this product line meets the sourcing requirements of the SFI program.
www.sfiprogram.org SGS-SFI/COC-US10/81072

WHAT CAME BEFORE

IT BEGAN WITH AN EPIC BATTLE BETWEEN EARTH'S GREATEST HERO, SUPERMAN, AND THE EVIL ALIEN BRAINIAC. DURING THAT CLASH, SUPERMAN DISCOVERED THE LOST CITY OF KANDOR TRAPPED IN THE DEPTHS OF THE ALIEN'S SHIP, 100,000 KRYPTONIAN INHABITANTS INSIDE. SUPERMAN WAS REUNITED WITH HIS PEOPLE, BUT AT A HUGE PERSONAL COST: HE WAS UNABLE TO SAVE THE LIFE OF HIS ADOPTIVE FATHER, JONATHAN KENT.

KANDOR WAS FREED AND RELOCATED TO EARTH, BUT THE UNEASY ALLIANCE BETWEEN HUMANS AND KRYPTONIANS QUICKLY DEGENERATED INTO VIOLENCE AND TRAGEDY. A SECRET GOVERNMENT ORGANIZATION, PROJECT 7734, HELPED ORCHESTRATE THE AGGRESSION BETWEEN THE TWO RACES. 7734'S LEADER IS GENERAL SAM LANE, A MAN THOUGHT LONG DEAD, AND HE GAVE THE ORDER TO ASSASSINATE ZOR-EL, SUPERGIRL'S FATHER AND THE LEADER OF THE KRYPTONIANS. MEANWHILE, A TEAM OF KRYPTONIANS BRUTALLY MURDERED SEVERAL OF METROPOLIS'S SCIENCE POLICE ON AMERICAN SOIL.

IN AN EFFORT TO RESOLVE THE GROWING CONFLICT, ZOR-EL'S WIDOW, ALURA, TOOK CHARGE OF THE KRYPTONIANS AND COMBINED BRAINIAC'S TECHNOLOGY WITH KANDOR'S TO CREATE A NEW PLANET — NEW KRYPTON. THE PLANET ESTABLISHED AN ORBIT OPPOSITE EARTH'S OWN. IT APPEARED THAT THE CONFLICT HAD ENDED...BUT LOOKS CAN BE DECEIVING.

WHEN ALURA RELEASED GENERAL ZOD FROM THE PHANTOM ZONE AND GAVE HIM COMMAND OF NEW KRYPTON'S ARMY, SUPERMAN WAS FORCED TO MAKE THE HARDEST DECISION OF HIS LIFE: HE WOULD MOVE TO NEW KRYPTON TO KEEP ZOD IN CHECK...

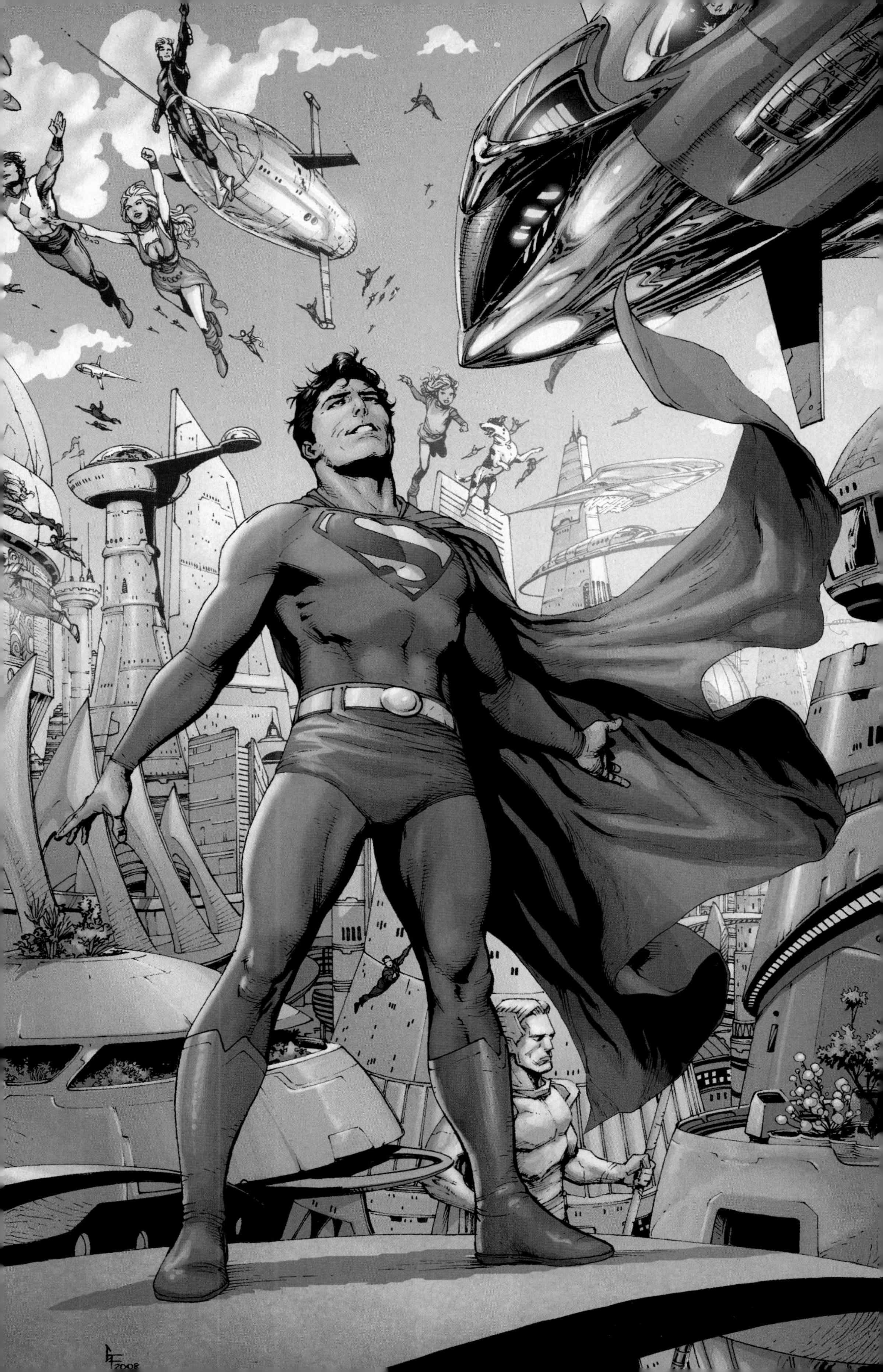

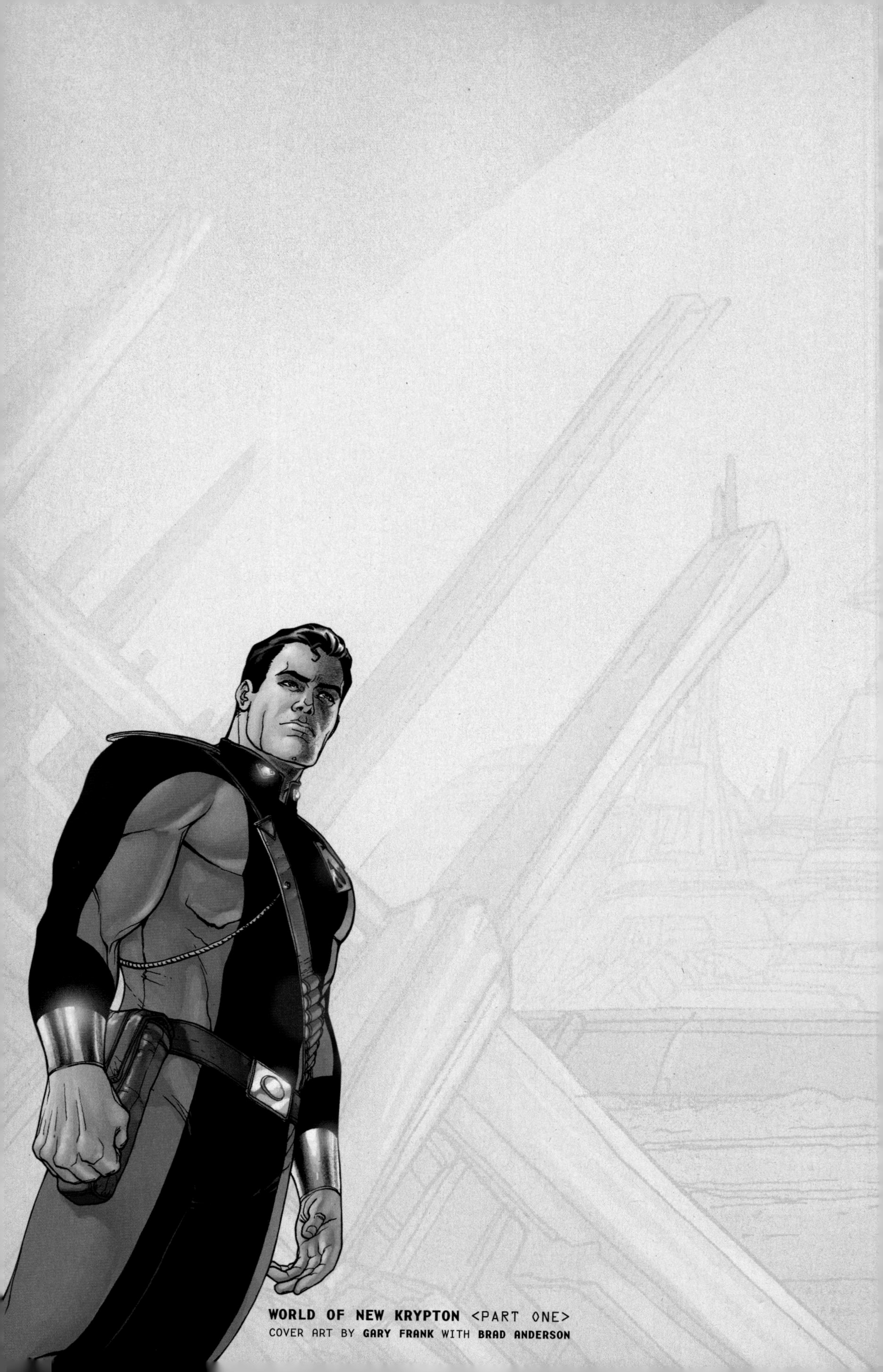

WORLD OF NEW KRYPTON <PART ONE>

COVER ART BY **GARY FRANK** WITH **BRAD ANDERSON**

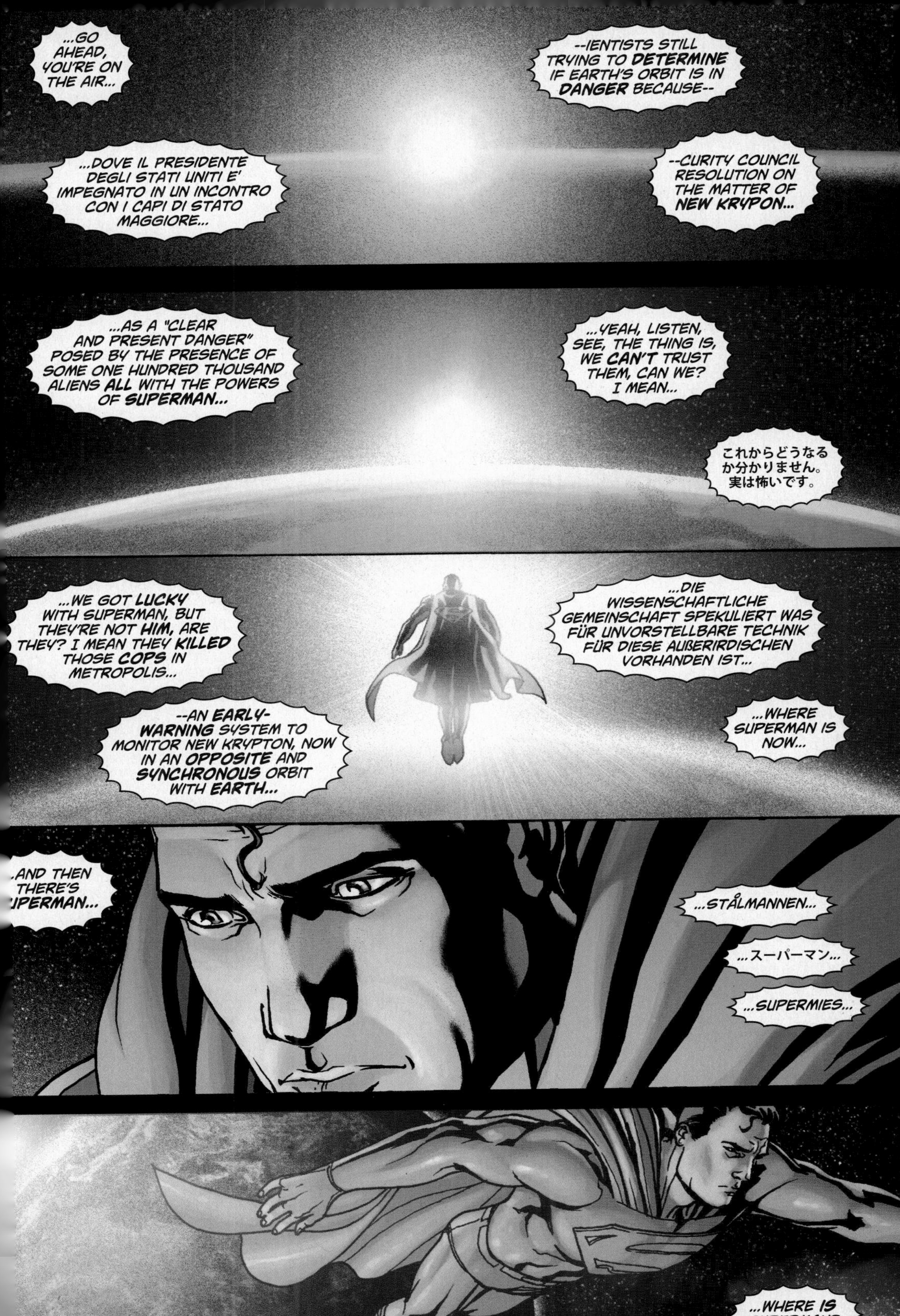
...GO AHEAD, YOU'RE ON THE AIR...
--IENTISTS STILL TRYING TO DETERMINE IF EARTH'S ORBIT IS IN DANGER BECAUSE--
...DOVE IL PRESIDENTE DEGLI STATI UNITI E' IMPEGNATO IN UN INCONTRO CON I CAPI DI STATO MAGGIORE...
--CURITY COUNCIL RESOLUTION ON THE MATTER OF NEW KRYPON...
...AS A "CLEAR AND PRESENT DANGER" POSED BY THE PRESENCE OF SOME ONE HUNDRED THOUSAND ALIENS ALL WITH THE POWERS OF SUPERMAN...
...YEAH, LISTEN, SEE, THE THING IS, WE CAN'T TRUST THEM, CAN WE? I MEAN...
これからどうなるか分かりません。実は怖いです。
...WE GOT LUCKY WITH SUPERMAN, BUT THEY'RE NOT HIM, ARE THEY? I MEAN THEY KILLED THOSE COPS IN METROPOLIS...
...DIE WISSENSCHAFTLICHE GEMEINSCHAFT SPEKULIERT WAS FÜR UNVORSTELLBARE TECHNIK FÜR DIESE AUßERIRDISCHEN VORHANDEN IST...
--AN EARLY-WARNING SYSTEM TO MONITOR NEW KRYPTON, NOW IN AN OPPOSITE AND SYNCHRONOUS ORBIT WITH EARTH...
...WHERE SUPERMAN IS NOW...
.AND THEN THERE'S SUPERMAN...
...STÅLMANNEN...
...スーパーマン...
...SUPERMIES...
...WHERE IS SUPERMAN?

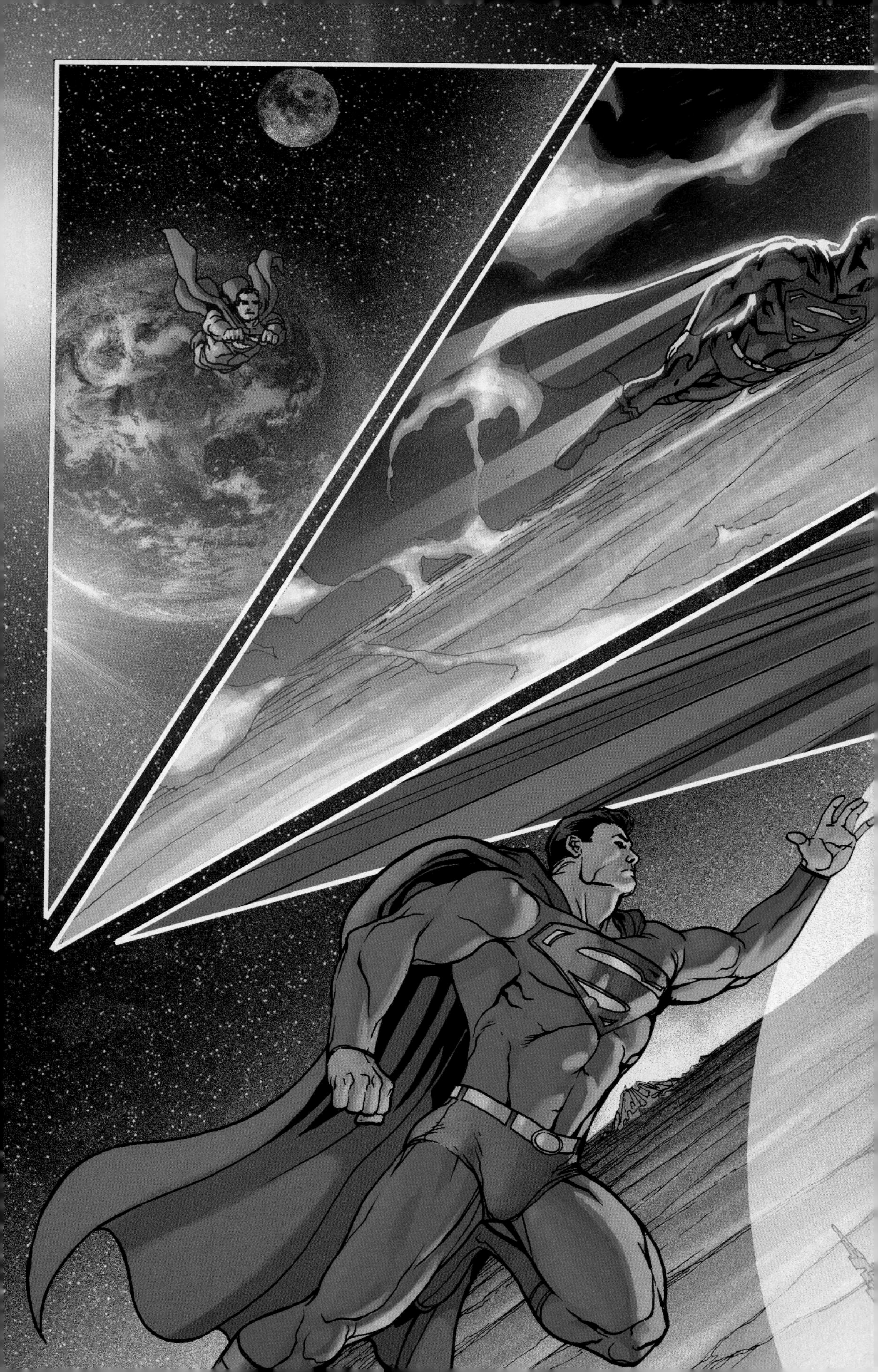

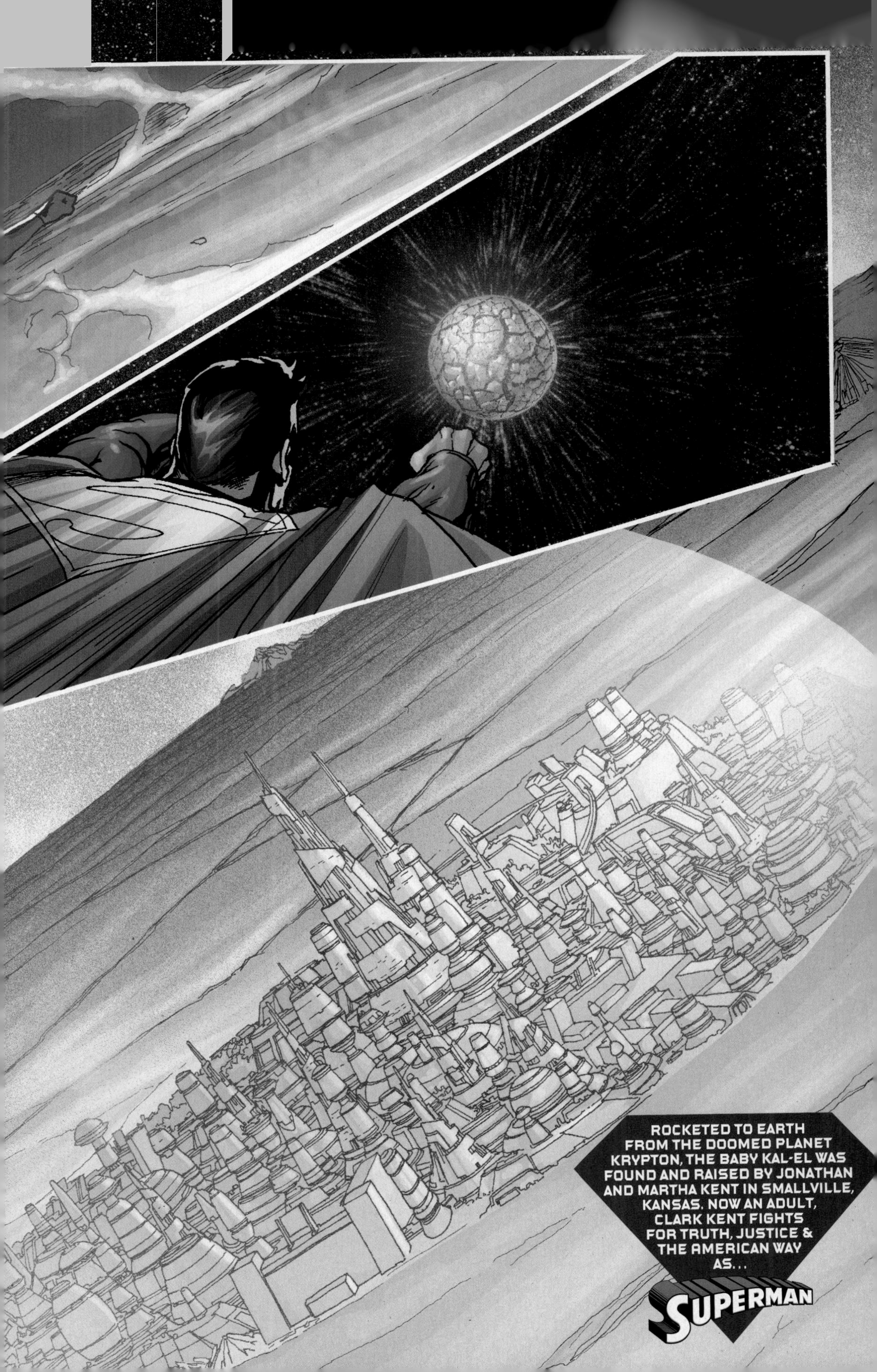
ROCKETED TO EARTH FROM THE DOOMED PLANET KRYPTON, THE BABY KAL-EL WAS FOUND AND RAISED BY JONATHAN AND MARTHA KENT IN SMALLVILLE, KANSAS. NOW AN ADULT, CLARK KENT FIGHTS FOR TRUTH, JUSTICE & THE AMERICAN WAY AS...
SUPERMAN

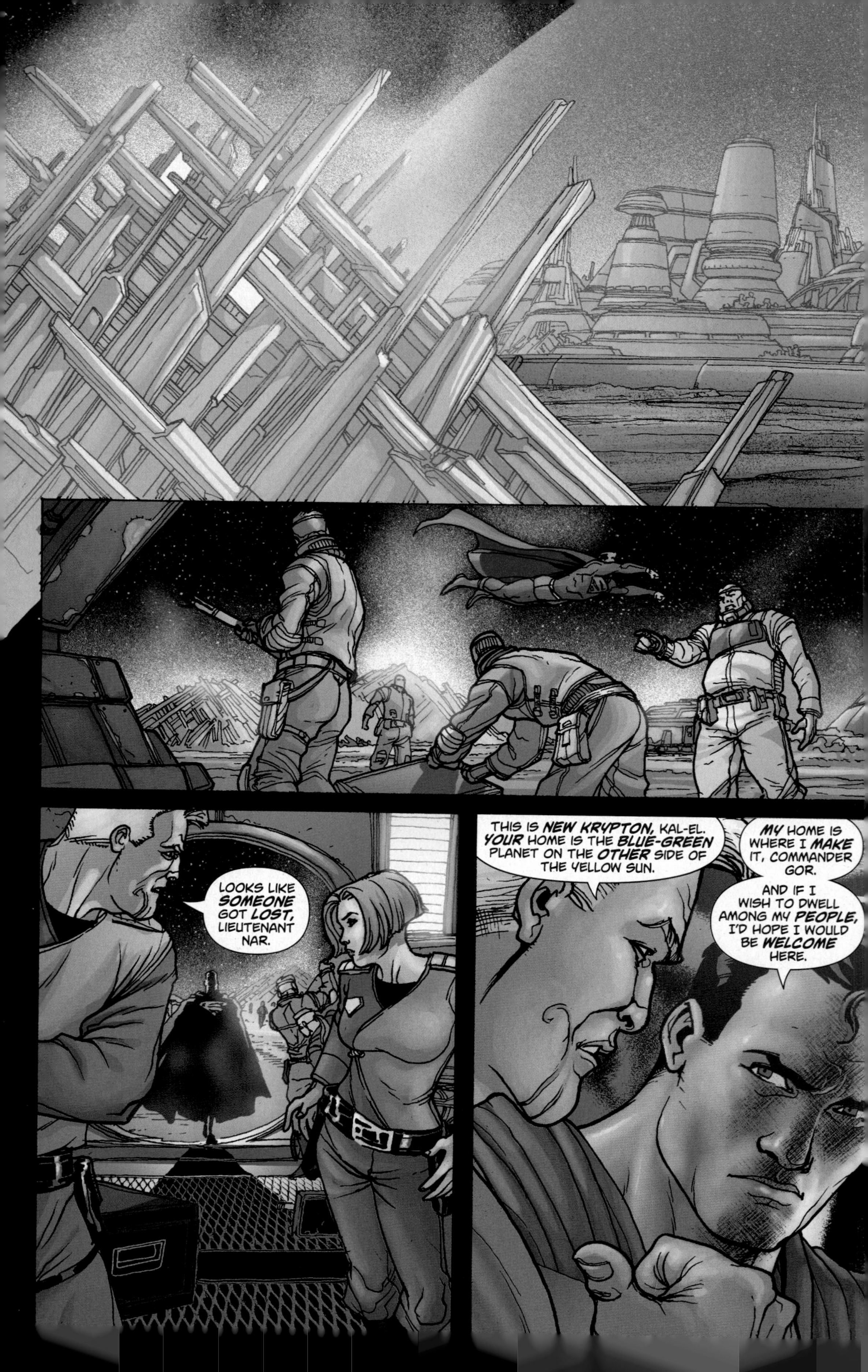
LOOKS LIKE SOMEONE GOT LOST, LIEUTENANT NAR.
THIS IS NEW KRYPTON, KAL-EL. YOUR HOME IS THE BLUE-GREEN PLANET ON THE OTHER SIDE OF THE YELLOW SUN.
MY HOME IS WHERE I MAKE IT, COMMANDER GOR.
AND IF I WISH TO DWELL AMONG MY PEOPLE, I'D HOPE I WOULD BE WELCOME HERE.

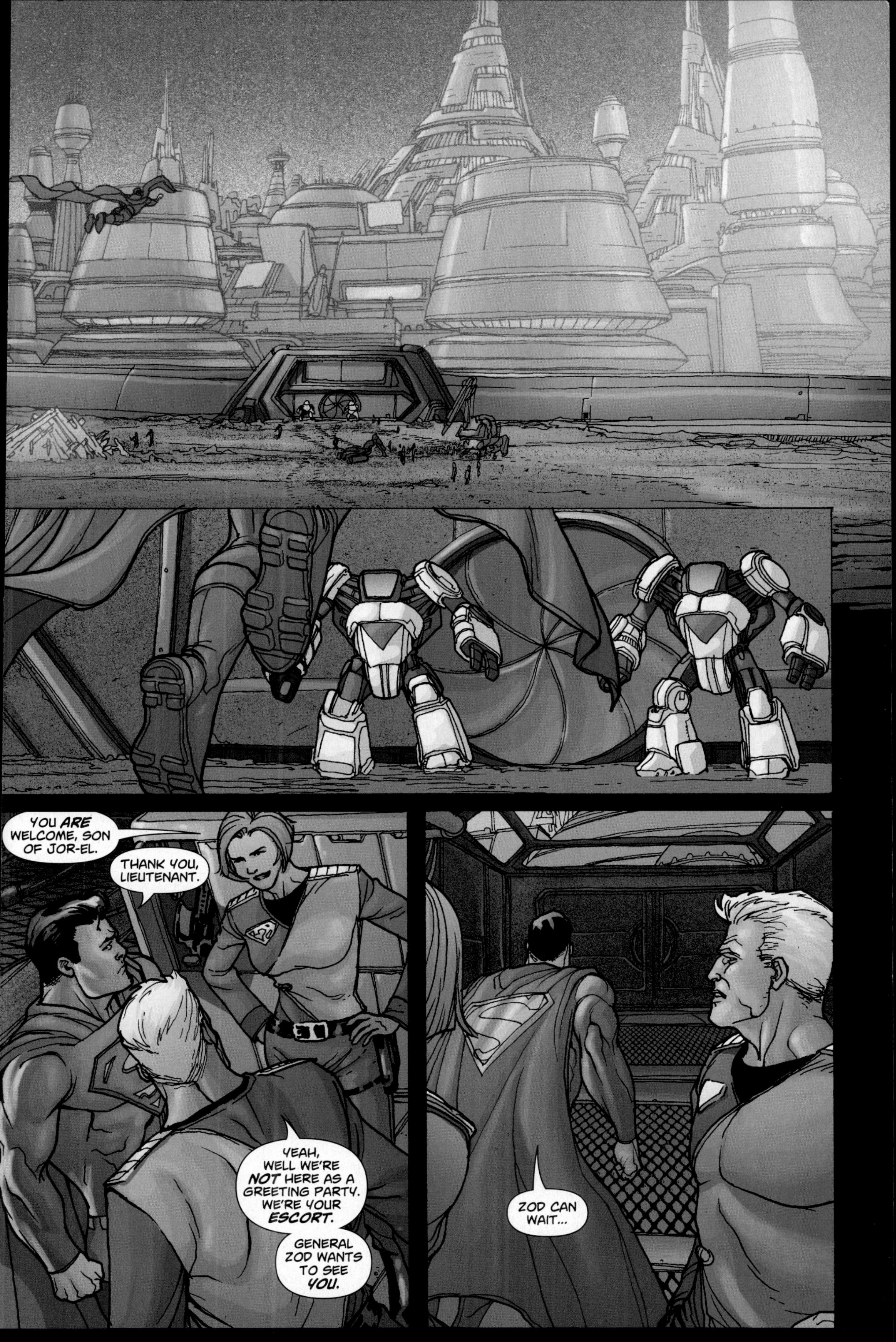
YOU ARE WELCOME, SON OF JOR-EL.
THANK YOU, LIEUTENANT.
YEAH, WELL WE'RE NOT HERE AS A GREETING PARTY. WE'RE YOUR ESCORT.
GENERAL ZOD WANTS TO SEE YOU.
ZOD CAN WAIT...

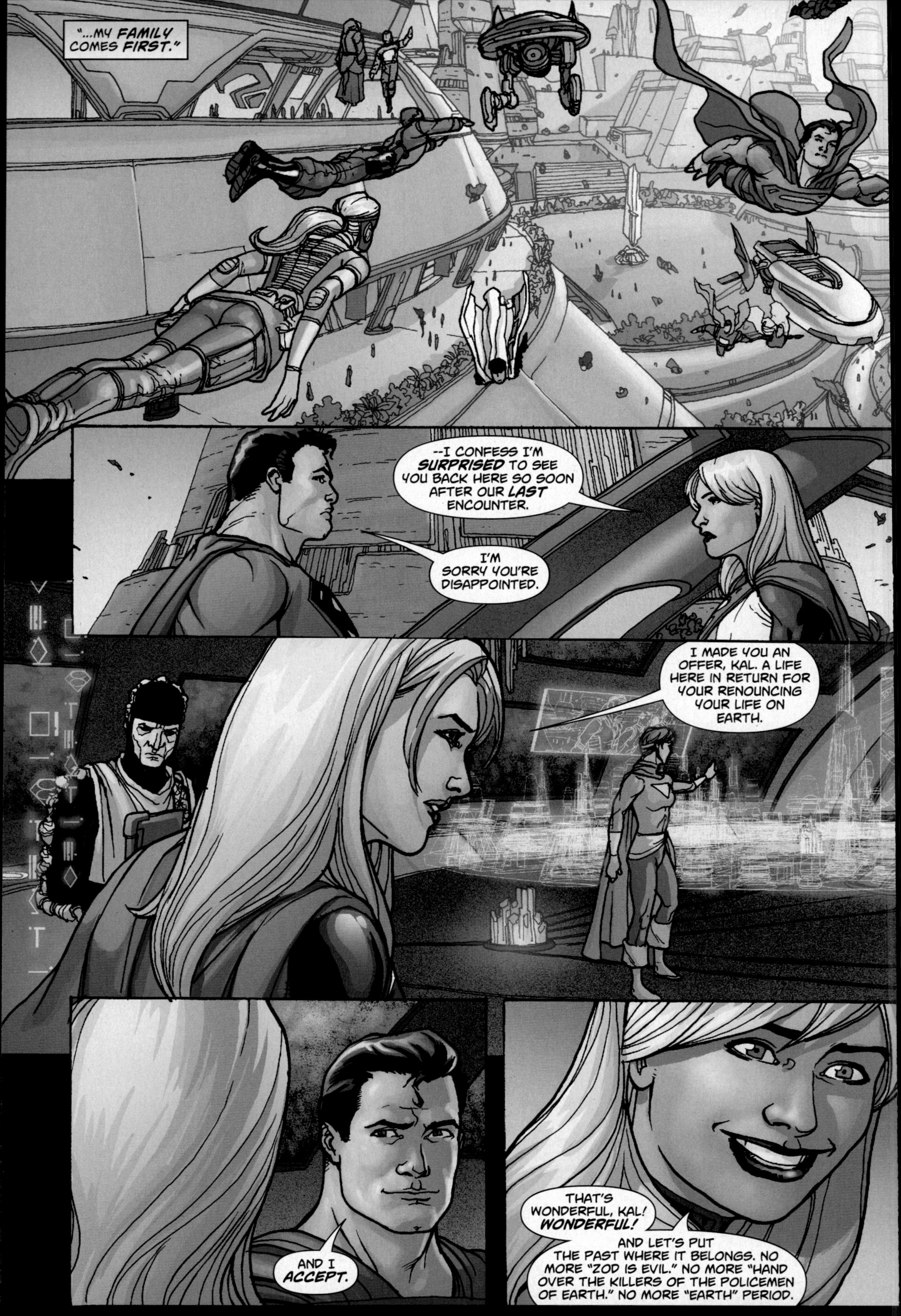
"...MY FAMILY COMES FIRST."
--I CONFESS I'M SURPRISED TO SEE YOU BACK HERE SO SOON AFTER OUR LAST ENCOUNTER.
I'M SORRY YOU'RE DISAPPOINTED.
I MADE YOU AN OFFER, KAL. A LIFE HERE IN RETURN FOR YOUR RENOUNCING YOUR LIFE ON EARTH.
AND I ACCEPT.
THAT'S WONDERFUL, KAL! WONDERFUL!
AND LET'S PUT THE PAST WHERE IT BELONGS. NO MORE "ZOD IS EVIL." NO MORE "HAND OVER THE KILLERS OF THE POLICEMEN OF EARTH." NO MORE "EARTH" PERIOD.

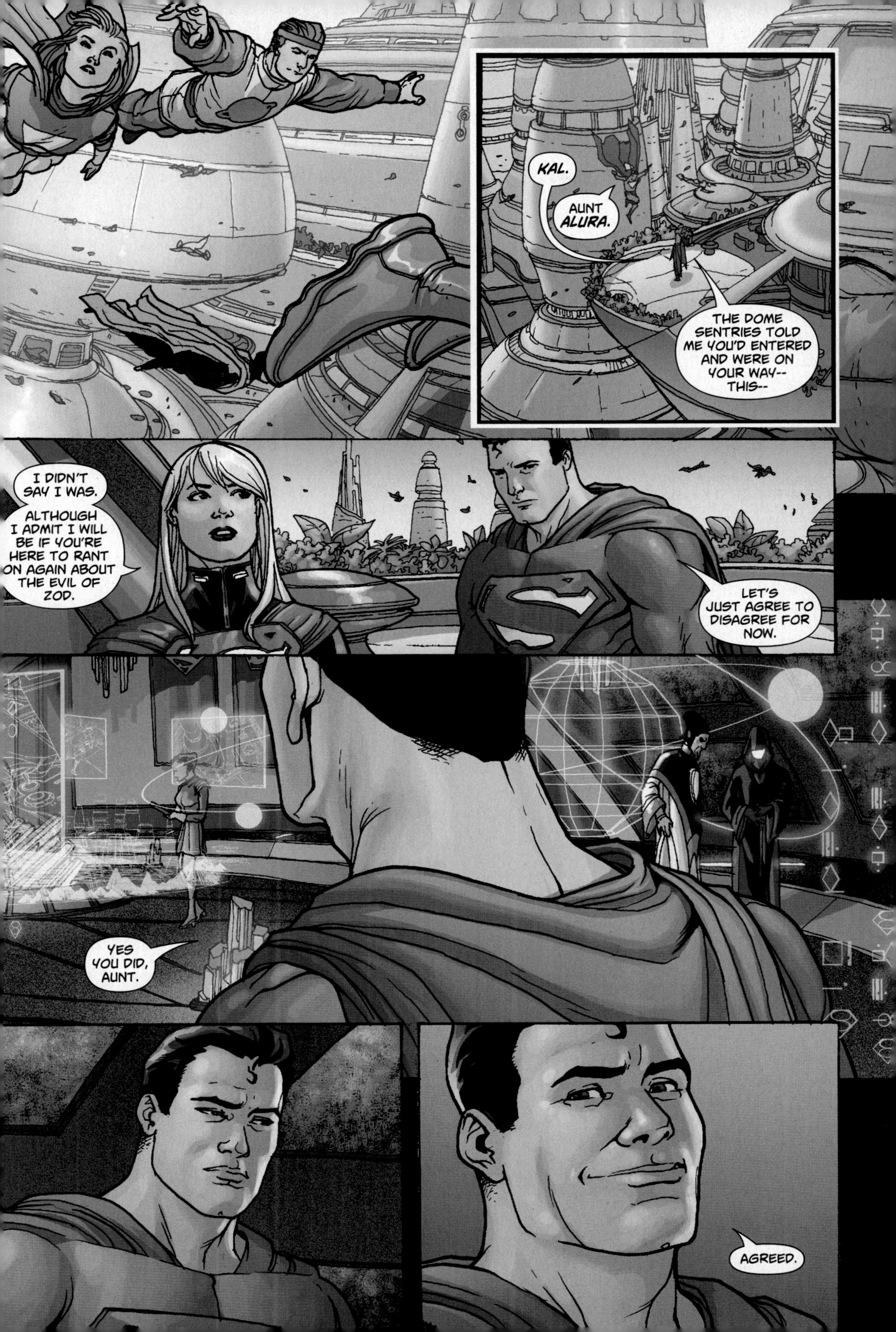
KAL.
AUNT ALURA.
THE DOME SENTRIES TOLD ME YOU'D ENTERED AND WERE ON YOUR WAY-- THIS--
I DIDN'T SAY I WAS.
ALTHOUGH I ADMIT I WILL BE IF YOU'RE HERE TO RANT ON AGAIN ABOUT THE EVIL OF ZOD.
LET'S JUST AGREE TO DISAGREE FOR NOW.
YES YOU DID, AUNT.
AGREED.

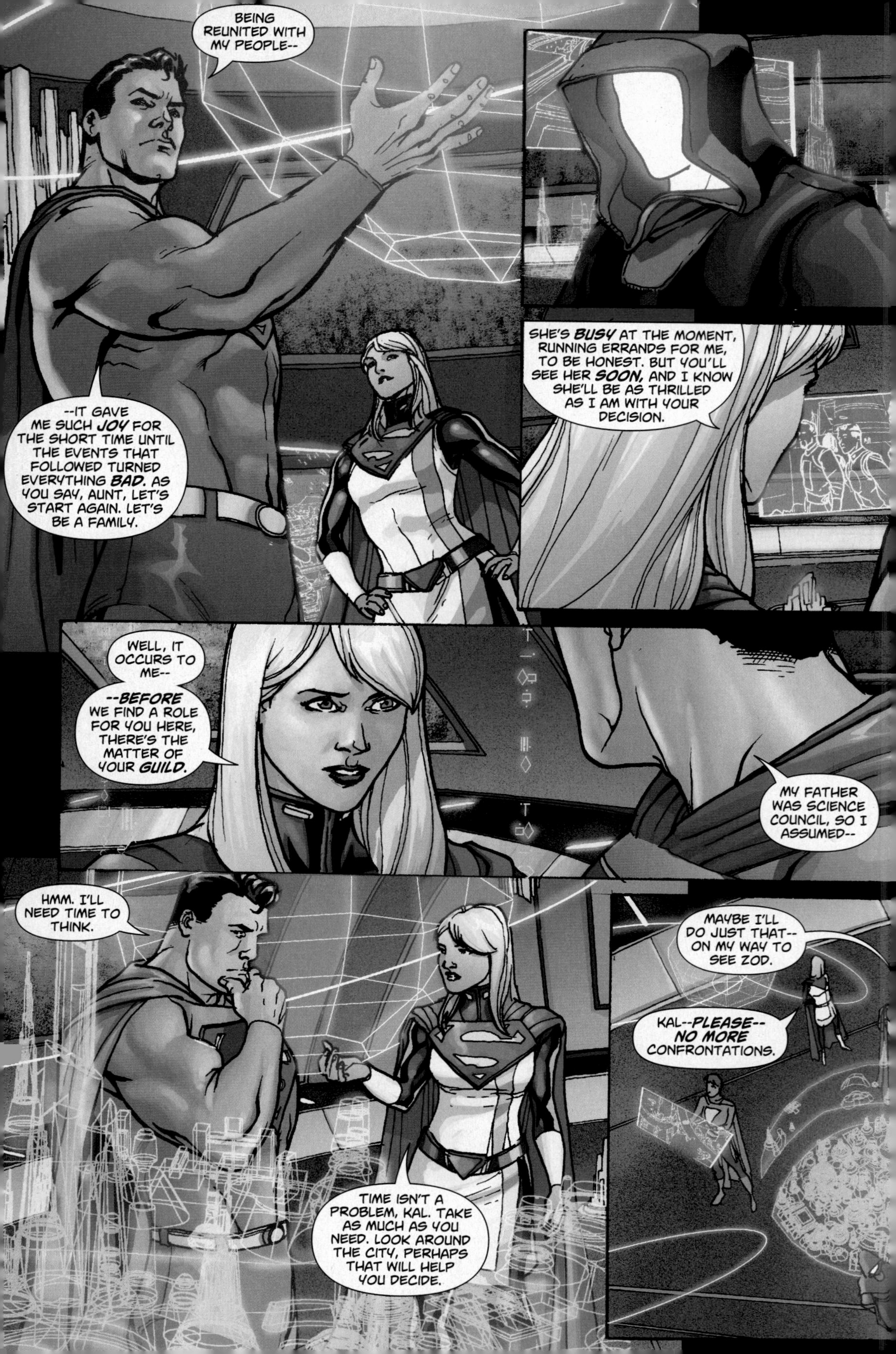
BEING REUNITED WITH MY PEOPLE--
--IT GAVE ME SUCH JOY FOR THE SHORT TIME UNTIL THE EVENTS THAT FOLLOWED TURNED EVERYTHING BAD. AS YOU SAY, AUNT, LET'S START AGAIN. LET'S BE A FAMILY.
SHE'S BUSY AT THE MOMENT, RUNNING ERRANDS FOR ME, TO BE HONEST. BUT YOU'LL SEE HER SOON, AND I KNOW SHE'LL BE AS THRILLED AS I AM WITH YOUR DECISION.
WELL, IT OCCURS TO ME--
--BEFORE WE FIND A ROLE FOR YOU HERE, THERE'S THE MATTER OF YOUR GUILD.
MY FATHER WAS SCIENCE COUNCIL, SO I ASSUMED--
HMM. I'LL NEED TIME TO THINK.
TIME ISN'T A PROBLEM, KAL. TAKE AS MUCH AS YOU NEED. LOOK AROUND THE CITY, PERHAPS THAT WILL HELP YOU DECIDE.
MAYBE I'LL DO JUST THAT--ON MY WAY TO SEE ZOD.
KAL--PLEASE--NO MORE CONFRONTATIONS.

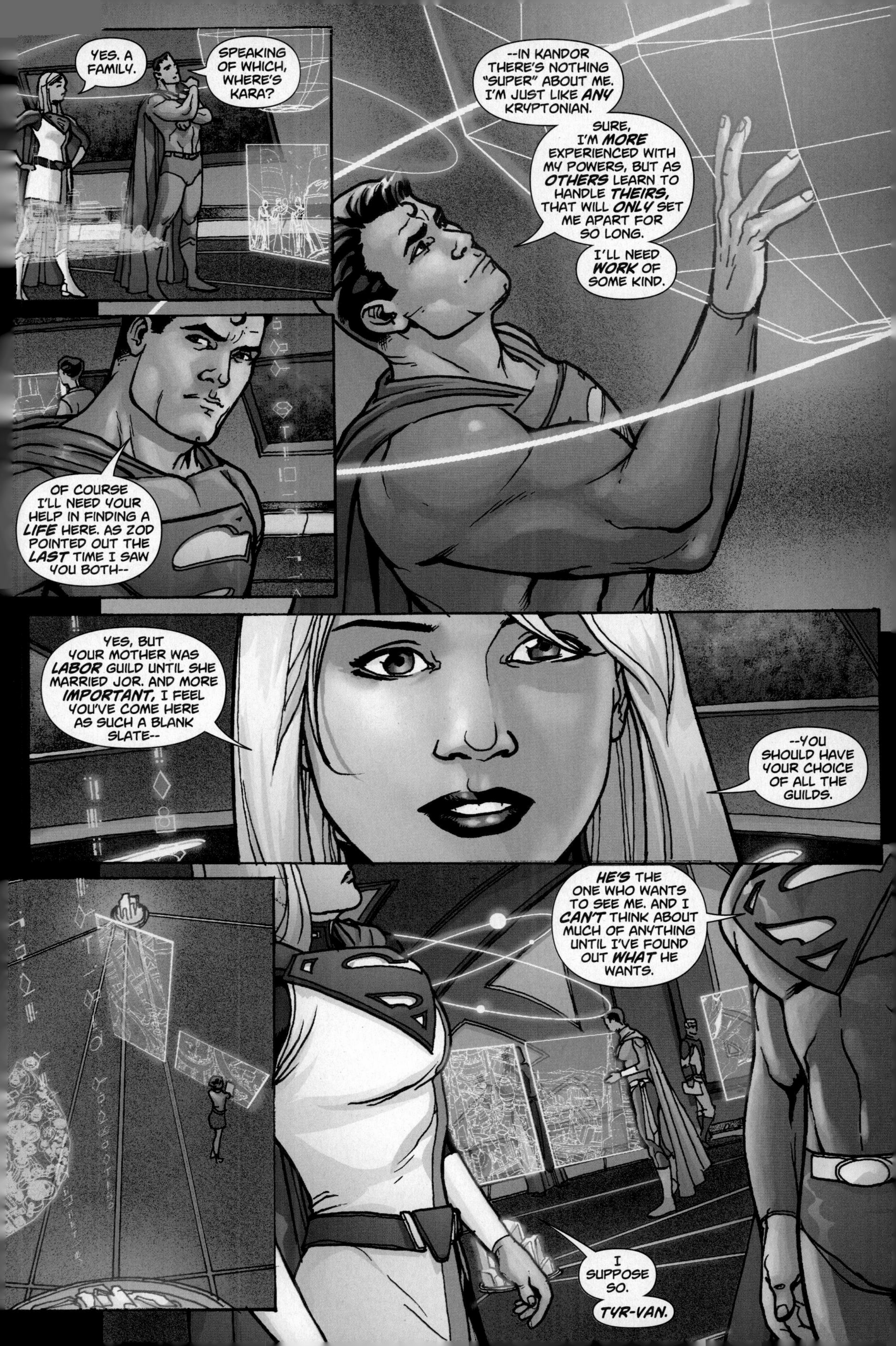
YES. A FAMILY.
SPEAKING OF WHICH, WHERE'S KARA?
--IN KANDOR THERE'S NOTHING "SUPER" ABOUT ME. I'M JUST LIKE ANY KRYPTONIAN.
SURE, I'M MORE EXPERIENCED WITH MY POWERS, BUT AS OTHERS LEARN TO HANDLE THEIRS, THAT WILL ONLY SET ME APART FOR SO LONG.
I'LL NEED WORK OF SOME KIND.
OF COURSE I'LL NEED YOUR HELP IN FINDING A LIFE HERE. AS ZOD POINTED OUT THE LAST TIME I SAW YOU BOTH--
YES, BUT YOUR MOTHER WAS LABOR GUILD UNTIL SHE MARRIED JOR. AND MORE IMPORTANT, I FEEL YOU'VE COME HERE AS SUCH A BLANK SLATE--
--YOU SHOULD HAVE YOUR CHOICE OF ALL THE GUILDS.
HE'S THE ONE WHO WANTS TO SEE ME. AND I CAN'T THINK ABOUT MUCH OF ANYTHING UNTIL I'VE FOUND OUT WHAT HE WANTS.
I SUPPOSE SO.
TYR-VAN.

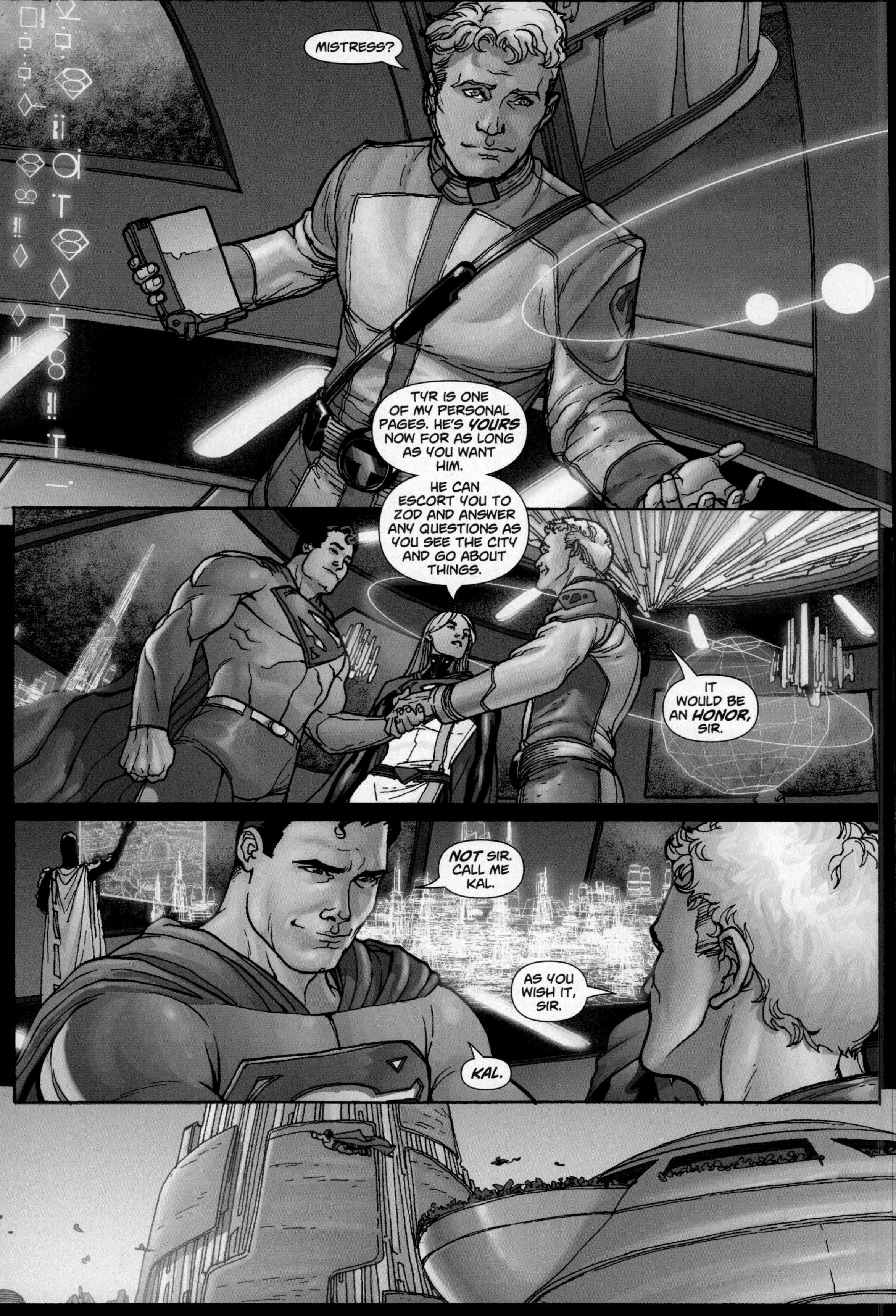
MISTRESS?
TYR IS ONE OF MY PERSONAL PAGES. HE'S YOURS NOW FOR AS LONG AS YOU WANT HIM.
HE CAN ESCORT YOU TO ZOD AND ANSWER ANY QUESTIONS AS YOU SEE THE CITY AND GO ABOUT THINGS.
IT WOULD BE AN HONOR, SIR.
NOT SIR. CALL ME KAL.
AS YOU WISH IT, SIR.
KAL.

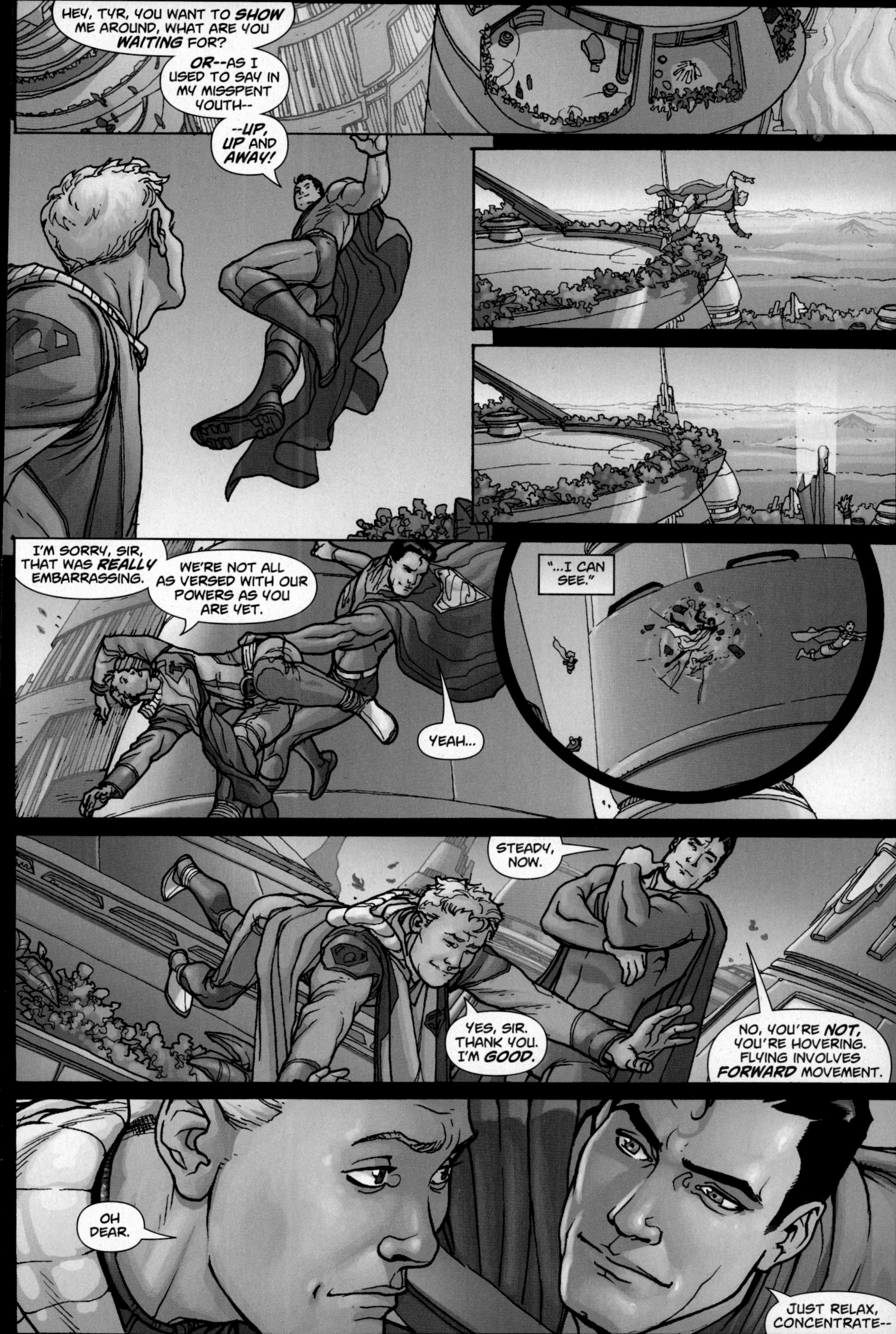
HEY, TYR, YOU WANT TO SHOW ME AROUND, WHAT ARE YOU WAITING FOR?
OR--AS I USED TO SAY IN MY MISSPENT YOUTH--
--UP, UP AND AWAY!
I'M SORRY, SIR, THAT WAS REALLY EMBARRASSING.
WE'RE NOT ALL AS VERSED WITH OUR POWERS AS YOU ARE YET.
YEAH...
"...I CAN SEE."
STEADY, NOW.
YES, SIR. THANK YOU. I'M GOOD.
NO, YOU'RE NOT, YOU'RE HOVERING. FLYING INVOLVES FORWARD MOVEMENT.
OH DEAR.
JUST RELAX, CONCENTRATE--

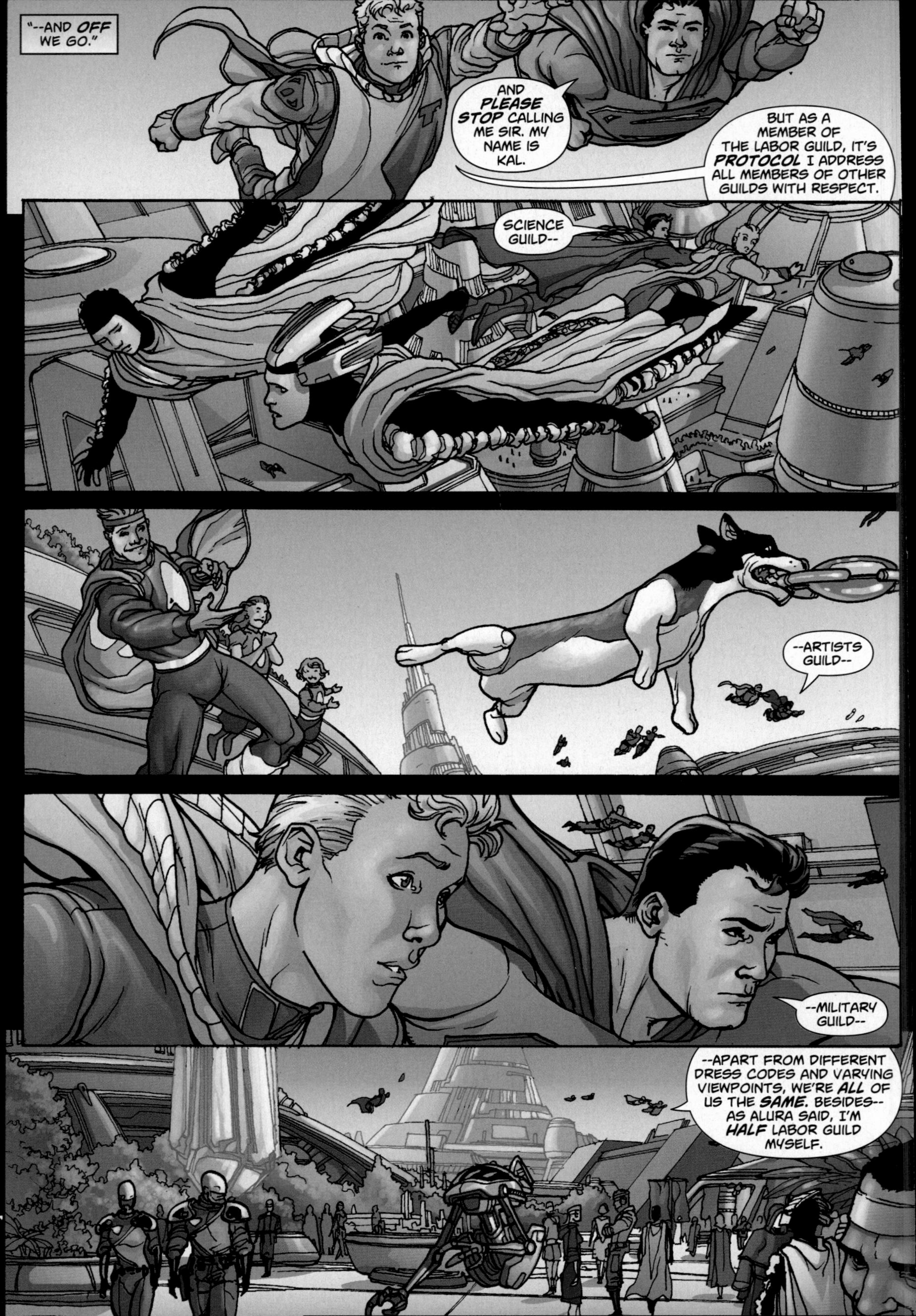
"--AND OFF WE GO."
AND PLEASE STOP CALLING ME SIR. MY NAME IS KAL.
BUT AS A MEMBER OF THE LABOR GUILD, IT'S PROTOCOL I ADDRESS ALL MEMBERS OF OTHER GUILDS WITH RESPECT.
SCIENCE GUILD--
--ARTISTS GUILD--
--MILITARY GUILD--
--APART FROM DIFFERENT DRESS CODES AND VARYING VIEWPOINTS, WE'RE ALL OF US THE SAME. BESIDES-- AS ALURA SAID, I'M HALF LABOR GUILD MYSELF.

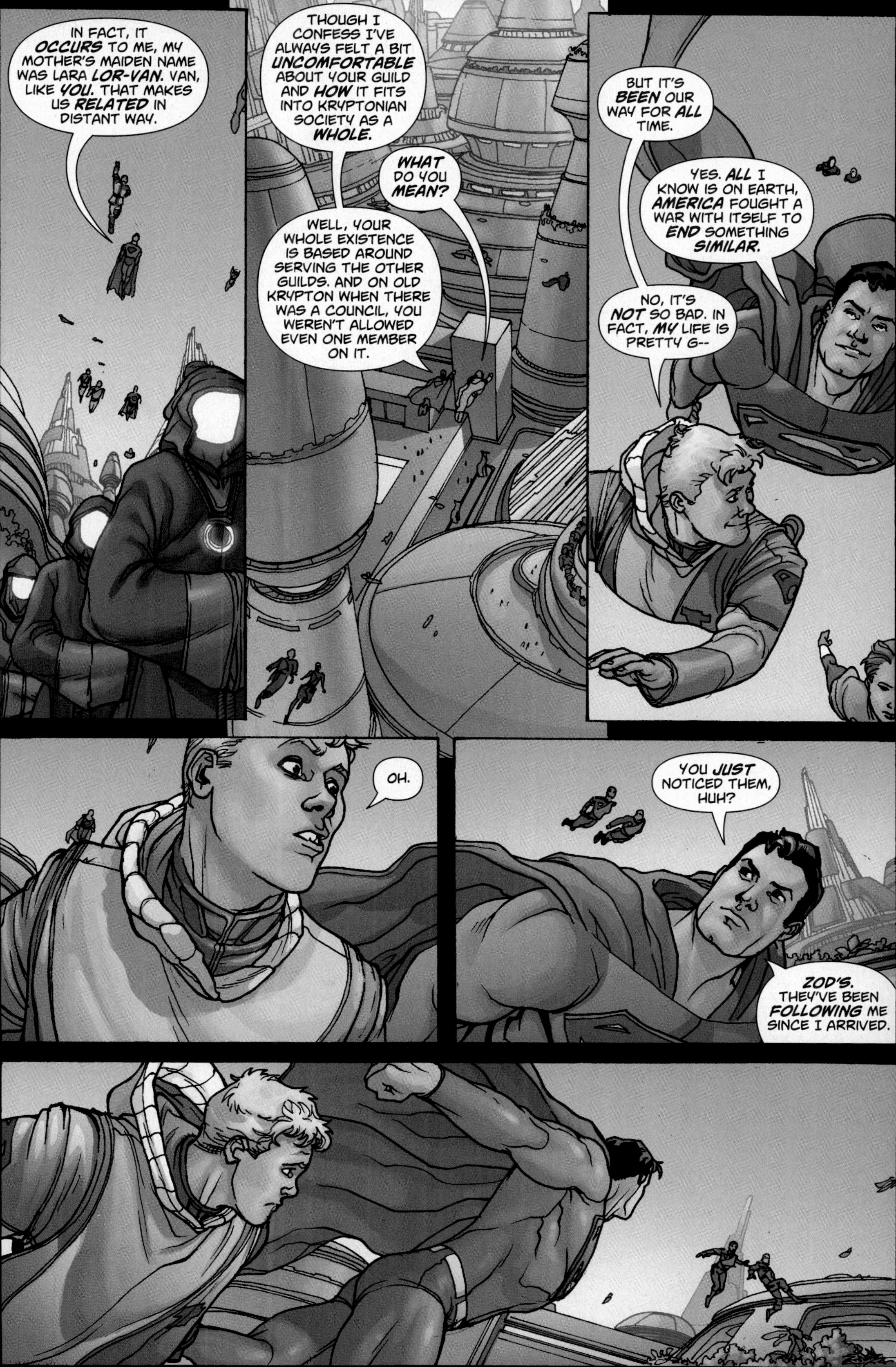

IN FACT, IT OCCURS TO ME, MY MOTHER'S MAIDEN NAME WAS LARA LOR-VAN. VAN, LIKE YOU. THAT MAKES US RELATED IN DISTANT WAY.
THOUGH I CONFESS I'VE ALWAYS FELT A BIT UNCOMFORTABLE ABOUT YOUR GUILD AND HOW IT FITS INTO KRYPTONIAN SOCIETY AS A WHOLE.
WHAT DO YOU MEAN?
WELL, YOUR WHOLE EXISTENCE IS BASED AROUND SERVING THE OTHER GUILDS. AND ON OLD KRYPTON WHEN THERE WAS A COUNCIL, YOU WEREN'T ALLOWED EVEN ONE MEMBER ON IT.
BUT IT'S BEEN OUR WAY FOR ALL TIME.
YES. ALL I KNOW IS ON EARTH, AMERICA FOUGHT A WAR WITH ITSELF TO END SOMETHING SIMILAR.
NO, IT'S NOT SO BAD. IN FACT, MY LIFE IS PRETTY G--
OH.
YOU JUST NOTICED THEM, HUH?
ZOD'S. THEY'VE BEEN FOLLOWING ME SINCE I ARRIVED.

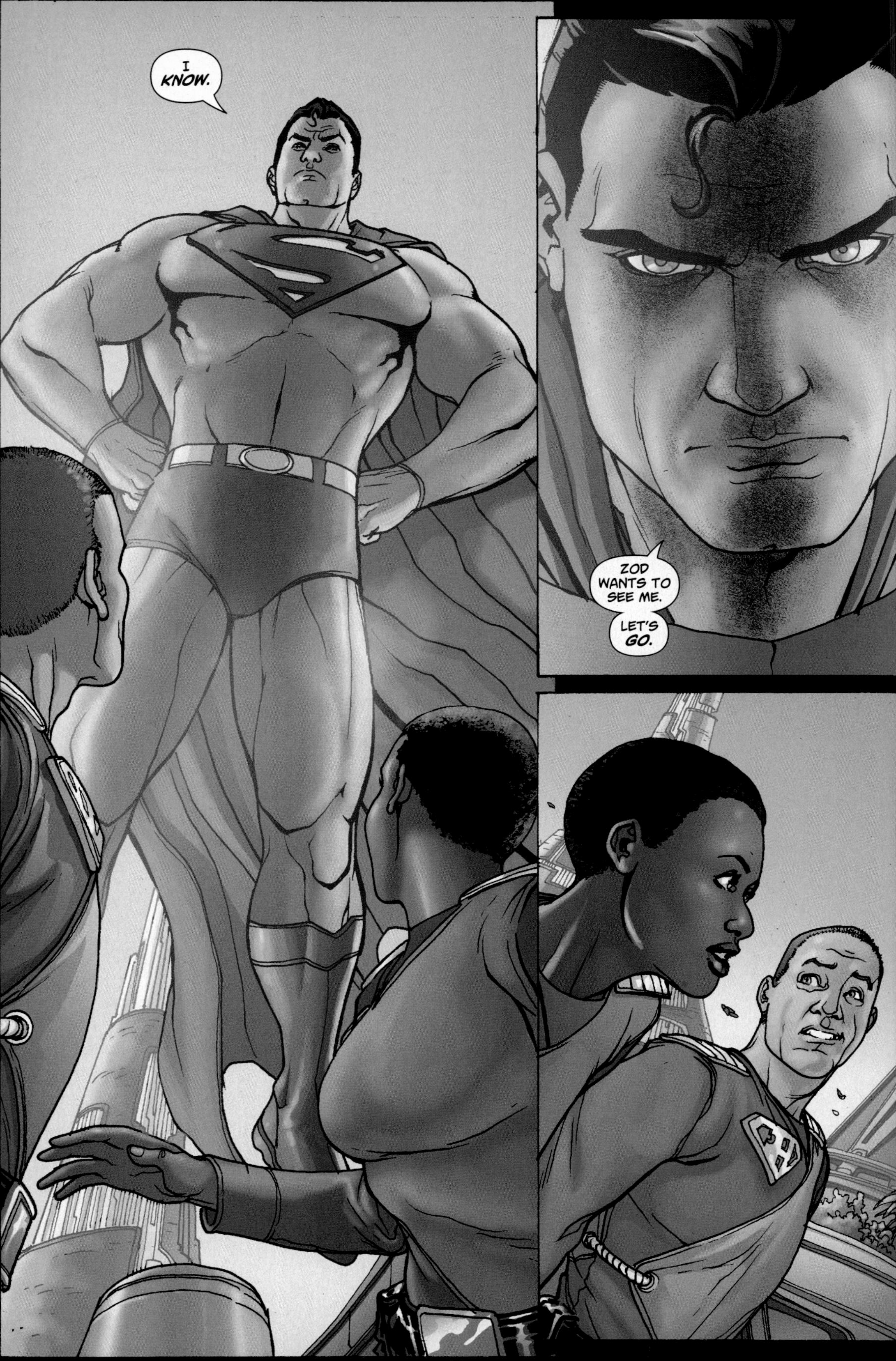
I KNOW.
ZOD WANTS TO SEE ME.
LET'S GO.

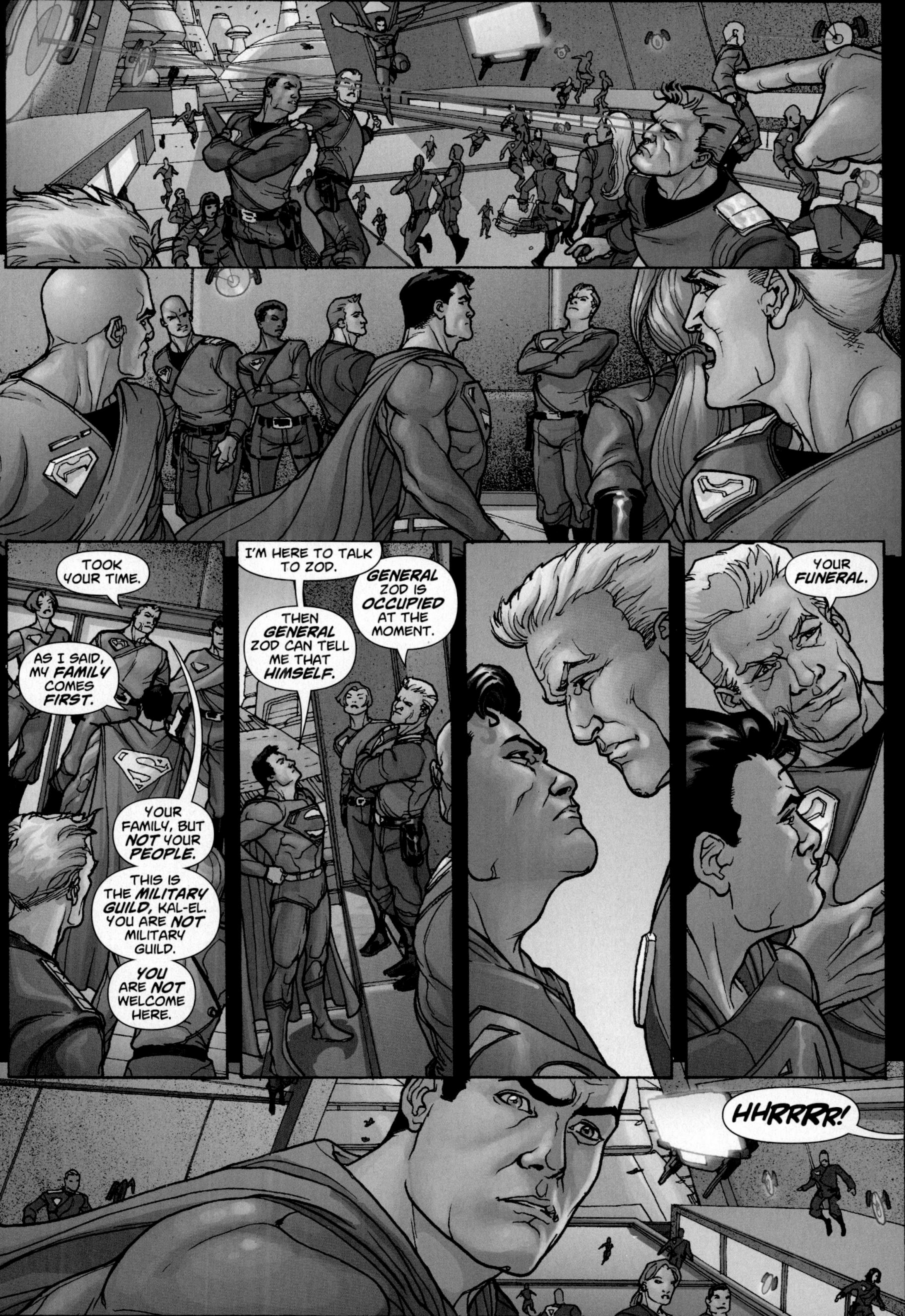
TOOK YOUR TIME.
AS I SAID, MY FAMILY COMES FIRST.
YOUR FAMILY, BUT NOT YOUR PEOPLE.
THIS IS THE MILITARY GUILD, KAL-EL. YOU ARE NOT MILITARY GUILD.
YOU ARE NOT WELCOME HERE.
I'M HERE TO TALK TO ZOD.
GENERAL ZOD IS OCCUPIED AT THE MOMENT.
THEN GENERAL ZOD CAN TELL ME THAT HIMSELF.
YOUR FUNERAL.
HHRRRR!

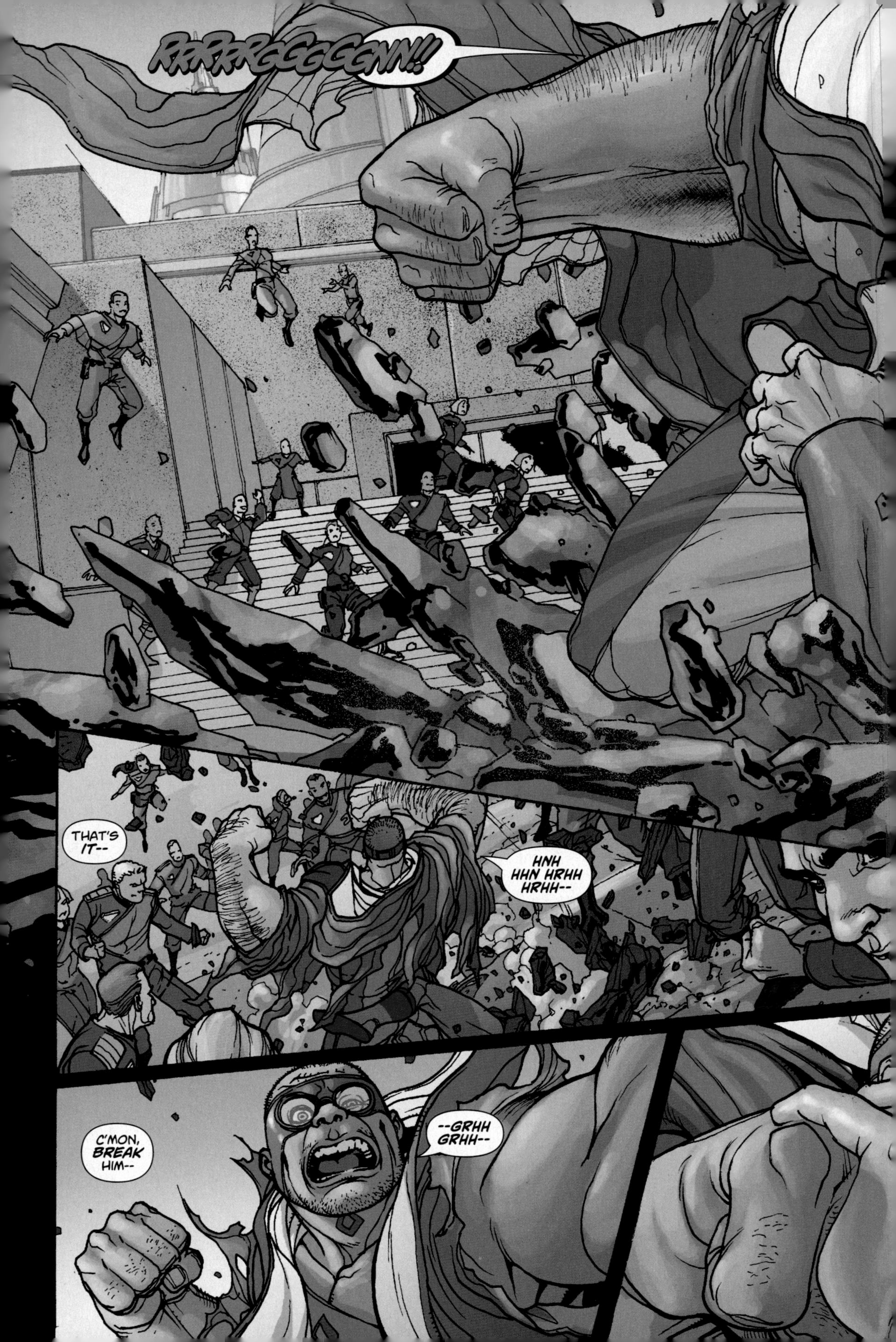
RRRRRGGGGGNN!!
THAT'S IT--
HNH HHN HRHH HRHH--
C'MON, BREAK HIM--
--GRHH GRHH--

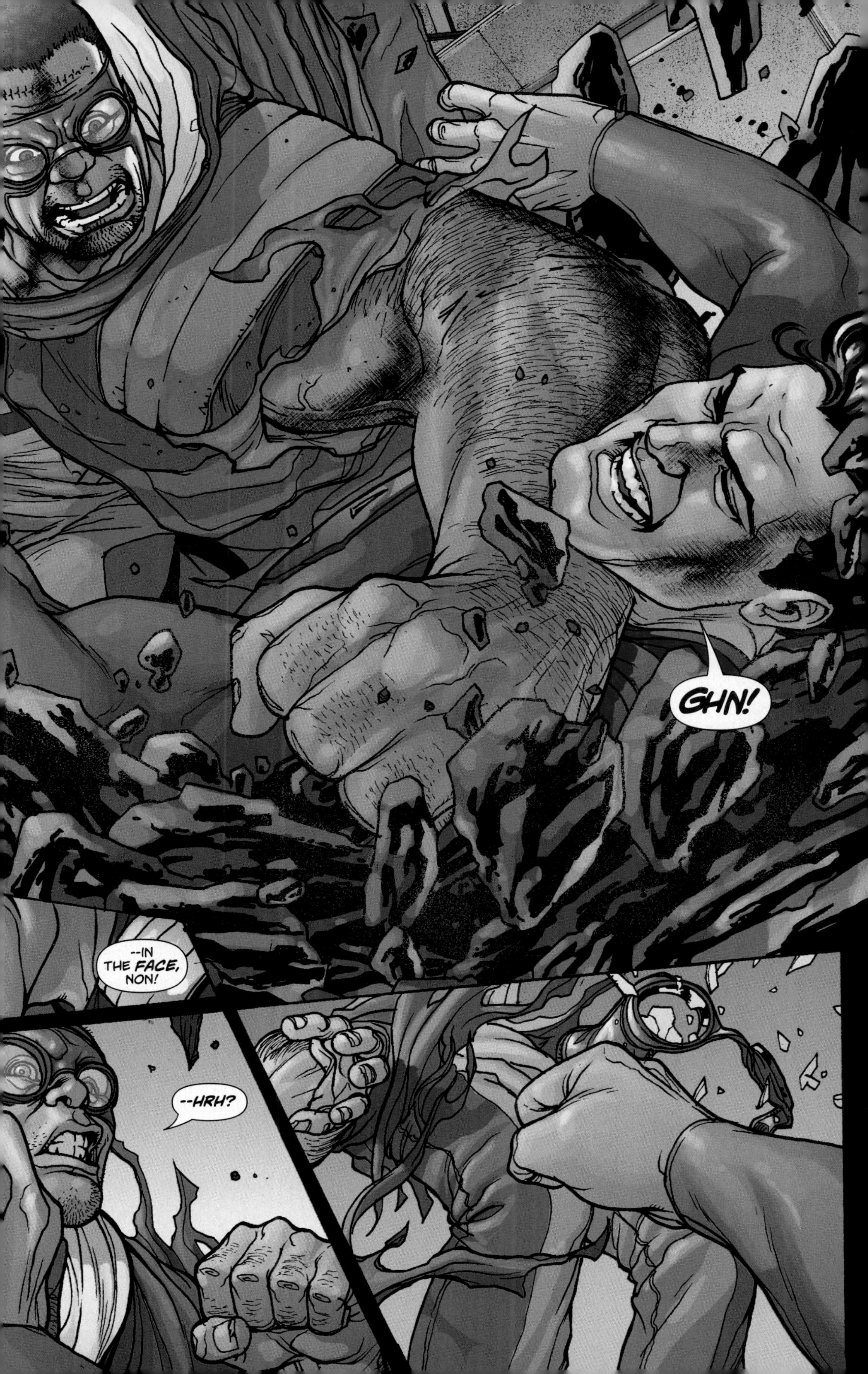
GHN!
--IN THE FACE, NON!
--HRH?

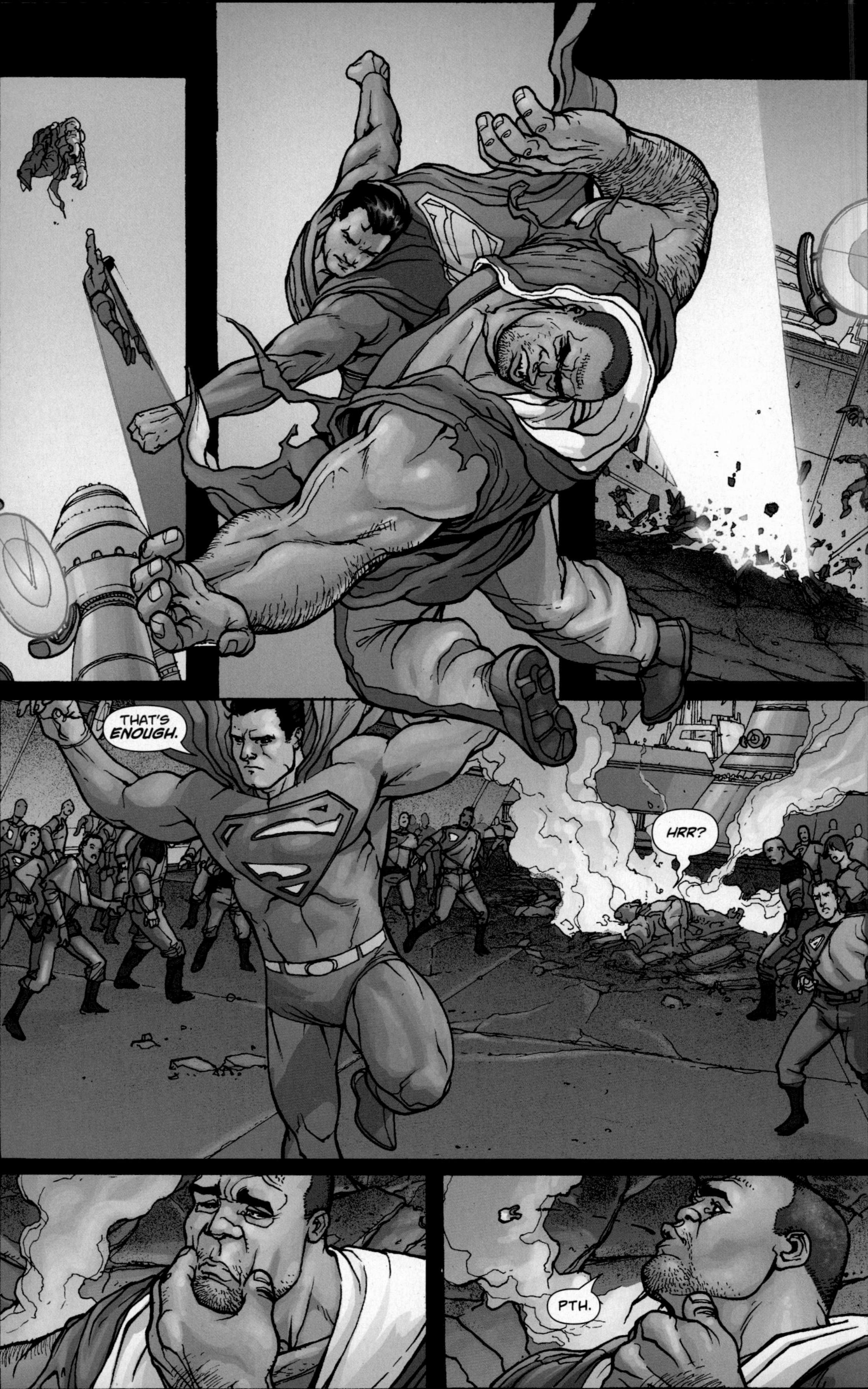
THAT'S ENOUGH.
HRR?
PTH.

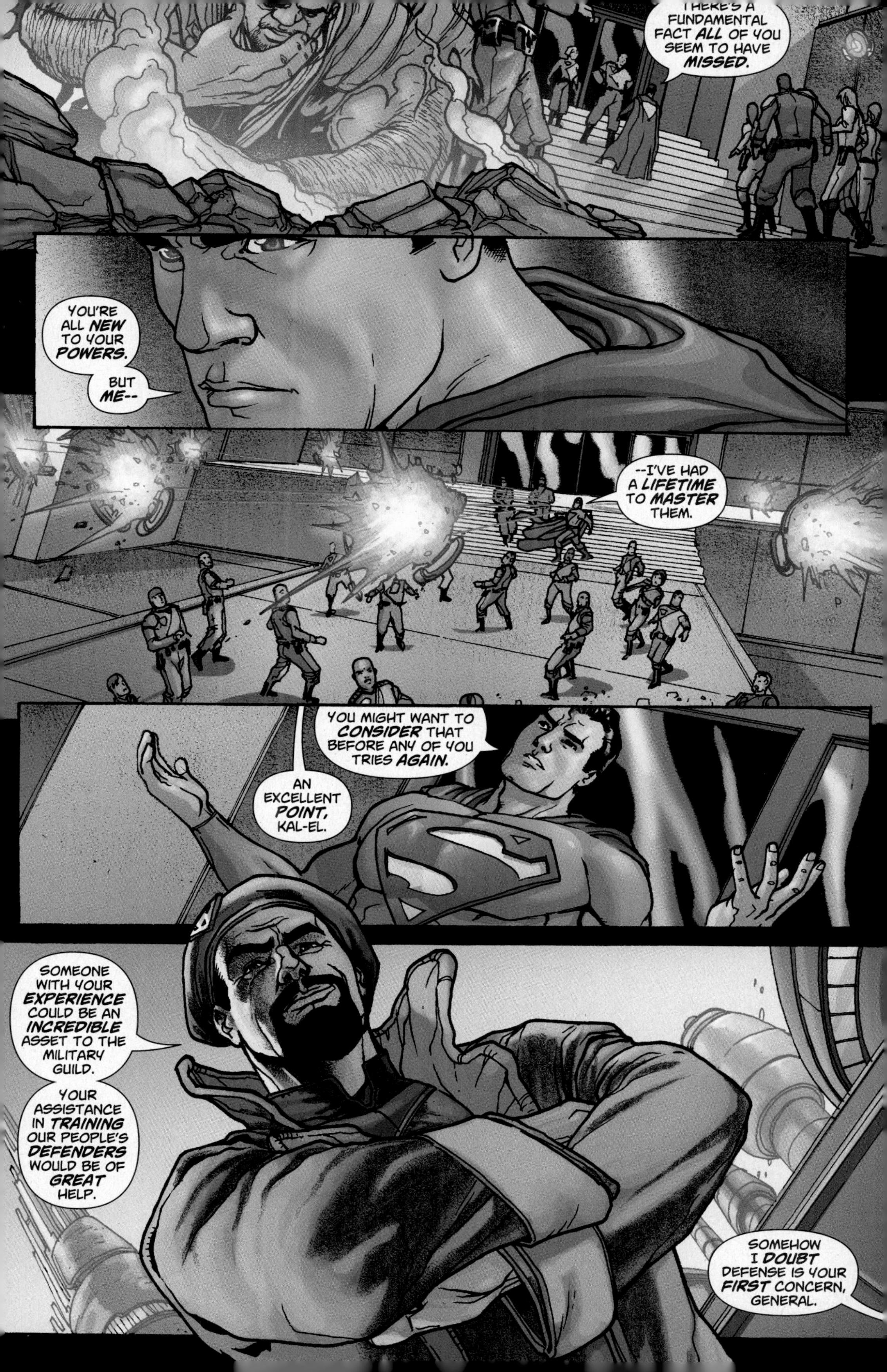
THERE'S A FUNDAMENTAL FACT ALL OF YOU SEEM TO HAVE MISSED.
YOU'RE ALL NEW TO YOUR POWERS.
BUT ME--
--I'VE HAD A LIFETIME TO MASTER THEM.
YOU MIGHT WANT TO CONSIDER THAT BEFORE ANY OF YOU TRIES AGAIN.
AN EXCELLENT POINT, KAL-EL.
SOMEONE WITH YOUR EXPERIENCE COULD BE AN INCREDIBLE ASSET TO THE MILITARY GUILD.
YOUR ASSISTANCE IN TRAINING OUR PEOPLE'S DEFENDERS WOULD BE OF GREAT HELP.
SOMEHOW I DOUBT DEFENSE IS YOUR FIRST CONCERN, GENERAL.

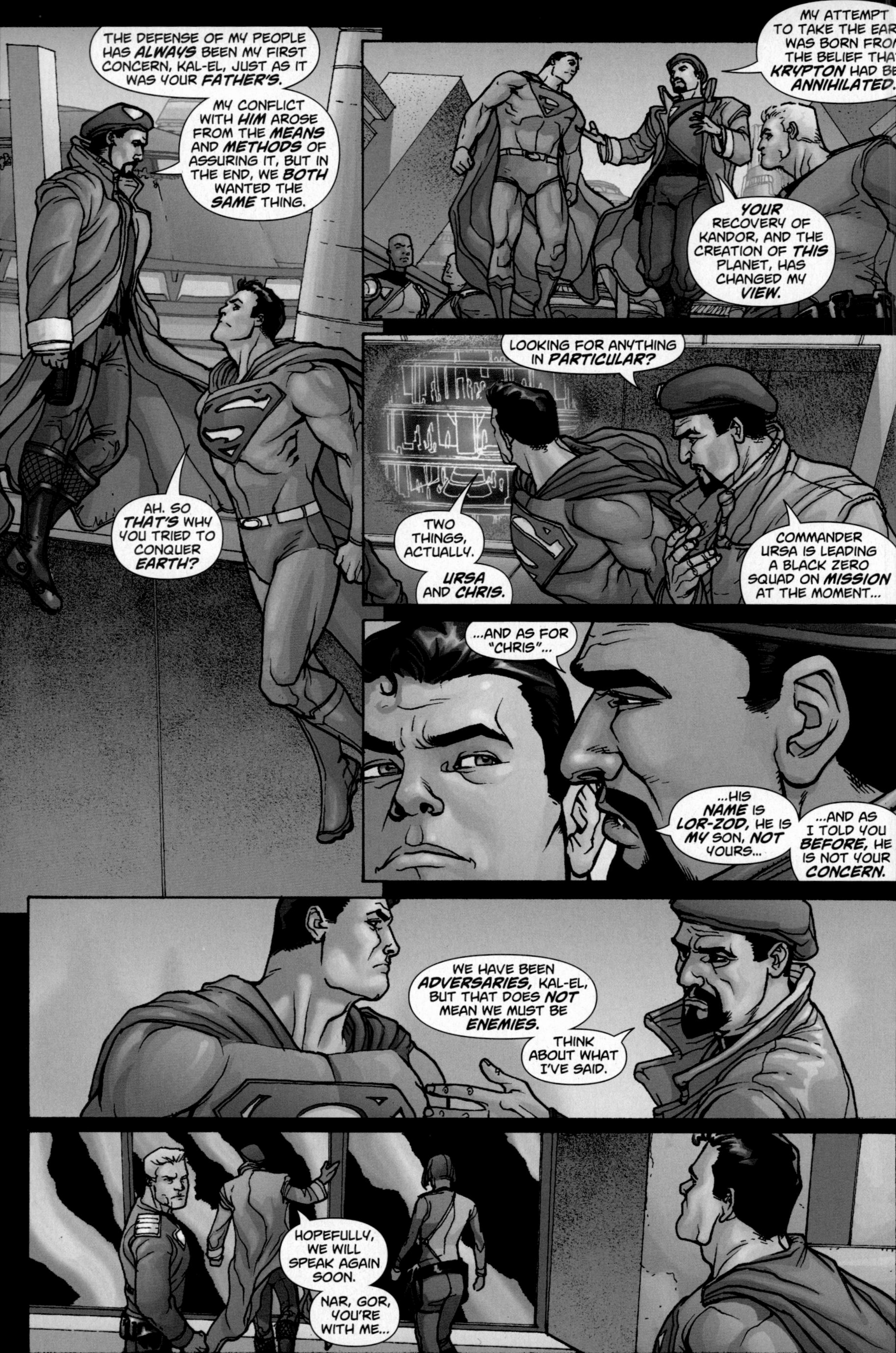
THE DEFENSE OF MY PEOPLE HAS ALWAYS BEEN MY FIRST CONCERN, KAL-EL, JUST AS IT WAS YOUR FATHER'S.
MY CONFLICT WITH HIM AROSE FROM THE MEANS AND METHODS OF ASSURING IT, BUT IN THE END, WE BOTH WANTED THE SAME THING.
AH. SO THAT'S WHY YOU TRIED TO CONQUER EARTH?
MY ATTEMPT TO TAKE THE EAR WAS BORN FROM THE BELIEF THAT KRYPTON HAD BE ANNIHILATED.
YOUR RECOVERY OF KANDOR, AND THE CREATION OF THIS PLANET, HAS CHANGED MY VIEW.
LOOKING FOR ANYTHING IN PARTICULAR?
TWO THINGS, ACTUALLY.
URSA AND CHRIS.
COMMANDER URSA IS LEADING A BLACK ZERO SQUAD ON MISSION AT THE MOMENT...
...AND AS FOR "CHRIS"...
...HIS NAME IS LOR-ZOD, HE IS MY SON, NOT YOURS...
...AND AS I TOLD YOU BEFORE, HE IS NOT YOUR CONCERN.
WE HAVE BEEN ADVERSARIES, KAL-EL, BUT THAT DOES NOT MEAN WE MUST BE ENEMIES.
THINK ABOUT WHAT I'VE SAID.
HOPEFULLY, WE WILL SPEAK AGAIN SOON.
NAR, GOR, YOU'RE WITH ME...

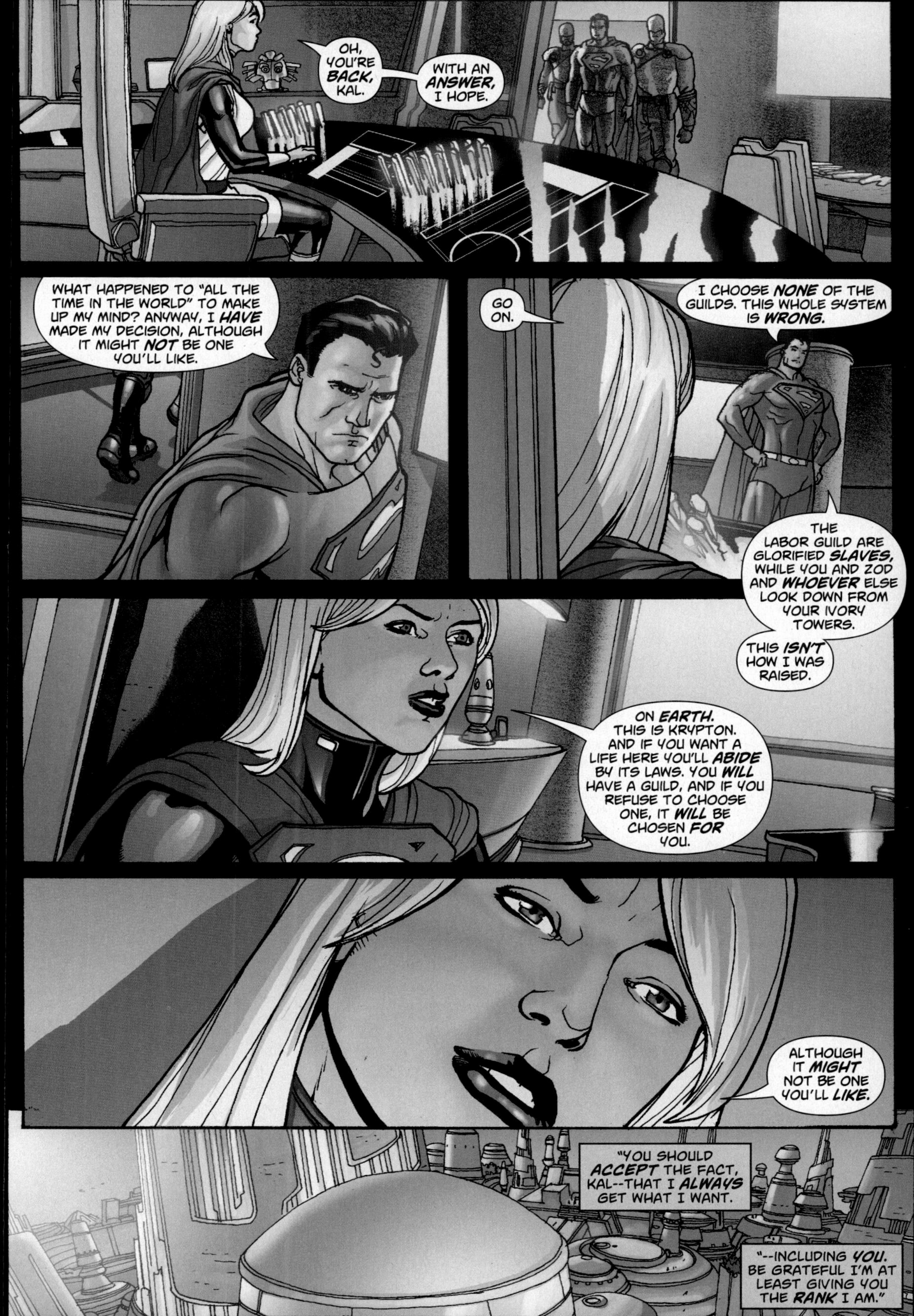

OH, YOU'RE BACK, KAL.
WITH AN ANSWER, I HOPE.
WHAT HAPPENED TO "ALL THE TIME IN THE WORLD" TO MAKE UP MY MIND? ANYWAY, I HAVE MADE MY DECISION, ALTHOUGH IT MIGHT NOT BE ONE YOU'LL LIKE.
GO ON.
I CHOOSE NONE OF THE GUILDS. THIS WHOLE SYSTEM IS WRONG.
THE LABOR GUILD ARE GLORIFIED SLAVES, WHILE YOU AND ZOD AND WHOEVER ELSE LOOK DOWN FROM YOUR IVORY TOWERS.
THIS ISN'T HOW I WAS RAISED.
ON EARTH. THIS IS KRYPTON. AND IF YOU WANT A LIFE HERE YOU'LL ABIDE BY ITS LAWS. YOU WILL HAVE A GUILD, AND IF YOU REFUSE TO CHOOSE ONE, IT WILL BE CHOSEN FOR YOU.
ALTHOUGH IT MIGHT NOT BE ONE YOU'LL LIKE.
"YOU SHOULD ACCEPT THE FACT, KAL--THAT I ALWAYS GET WHAT I WANT.
"--INCLUDING YOU. BE GRATEFUL I'M AT LEAST GIVING YOU THE RANK I AM."

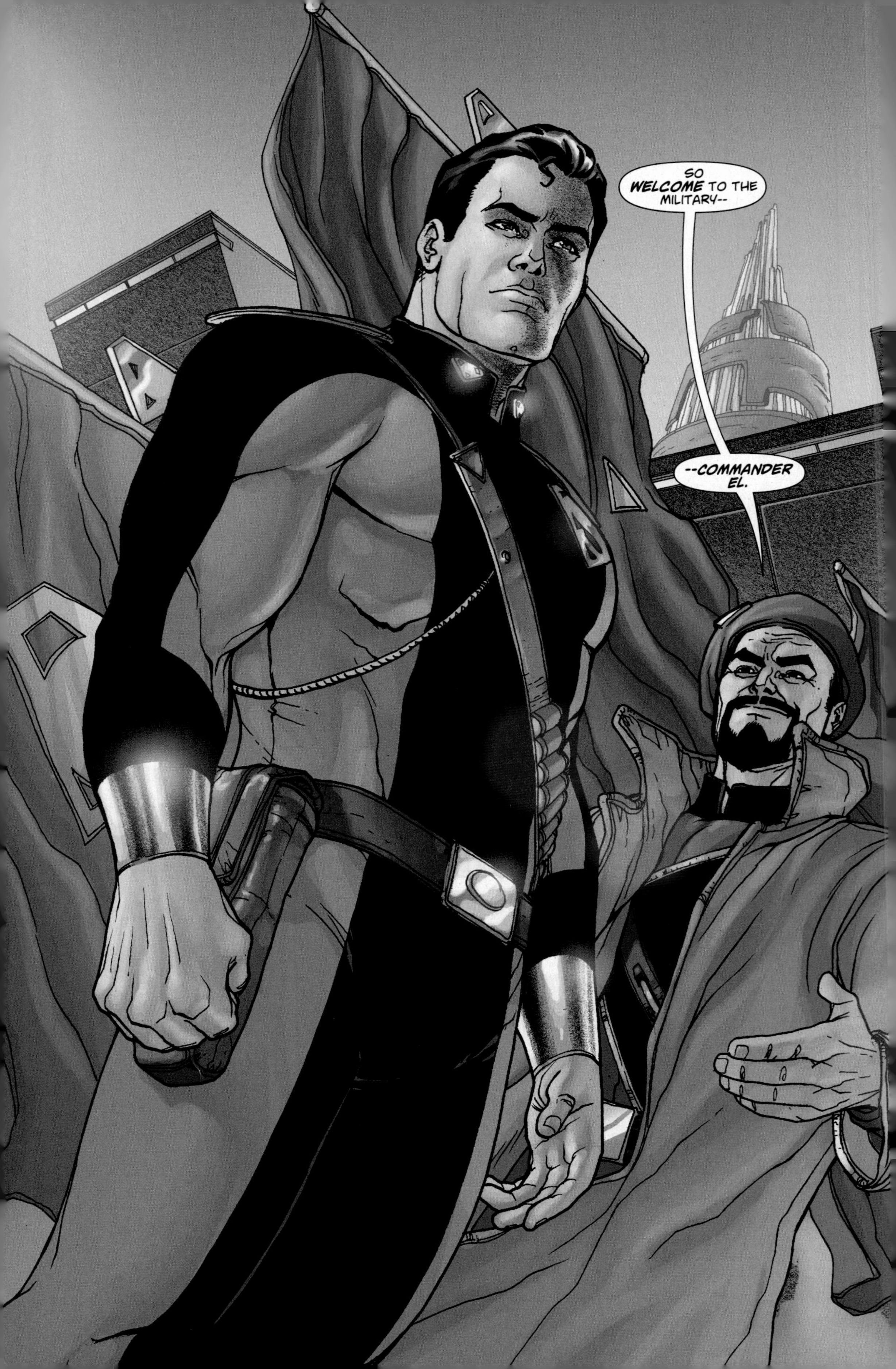
SO WELCOME TO THE MILITARY--
--COMMANDER EL.

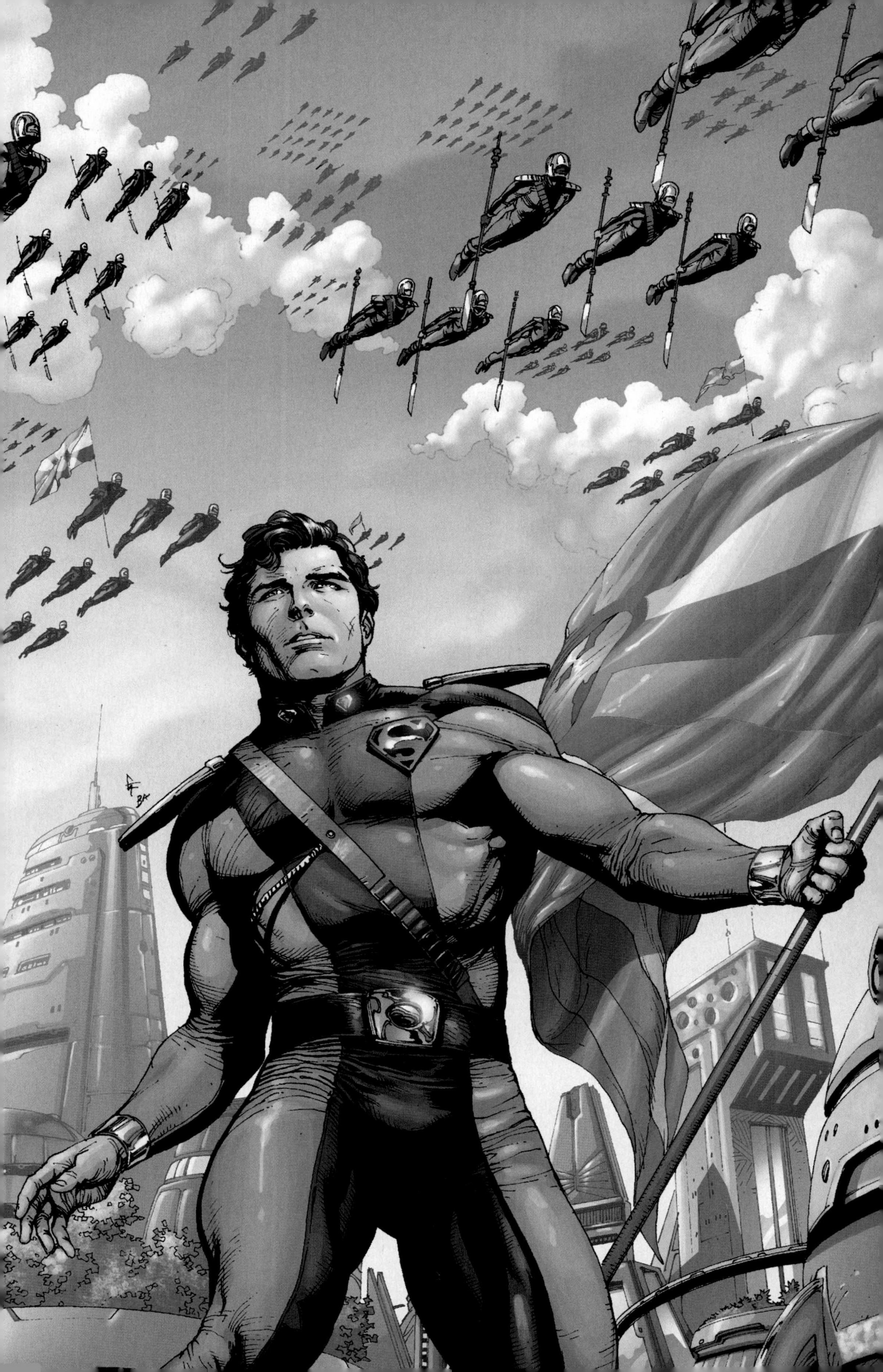

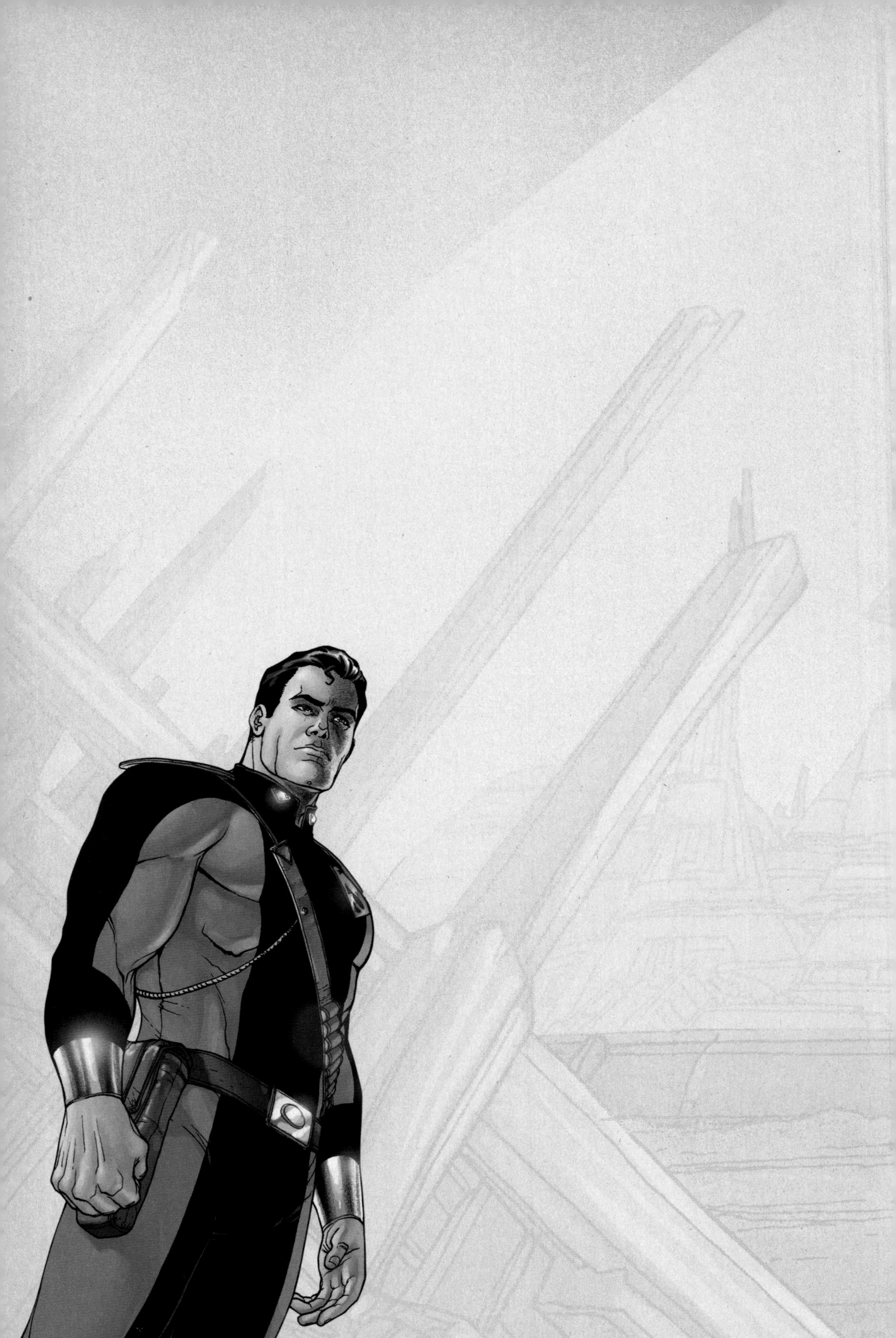

WORLD OF NEW KRYPTON <PART TWO>
COVER BY **GARY FRANK** WITH **BRAD ANDERSON**

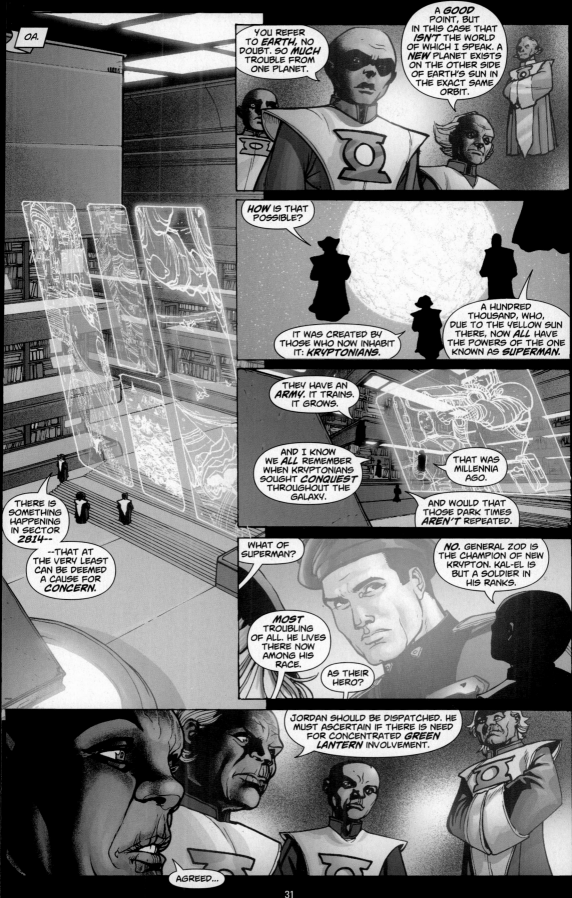

YOU REFER TO *EARTH*, NO DOUBT. SO *MUCH* TROUBLE FROM ONE PLANET.

A *GOOD* POINT, BUT IN THIS CASE THAT *ISN'T* THE WORLD OF WHICH I SPEAK. A *NEW* PLANET EXISTS ON THE OTHER SIDE OF EARTH'S SUN IN THE EXACT SAME ORBIT.

HOW IS THAT POSSIBLE?

IT WAS CREATED BY THOSE WHO NOW INHABIT IT: *KRYPTONIANS.*

A HUNDRED THOUSAND, WHO, DUE TO THE YELLOW SUN THERE, NOW *ALL* HAVE THE POWERS OF THE ONE KNOWN AS *SUPERMAN.*

THEY HAVE AN *ARMY.* IT TRAINS. IT GROWS.

AND I KNOW WE *ALL* REMEMBER WHEN KRYPTONIANS SOUGHT *CONQUEST* THROUGHOUT THE GALAXY.

THAT WAS *MILLENNIA* AGO.

AND WOULD THAT THOSE DARK TIMES *AREN'T* REPEATED.

THERE IS SOMETHING HAPPENING IN SECTOR 2814--

--THAT AT THE VERY LEAST CAN BE DEEMED A CAUSE FOR *CONCERN.*

WHAT OF SUPERMAN?

NO. GENERAL ZOD IS THE CHAMPION OF NEW KRYPTON. KAL-EL IS BUT A SOLDIER IN HIS RANKS.

MOST TROUBLING OF ALL. HE LIVES THERE NOW AMONG HIS RACE.

AS THEIR HERO?

JORDAN SHOULD BE DISPATCHED. HE MUST ASCERTAIN IF THERE IS NEED FOR CONCENTRATED *GREEN LANTERN* INVOLVEMENT.

AGREED...

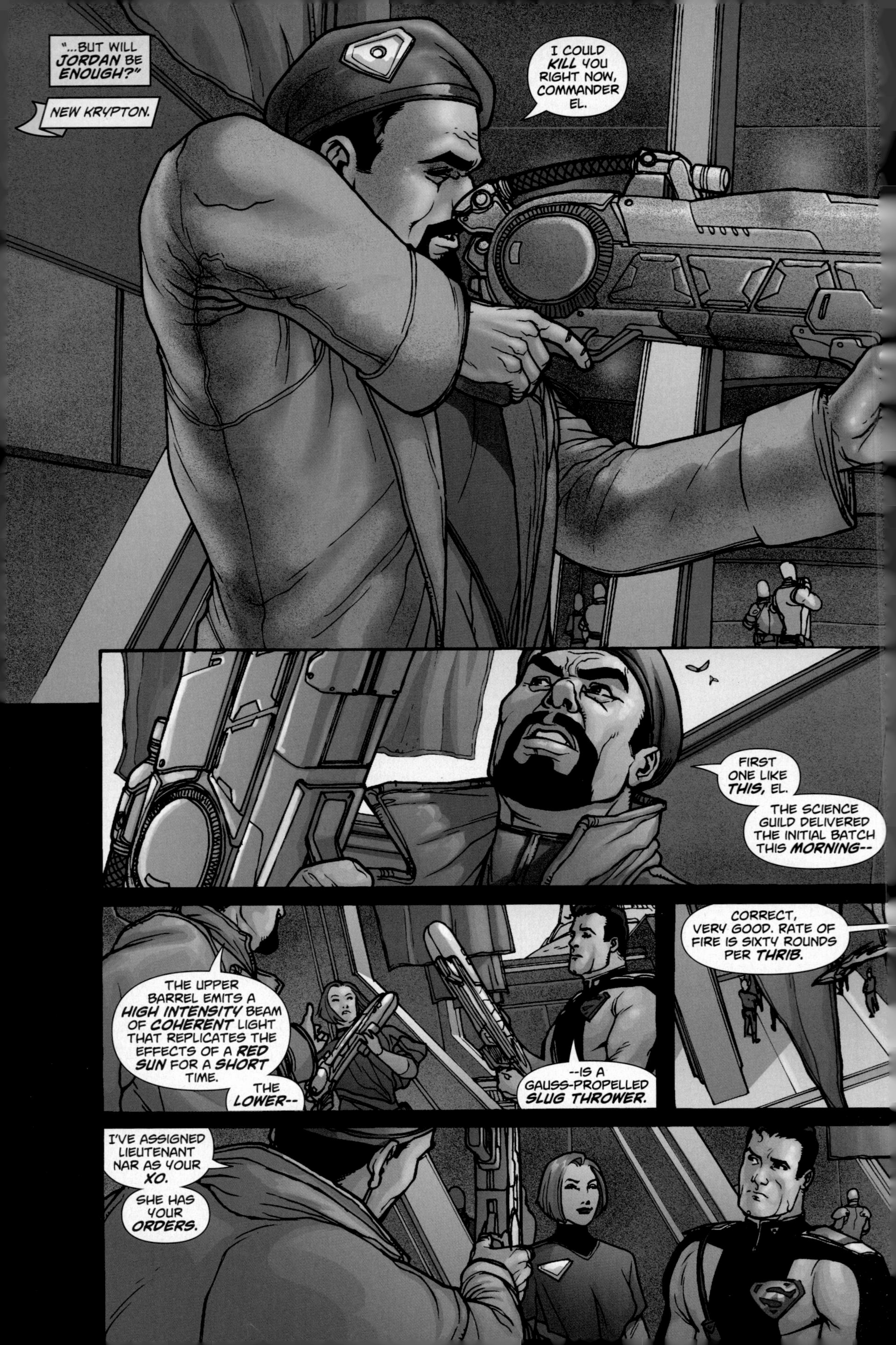
"...BUT WILL JORDAN BE ENOUGH?"
NEW KRYPTON.
I COULD KILL YOU RIGHT NOW, COMMANDER EL.
FIRST ONE LIKE THIS, EL.
THE SCIENCE GUILD DELIVERED THE INITIAL BATCH THIS MORNING--
THE UPPER BARREL EMITS A HIGH INTENSITY BEAM OF COHERENT LIGHT THAT REPLICATES THE EFFECTS OF A RED SUN FOR A SHORT TIME.
THE LOWER--
--IS A GAUSS-PROPELLED SLUG THROWER.
CORRECT, VERY GOOD. RATE OF FIRE IS SIXTY ROUNDS PER THRIB.
I'VE ASSIGNED LIEUTENANT NAR AS YOUR XO.
SHE HAS YOUR ORDERS.

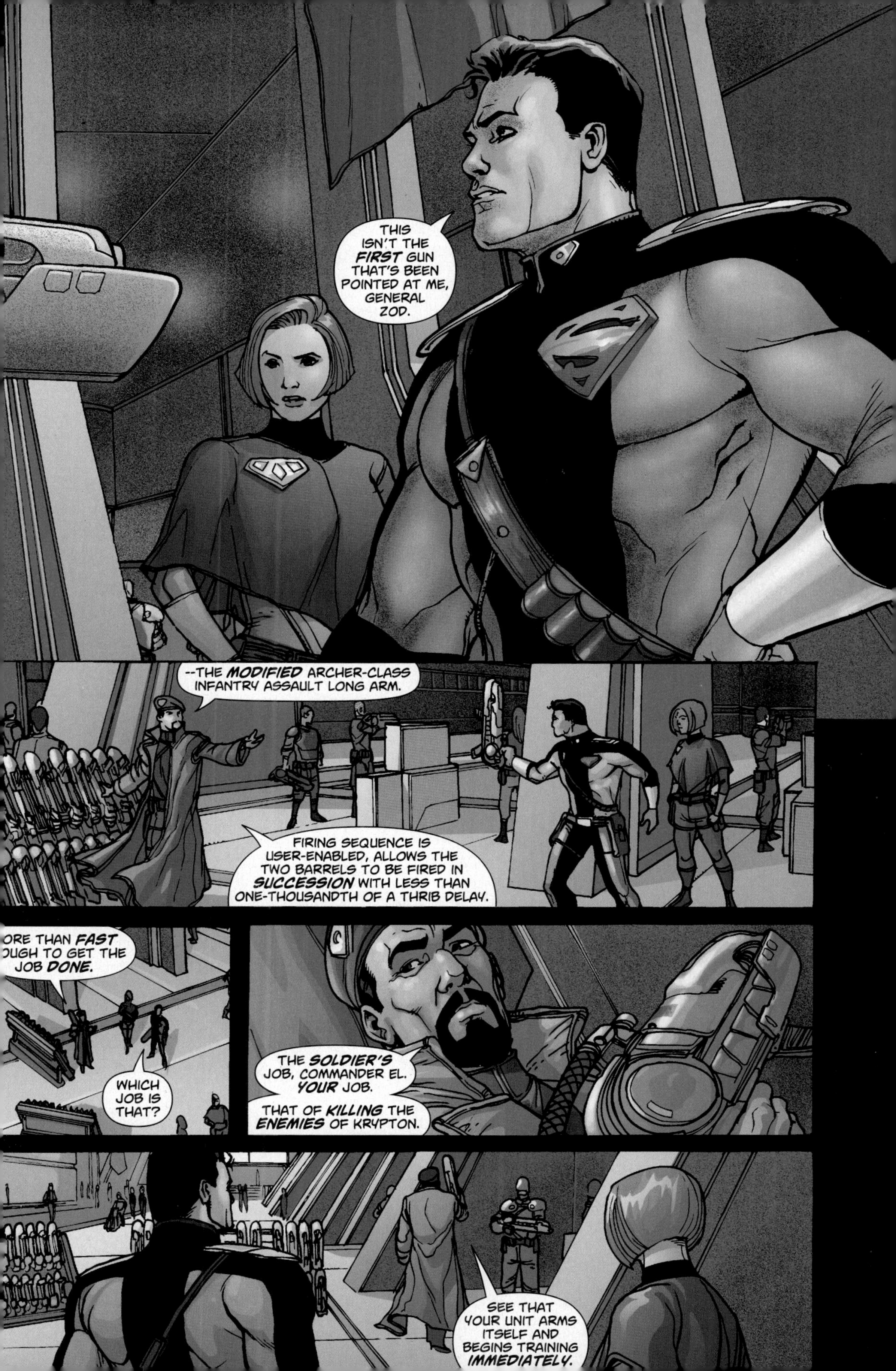

THIS ISN'T THE FIRST GUN THAT'S BEEN POINTED AT ME, GENERAL ZOD.
--THE MODIFIED ARCHER-CLASS INFANTRY ASSAULT LONG ARM.
FIRING SEQUENCE IS USER-ENABLED, ALLOWS THE TWO BARRELS TO BE FIRED IN SUCCESSION WITH LESS THAN ONE-THOUSANDTH OF A THRIB DELAY.
ORE THAN FAST OUGH TO GET THE JOB DONE.
WHICH JOB IS THAT?
THE SOLDIER'S JOB, COMMANDER EL. YOUR JOB.
THAT OF KILLING THE ENEMIES OF KRYPTON.
SEE THAT YOUR UNIT ARMS ITSELF AND BEGINS TRAINING IMMEDIATELY.

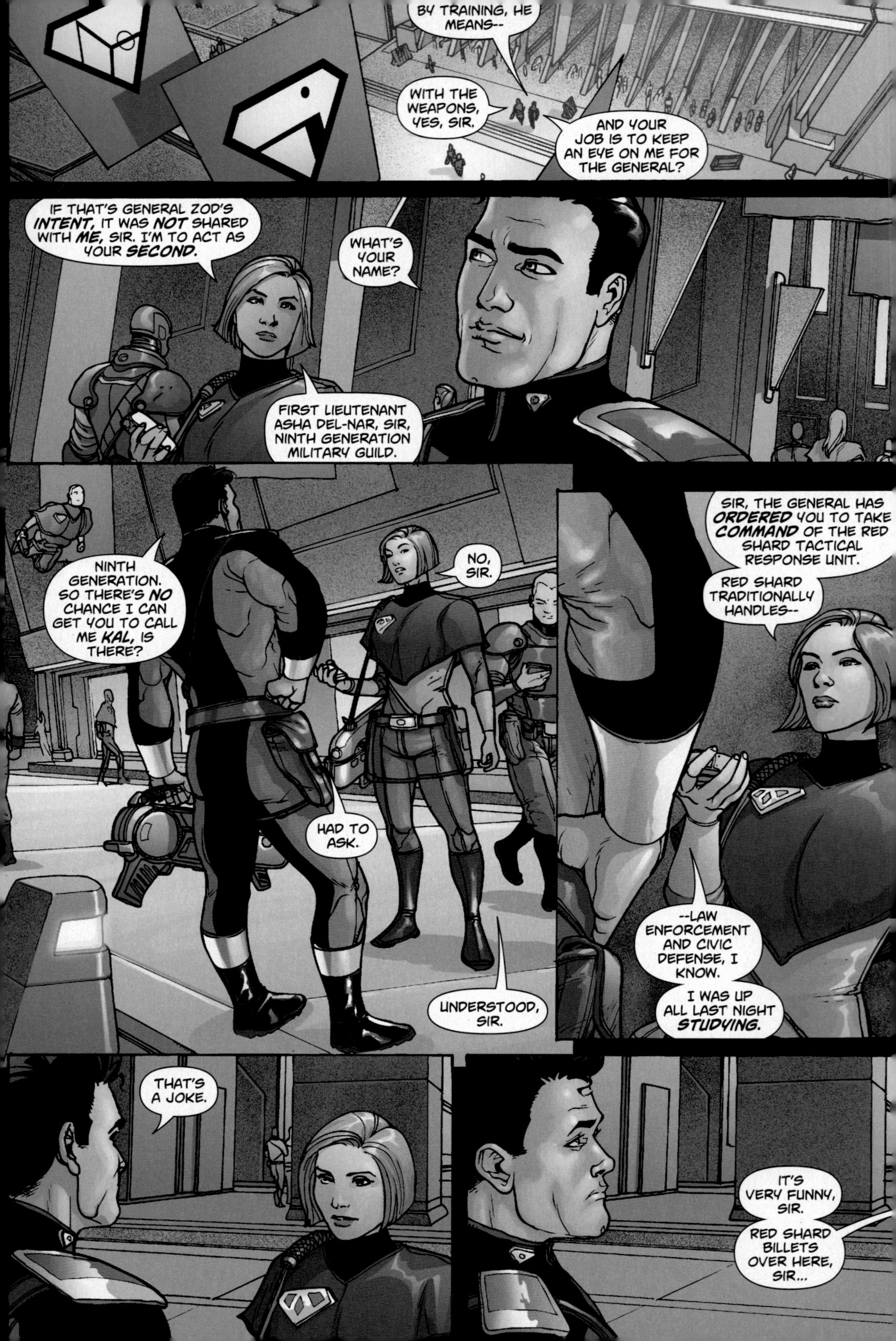
BY TRAINING, HE MEANS--
WITH THE WEAPONS, YES, SIR.
AND YOUR JOB IS TO KEEP AN EYE ON ME FOR THE GENERAL?
IF THAT'S GENERAL ZOD'S INTENT, IT WAS NOT SHARED WITH ME, SIR. I'M TO ACT AS YOUR SECOND.
WHAT'S YOUR NAME?
FIRST LIEUTENANT ASHA DEL-NAR, SIR, NINTH GENERATION MILITARY GUILD.
NINTH GENERATION. SO THERE'S NO CHANCE I CAN GET YOU TO CALL ME KAL, IS THERE?
NO, SIR.
HAD TO ASK.
UNDERSTOOD, SIR.
SIR, THE GENERAL HAS ORDERED YOU TO TAKE COMMAND OF THE RED SHARD TACTICAL RESPONSE UNIT.
RED SHARD TRADITIONALLY HANDLES--
--LAW ENFORCEMENT AND CIVIC DEFENSE, I KNOW.
I WAS UP ALL LAST NIGHT STUDYING.
THAT'S A JOKE.
IT'S VERY FUNNY, SIR.
RED SHARD BILLETS OVER HERE, SIR...

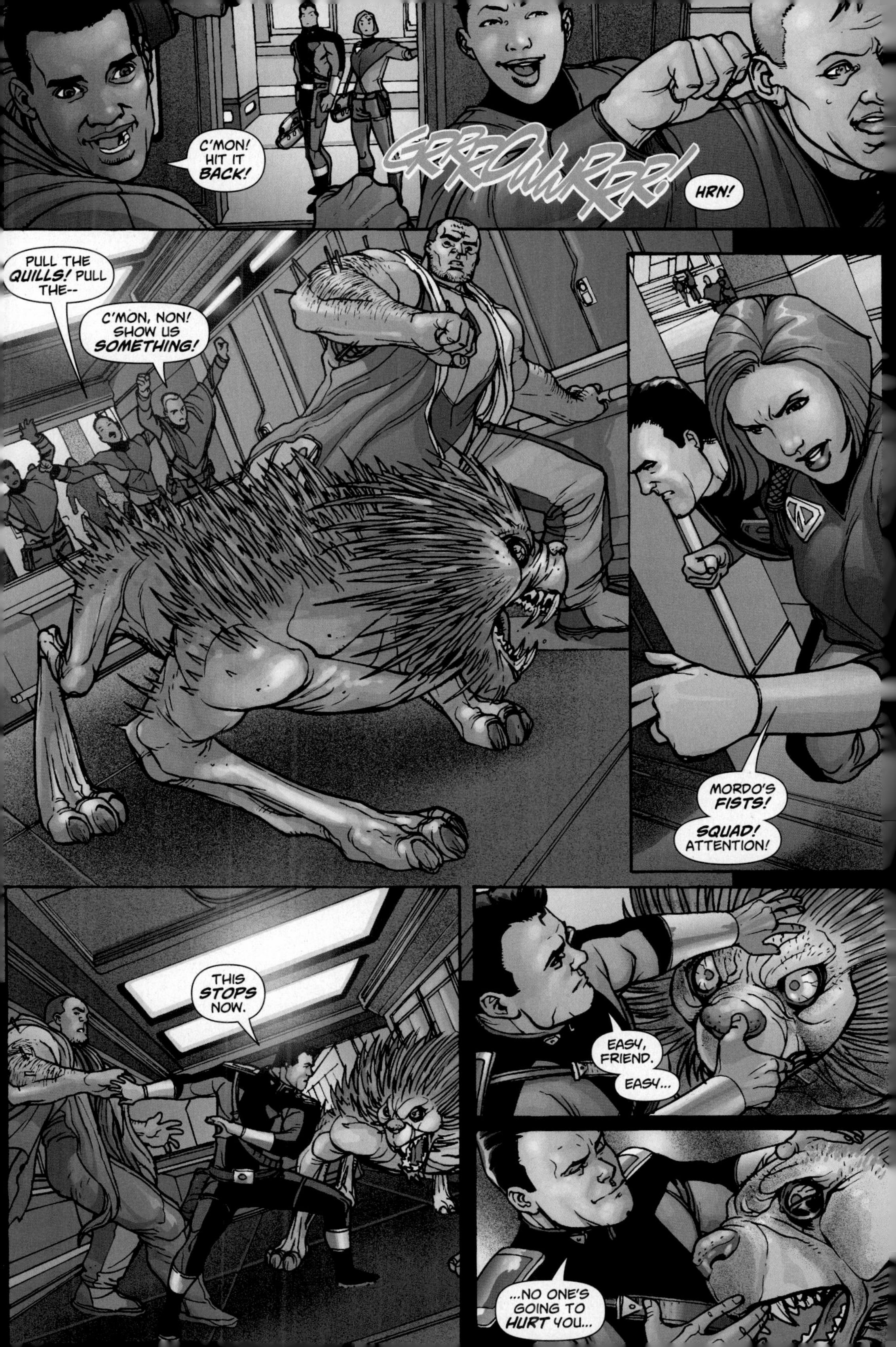
C'MON! HIT IT BACK!
GRRROWRRR!
HRN!
PULL THE QUILLS! PULL THE--
C'MON, NON! SHOW US SOMETHING!
MORDO'S FISTS!
SQUAD! ATTENTION!
THIS STOPS NOW.
EASY, FRIEND.
EASY...
...NO ONE'S GOING TO HURT YOU...

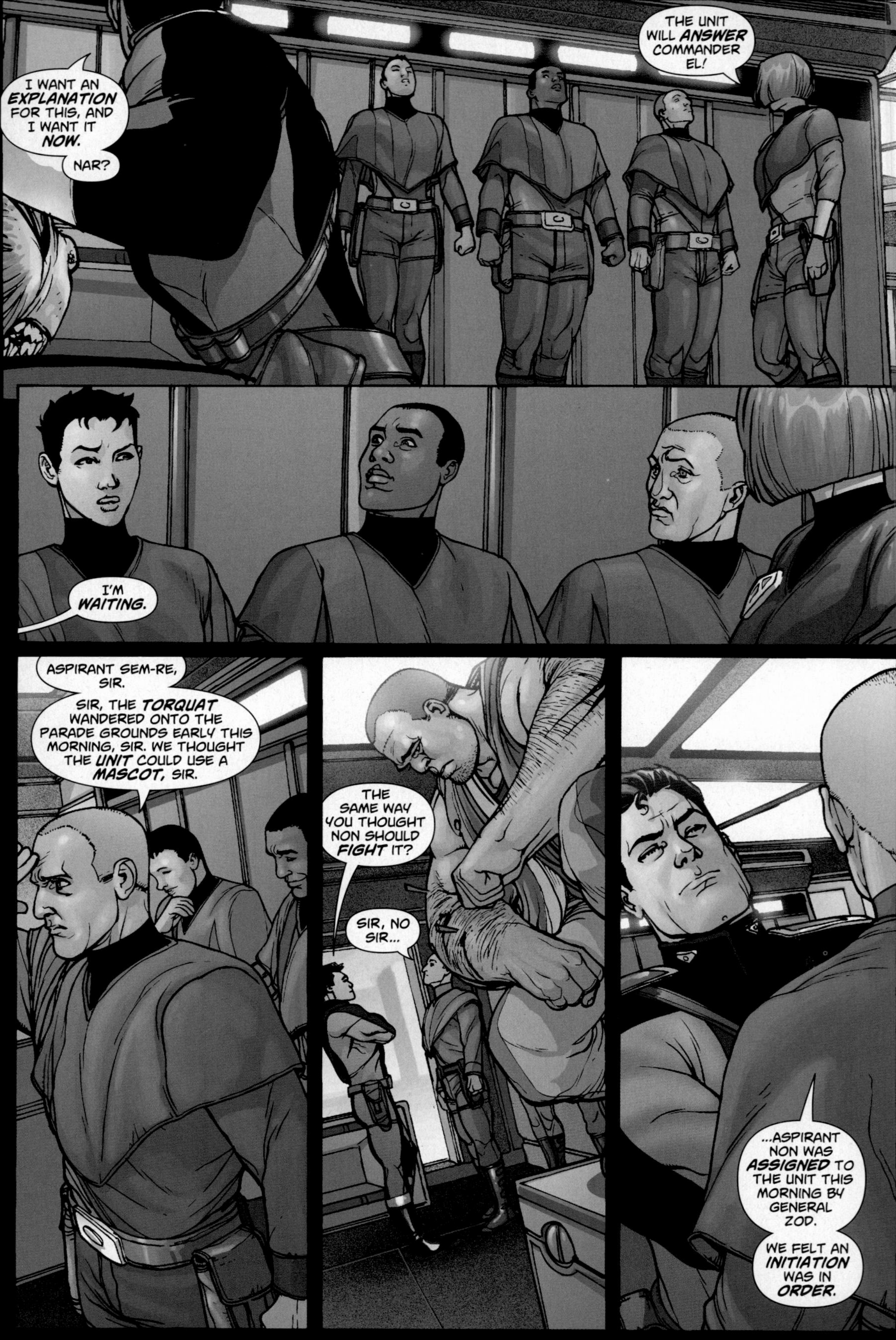
I WANT AN EXPLANATION FOR THIS, AND I WANT IT NOW.
NAR?
THE UNIT WILL ANSWER COMMANDER EL!
I'M WAITING.
ASPIRANT SEM-RE, SIR.
SIR, THE TORQUAT WANDERED ONTO THE PARADE GROUNDS EARLY THIS MORNING, SIR. WE THOUGHT THE UNIT COULD USE A MASCOT, SIR.
THE SAME WAY YOU THOUGHT NON SHOULD FIGHT IT?
SIR, NO SIR...
...ASPIRANT NON WAS ASSIGNED TO THE UNIT THIS MORNING BY GENERAL ZOD.
WE FELT AN INITIATION WAS IN ORDER.

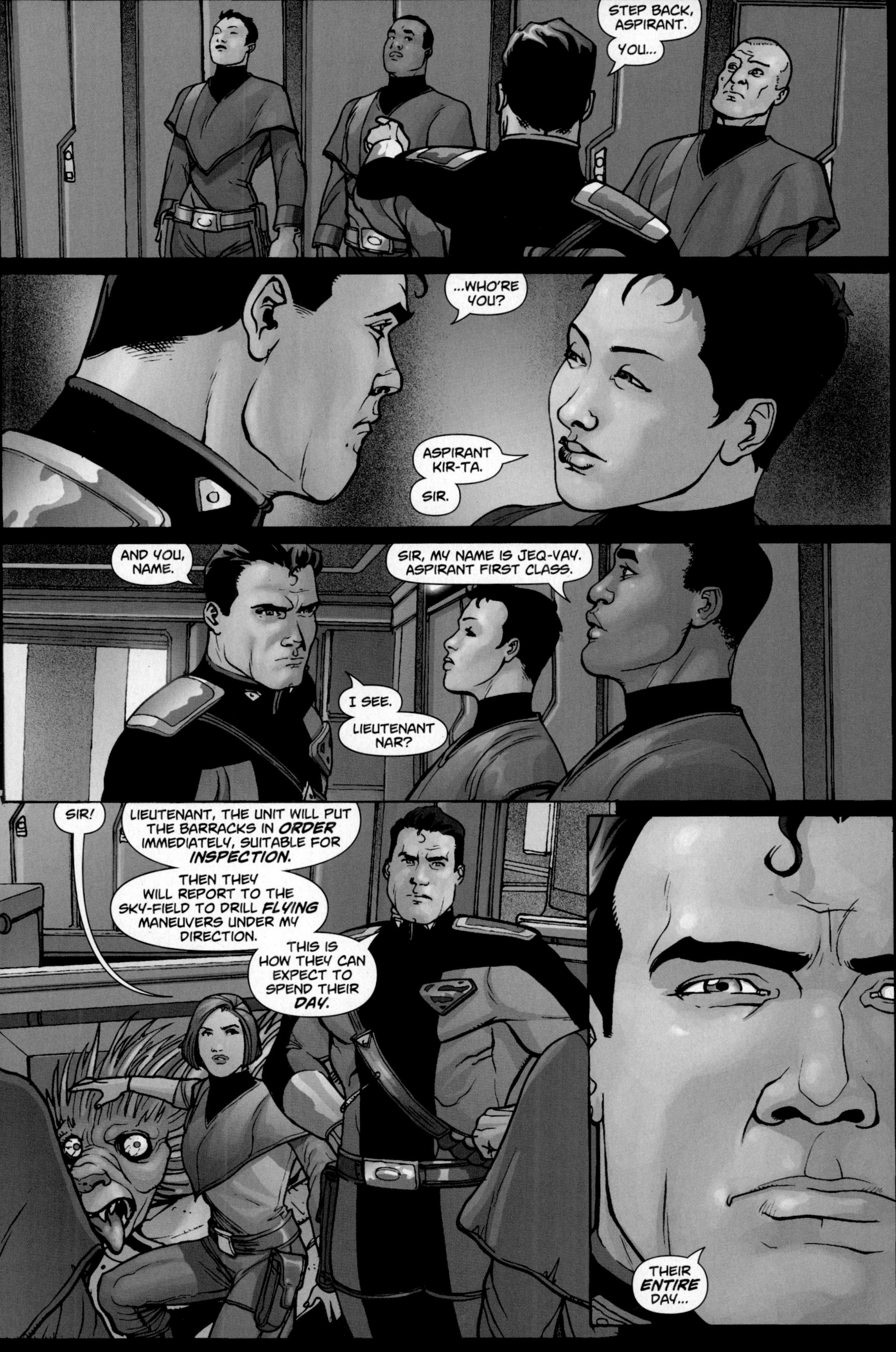
STEP BACK, ASPIRANT.
YOU...
...WHO'RE YOU?
ASPIRANT KIR-TA.
SIR.
AND YOU, NAME.
SIR, MY NAME IS JEQ-VAY. ASPIRANT FIRST CLASS.
I SEE.
LIEUTENANT NAR?
SIR!
LIEUTENANT, THE UNIT WILL PUT THE BARRACKS IN ORDER IMMEDIATELY, SUITABLE FOR INSPECTION.
THEN THEY WILL REPORT TO THE SKY-FIELD TO DRILL FLYING MANEUVERS UNDER MY DIRECTION.
THIS IS HOW THEY CAN EXPECT TO SPEND THEIR DAY.
THEIR ENTIRE DAY...

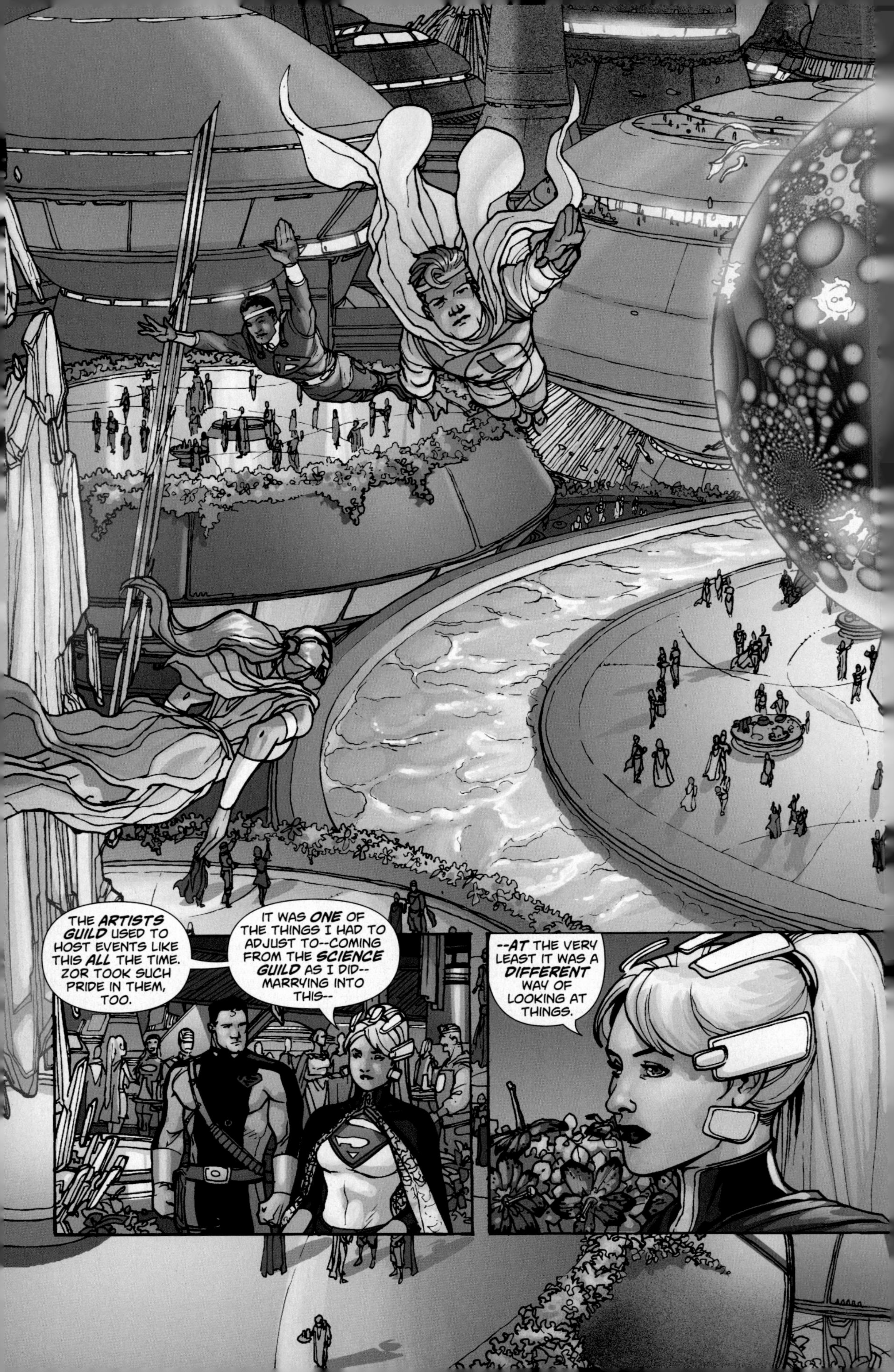
THE ARTISTS GUILD USED TO HOST EVENTS LIKE THIS ALL THE TIME. ZOR TOOK SUCH PRIDE IN THEM, TOO.
IT WAS ONE OF THE THINGS I HAD TO ADJUST TO--COMING FROM THE SCIENCE GUILD AS I DID--MARRYING INTO THIS--
--AT THE VERY LEAST IT WAS A DIFFERENT WAY OF LOOKING AT THINGS.

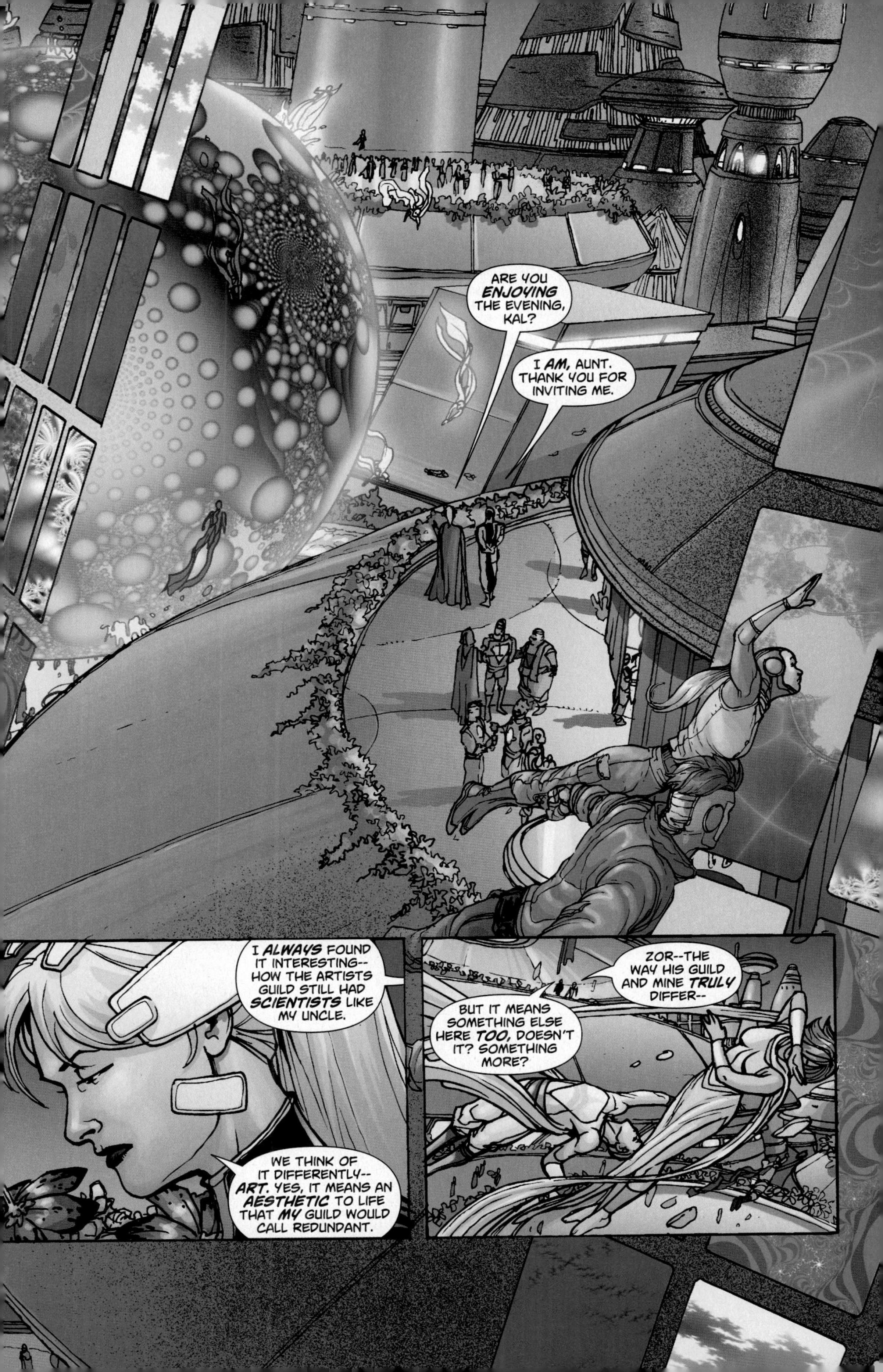
ARE YOU ENJOYING THE EVENING, KAL?
I AM, AUNT. THANK YOU FOR INVITING ME.
I ALWAYS FOUND IT INTERESTING-- HOW THE ARTISTS GUILD STILL HAD SCIENTISTS LIKE MY UNCLE.
WE THINK OF IT DIFFERENTLY-- ART. YES, IT MEANS AN AESTHETIC TO LIFE THAT MY GUILD WOULD CALL REDUNDANT.
BUT IT MEANS SOMETHING ELSE HERE TOO, DOESN'T IT? SOMETHING MORE?
ZOR--THE WAY HIS GUILD AND MINE TRULY DIFFER--

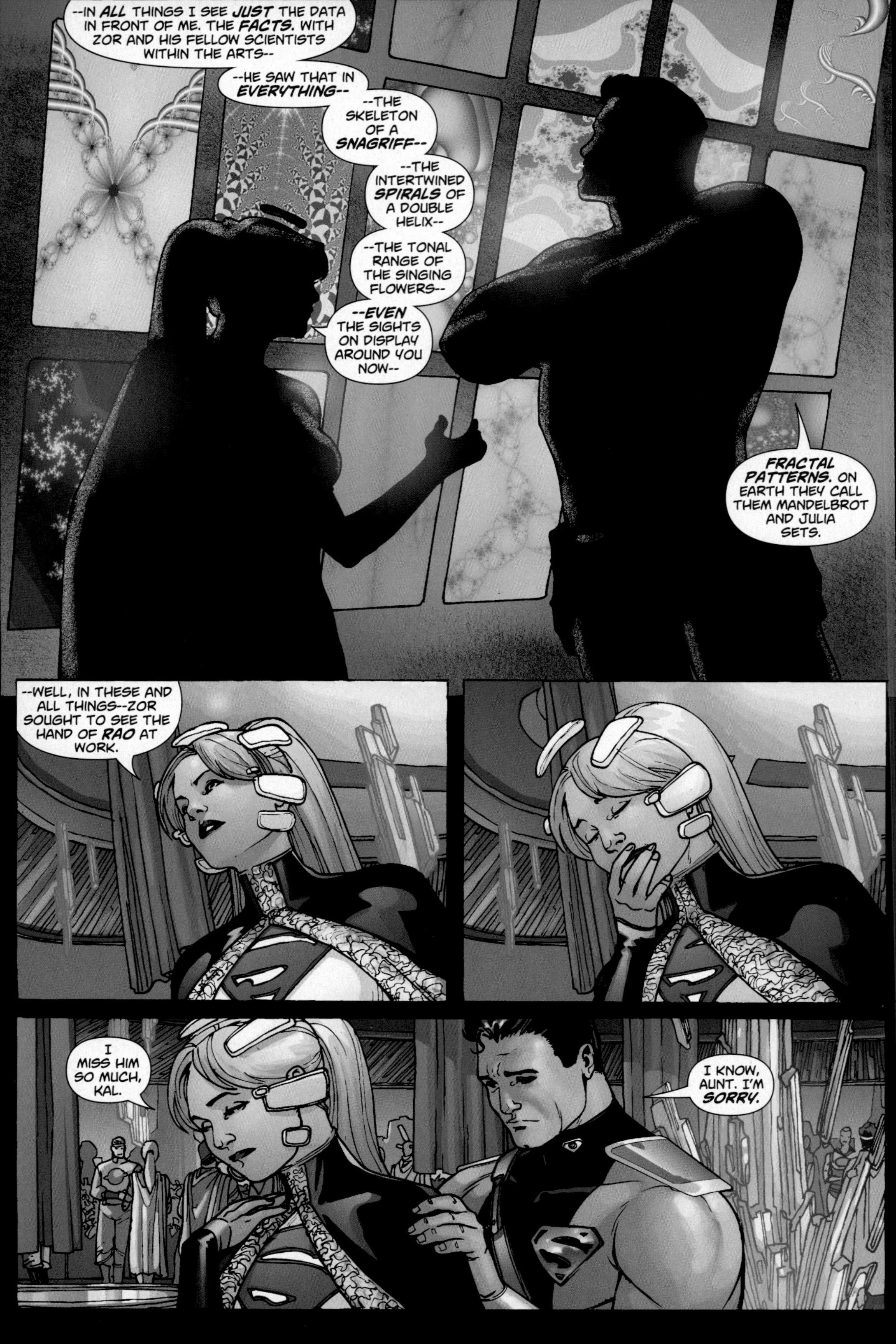
--IN ALL THINGS I SEE JUST THE DATA IN FRONT OF ME. THE FACTS. WITH ZOR AND HIS FELLOW SCIENTISTS WITHIN THE ARTS--
--HE SAW THAT IN EVERYTHING--
--THE SKELETON OF A SNAGRIFF--
--THE INTERTWINED SPIRALS OF A DOUBLE HELIX--
--THE TONAL RANGE OF THE SINGING FLOWERS--
--EVEN THE SIGHTS ON DISPLAY AROUND YOU NOW--
FRACTAL PATTERNS. ON EARTH THEY CALL THEM MANDELBROT AND JULIA SETS.
--WELL, IN THESE AND ALL THINGS--ZOR SOUGHT TO SEE THE HAND OF RAO AT WORK.
I MISS HIM SO MUCH, KAL.
I KNOW, AUNT. I'M SORRY.

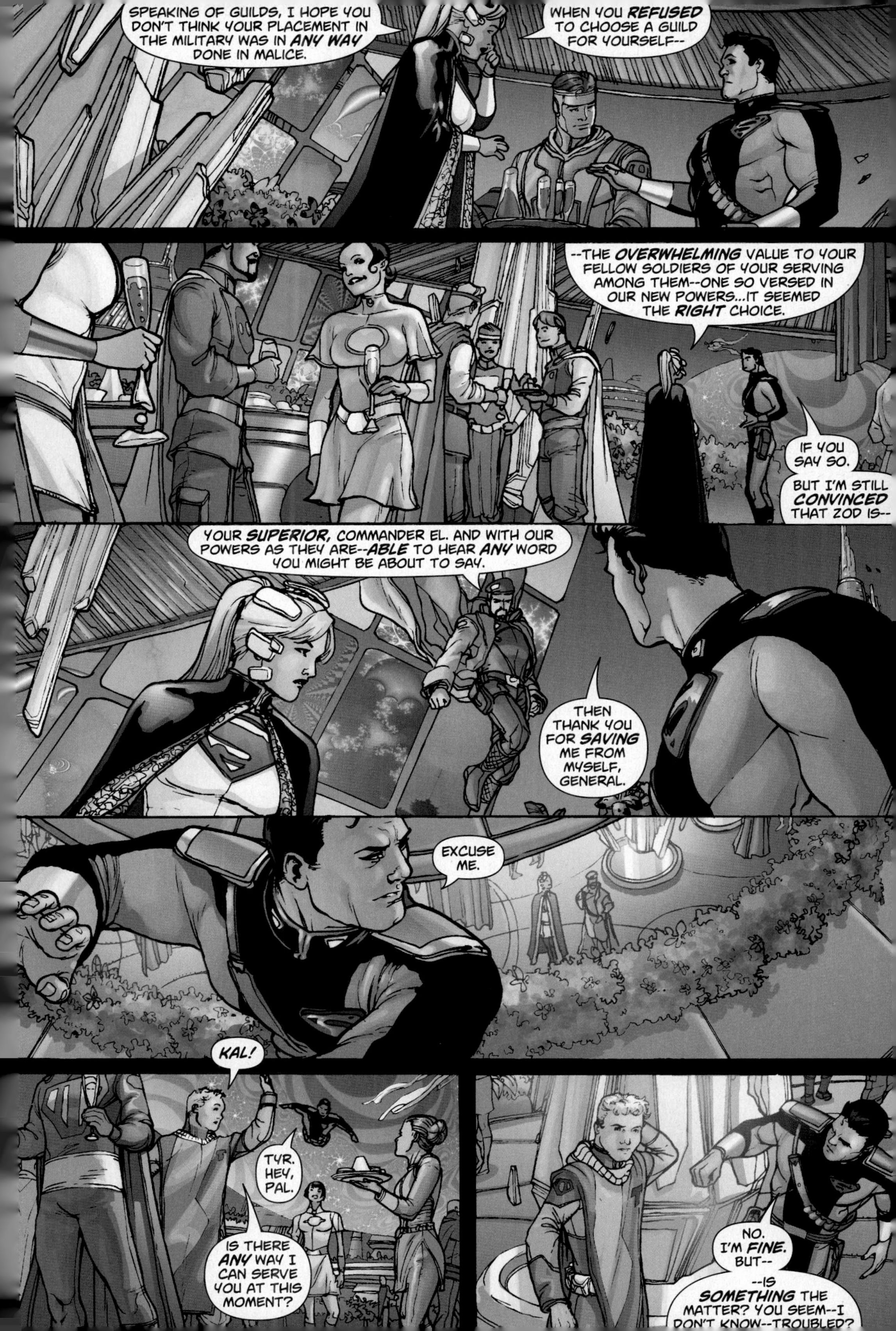
SPEAKING OF GUILDS, I HOPE YOU DON'T THINK YOUR PLACEMENT IN THE MILITARY WAS IN ANY WAY DONE IN MALICE.
WHEN YOU REFUSED TO CHOOSE A GUILD FOR YOURSELF--
--THE OVERWHELMING VALUE TO YOUR FELLOW SOLDIERS OF YOUR SERVING AMONG THEM--ONE SO VERSED IN OUR NEW POWERS...IT SEEMED THE RIGHT CHOICE.
IF YOU SAY SO.
BUT I'M STILL CONVINCED THAT ZOD IS--
YOUR SUPERIOR, COMMANDER EL. AND WITH OUR POWERS AS THEY ARE--ABLE TO HEAR ANY WORD YOU MIGHT BE ABOUT TO SAY.
THEN THANK YOU FOR SAVING ME FROM MYSELF, GENERAL.
EXCUSE ME.
KAL!
TYR. HEY, PAL.
IS THERE ANY WAY I CAN SERVE YOU AT THIS MOMENT?
NO. I'M FINE. BUT--
--IS SOMETHING THE MATTER? YOU SEEM--I DON'T KNOW--TROUBLED?

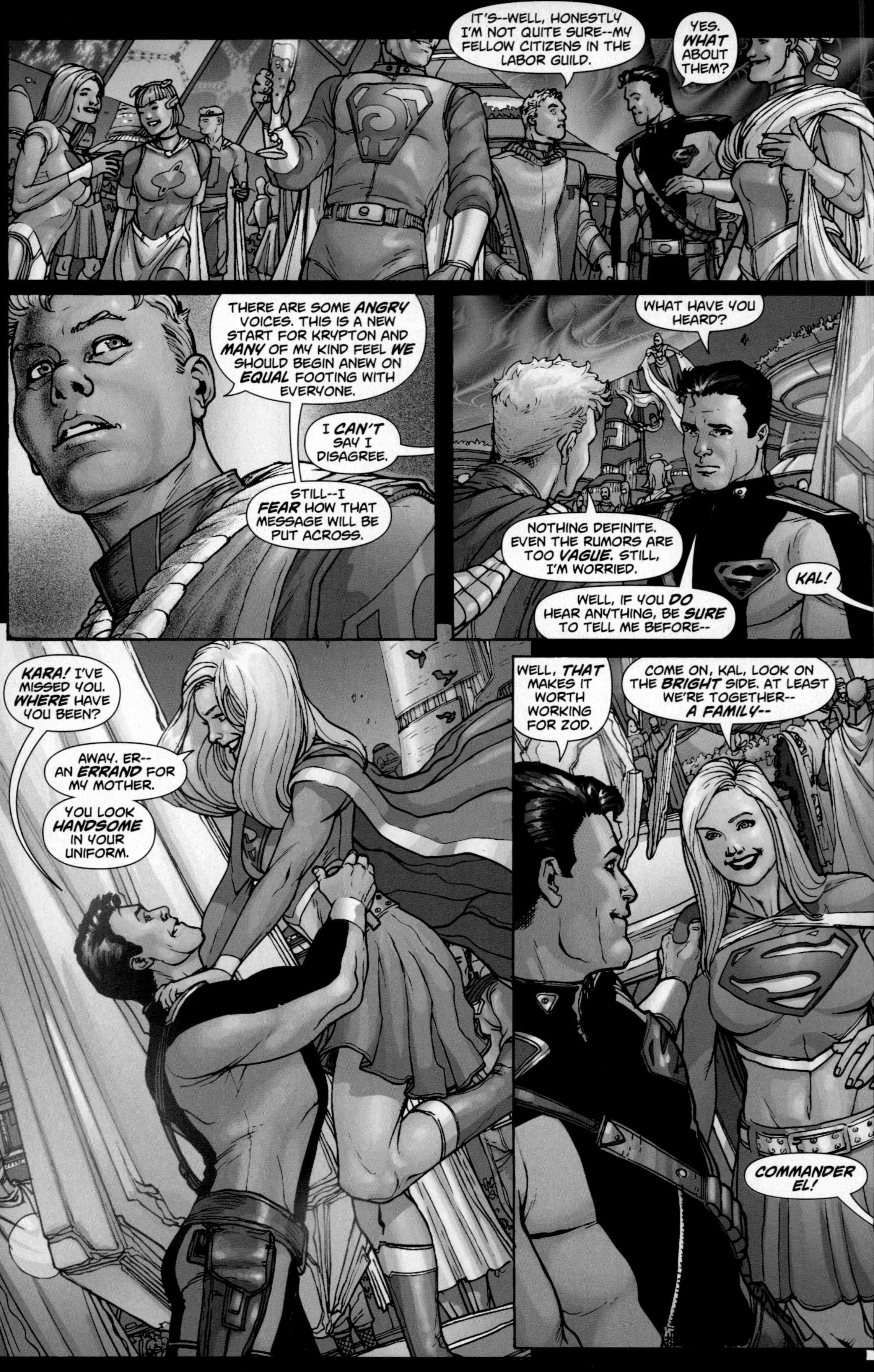
IT'S--WELL, HONESTLY I'M NOT QUITE SURE--MY FELLOW CITIZENS IN THE LABOR GUILD.
YES. WHAT ABOUT THEM?
THERE ARE SOME ANGRY VOICES. THIS IS A NEW START FOR KRYPTON AND MANY OF MY KIND FEEL WE SHOULD BEGIN ANEW ON EQUAL FOOTING WITH EVERYONE.
I CAN'T SAY I DISAGREE.
STILL--I FEAR HOW THAT MESSAGE WILL BE PUT ACROSS.
WHAT HAVE YOU HEARD?
NOTHING DEFINITE. EVEN THE RUMORS ARE TOO VAGUE. STILL, I'M WORRIED.
WELL, IF YOU DO HEAR ANYTHING, BE SURE TO TELL ME BEFORE--
KAL!
KARA! I'VE MISSED YOU. WHERE HAVE YOU BEEN?
AWAY. ER-- AN ERRAND FOR MY MOTHER.
YOU LOOK HANDSOME IN YOUR UNIFORM.
WELL, THAT MAKES IT WORTH WORKING FOR ZOD.
COME ON, KAL, LOOK ON THE BRIGHT SIDE. AT LEAST WE'RE TOGETHER-- A FAMILY--
COMMANDER EL!

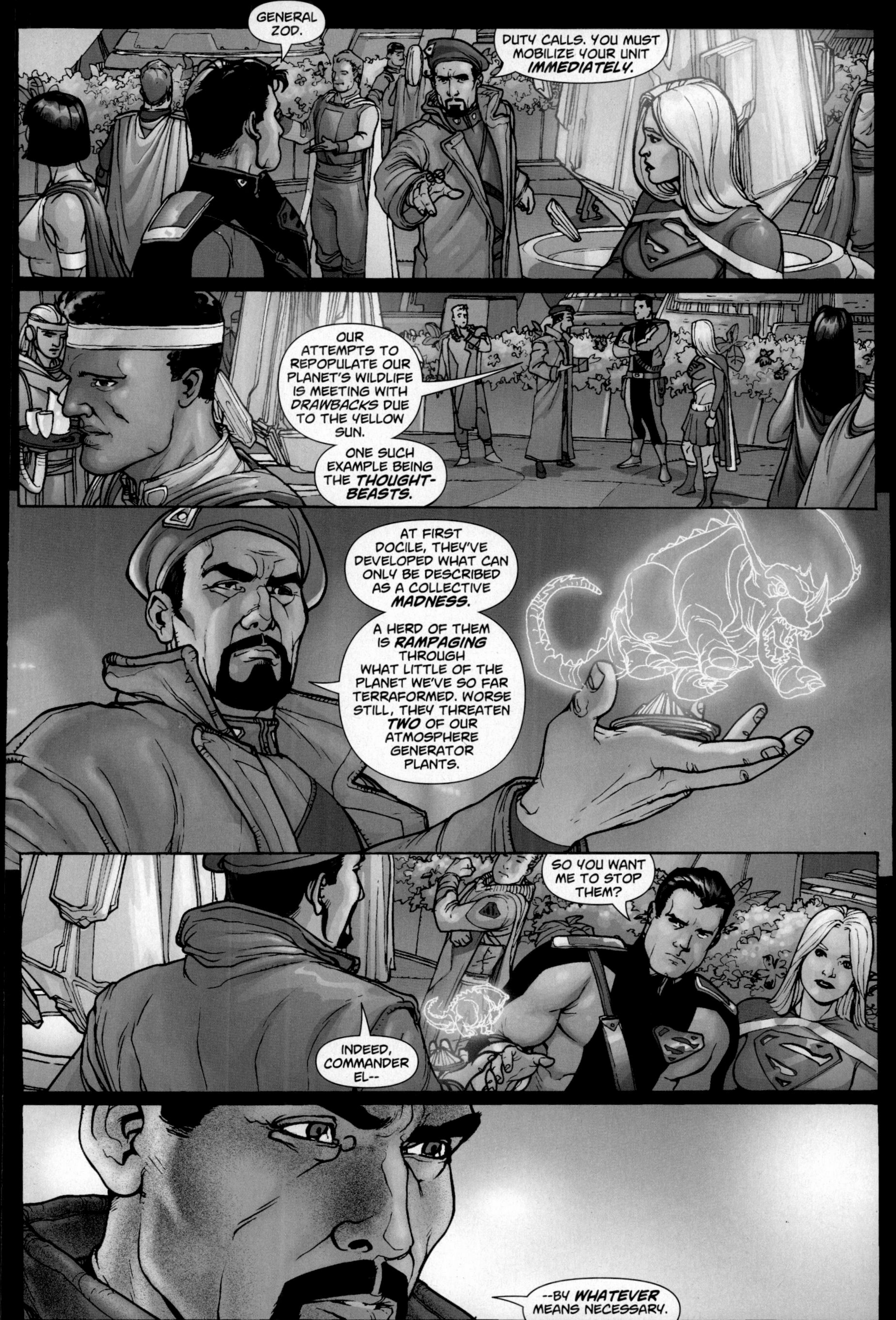
GENERAL ZOD.
DUTY CALLS. YOU MUST MOBILIZE YOUR UNIT IMMEDIATELY.
OUR ATTEMPTS TO REPOPULATE OUR PLANET'S WILDLIFE IS MEETING WITH DRAWBACKS DUE TO THE YELLOW SUN.
ONE SUCH EXAMPLE BEING THE THOUGHT-BEASTS.
AT FIRST DOCILE, THEY'VE DEVELOPED WHAT CAN ONLY BE DESCRIBED AS A COLLECTIVE MADNESS.
A HERD OF THEM IS RAMPAGING THROUGH WHAT LITTLE OF THE PLANET WE'VE SO FAR TERRAFORMED. WORSE STILL, THEY THREATEN TWO OF OUR ATMOSPHERE GENERATOR PLANTS.
SO YOU WANT ME TO STOP THEM?
INDEED, COMMANDER EL--
--BY WHATEVER MEANS NECESSARY.

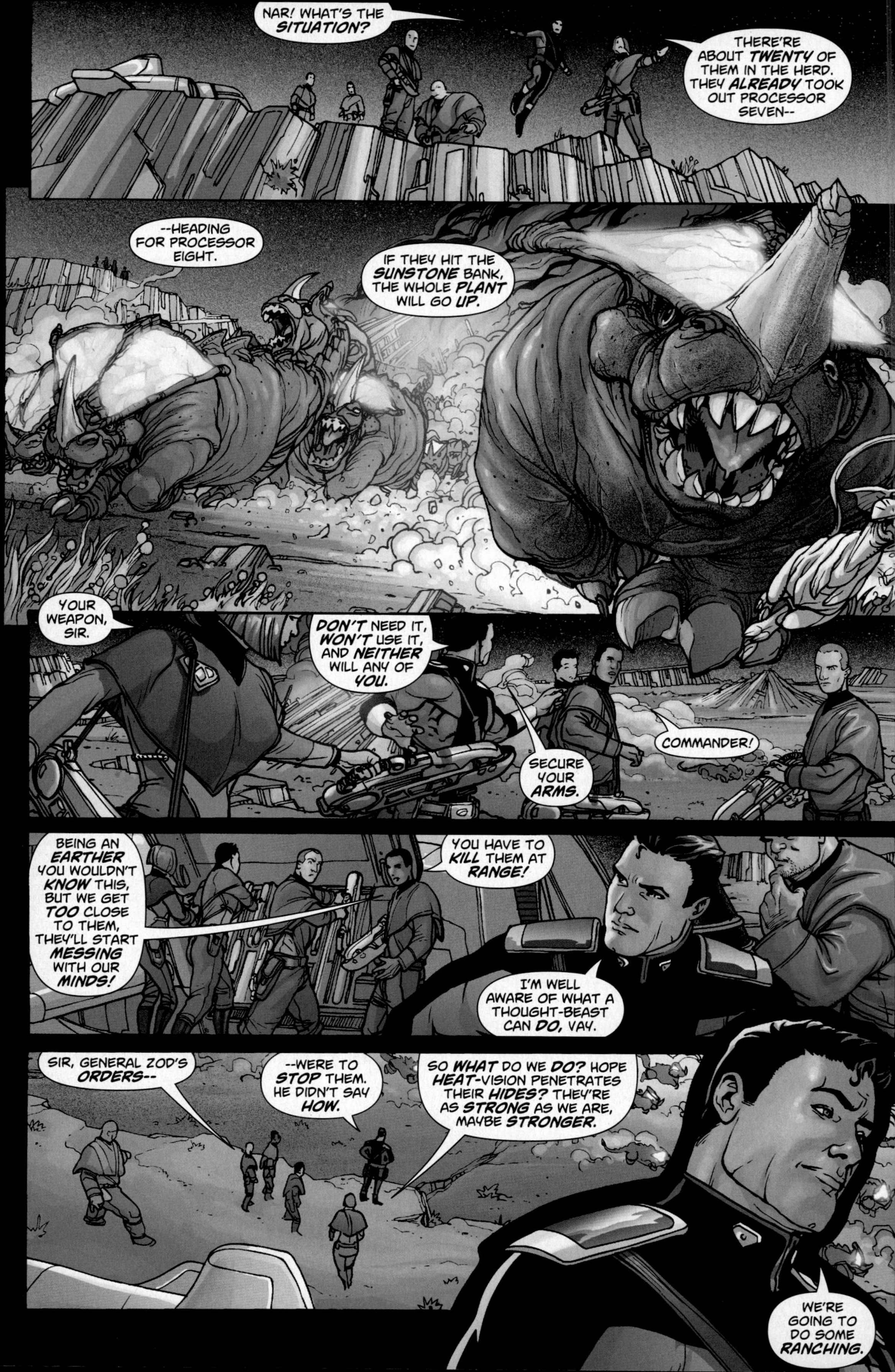
NAR! WHAT'S THE SITUATION?
THERE'RE ABOUT TWENTY OF THEM IN THE HERD. THEY ALREADY TOOK OUT PROCESSOR SEVEN--
--HEADING FOR PROCESSOR EIGHT.
IF THEY HIT THE SUNSTONE BANK, THE WHOLE PLANT WILL GO UP.
YOUR WEAPON, SIR.
DON'T NEED IT, WON'T USE IT, AND NEITHER WILL ANY OF YOU.
SECURE YOUR ARMS.
COMMANDER!
BEING AN EARTHER YOU WOULDN'T KNOW THIS, BUT WE GET TOO CLOSE TO THEM, THEY'LL START MESSING WITH OUR MINDS!
YOU HAVE TO KILL THEM AT RANGE!
I'M WELL AWARE OF WHAT A THOUGHT-BEAST CAN DO, VAY.
SIR, GENERAL ZOD'S ORDERS--
--WERE TO STOP THEM. HE DIDN'T SAY HOW.
SO WHAT DO WE DO? HOPE HEAT-VISION PENETRATES THEIR HIDES? THEY'RE AS STRONG AS WE ARE, MAYBE STRONGER.
WE'RE GOING TO DO SOME RANCHING.

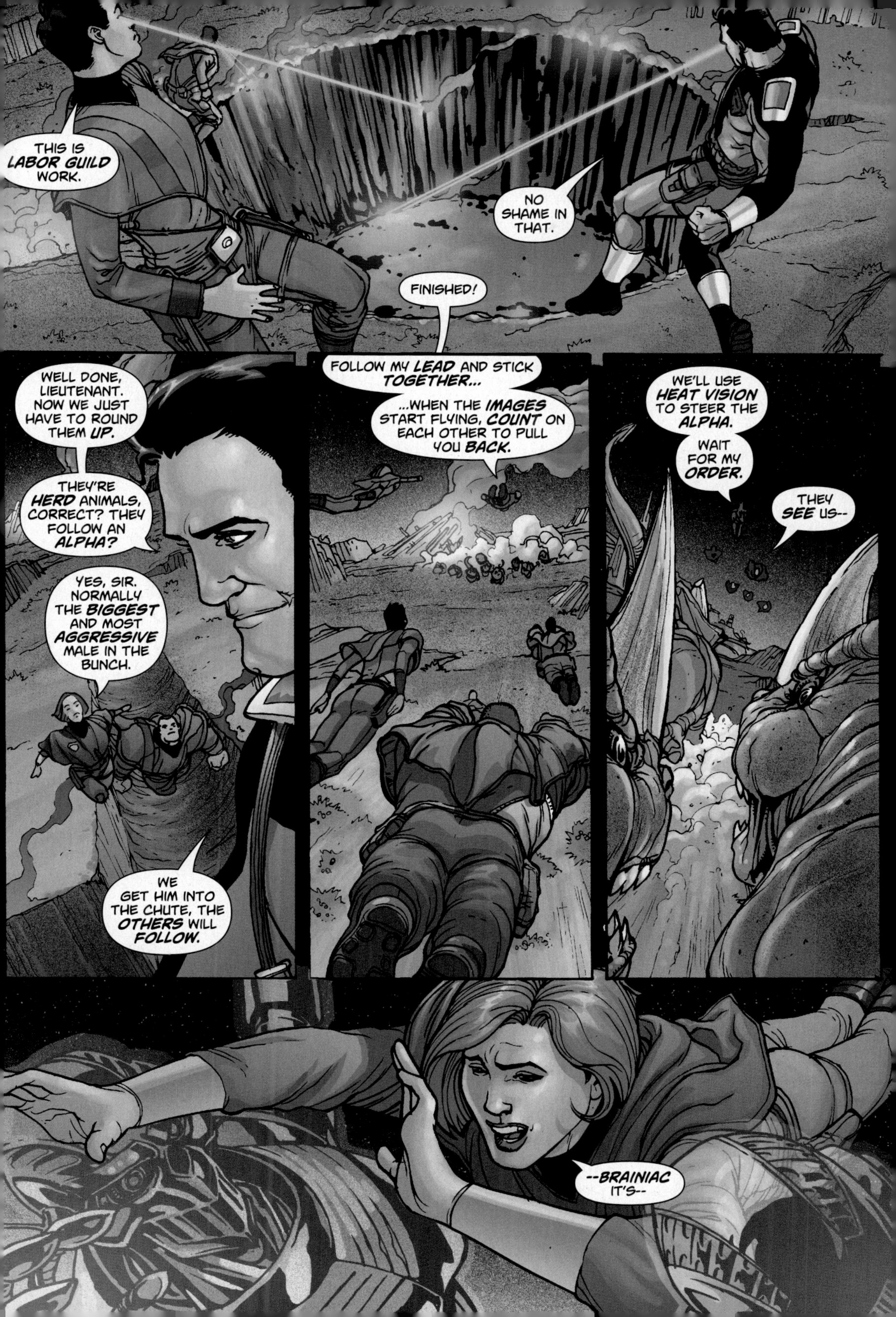
THIS IS LABOR GUILD WORK.
NO SHAME IN THAT.
FINISHED!
WELL DONE, LIEUTENANT. NOW WE JUST HAVE TO ROUND THEM UP.
THEY'RE HERD ANIMALS, CORRECT? THEY FOLLOW AN ALPHA?
YES, SIR. NORMALLY THE BIGGEST AND MOST AGGRESSIVE MALE IN THE BUNCH.
WE GET HIM INTO THE CHUTE, THE OTHERS WILL FOLLOW.
FOLLOW MY LEAD AND STICK TOGETHER...
...WHEN THE IMAGES START FLYING, COUNT ON EACH OTHER TO PULL YOU BACK.
WE'LL USE HEAT VISION TO STEER THE ALPHA.
WAIT FOR MY ORDER.
THEY SEE US--
--BRAINIAC IT'S--

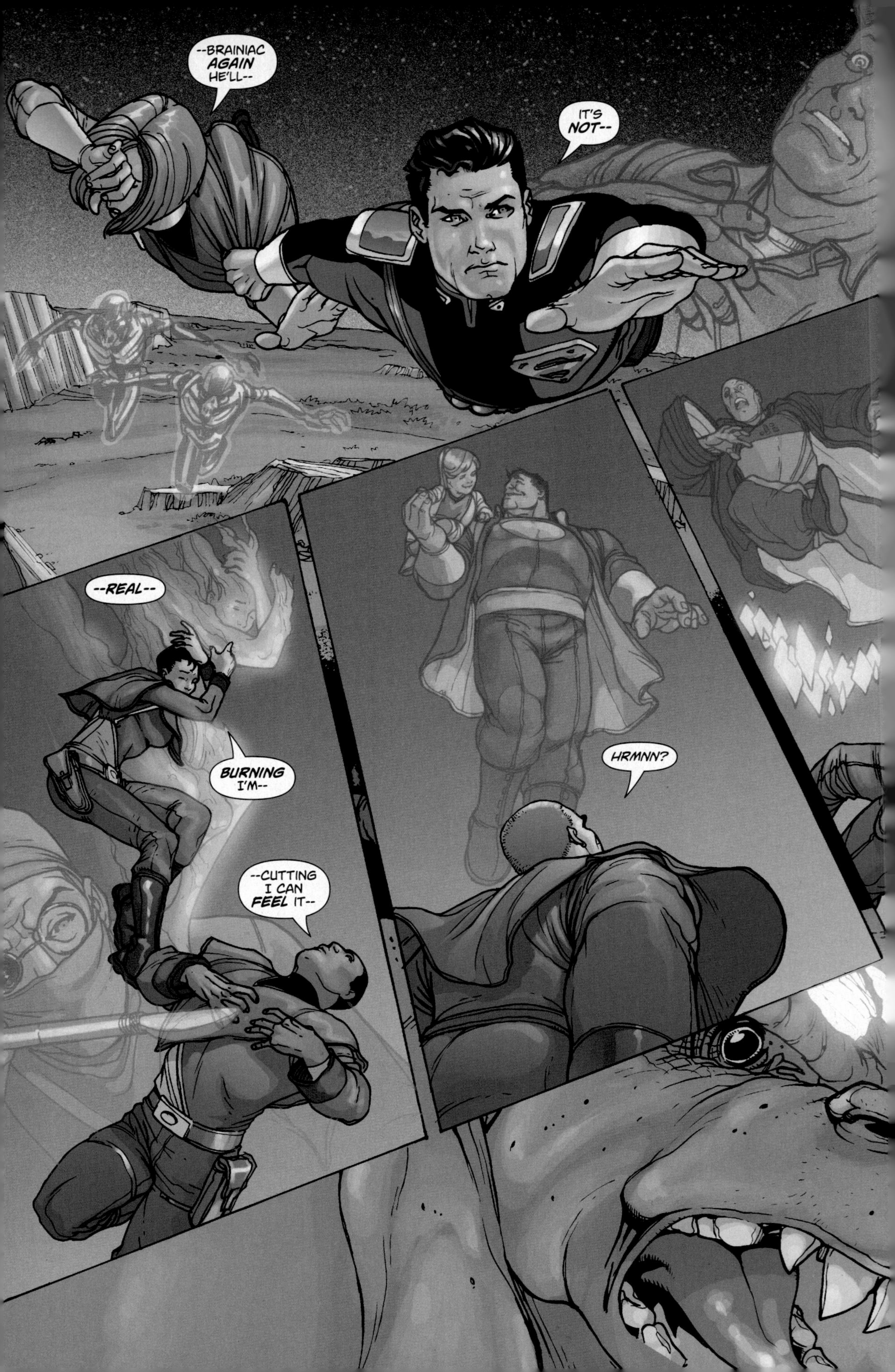
--BRAINIAC AGAIN HE'LL--
IT'S NOT--
--REAL--
BURNING I'M--
--CUTTING I CAN FEEL IT--
HRMNN?

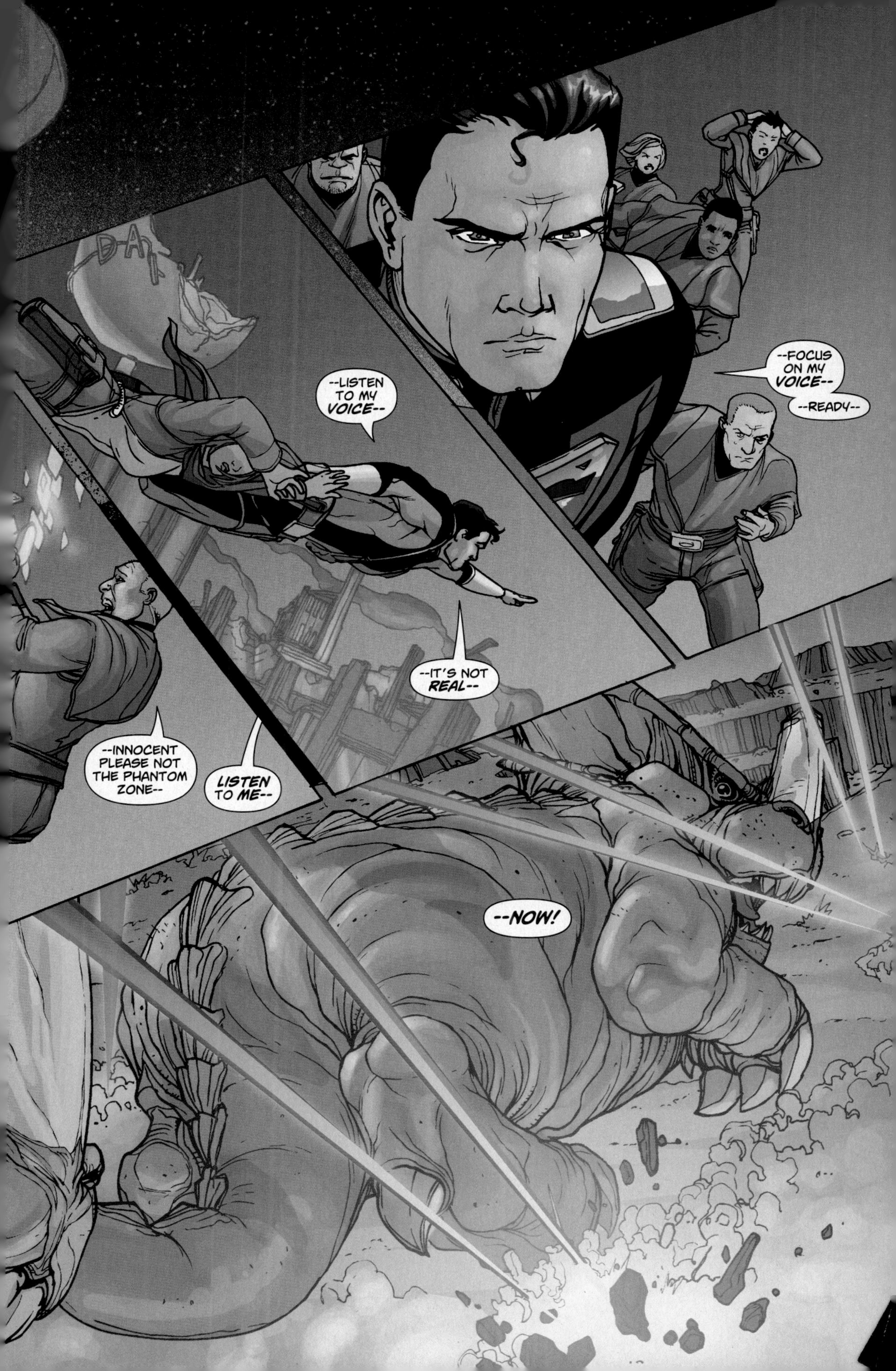
--FOCUS ON MY VOICE--
--READY--
--LISTEN TO MY VOICE--
--IT'S NOT REAL--
--INNOCENT PLEASE NOT THE PHANTOM ZONE--
LISTEN TO ME--
--NOW!

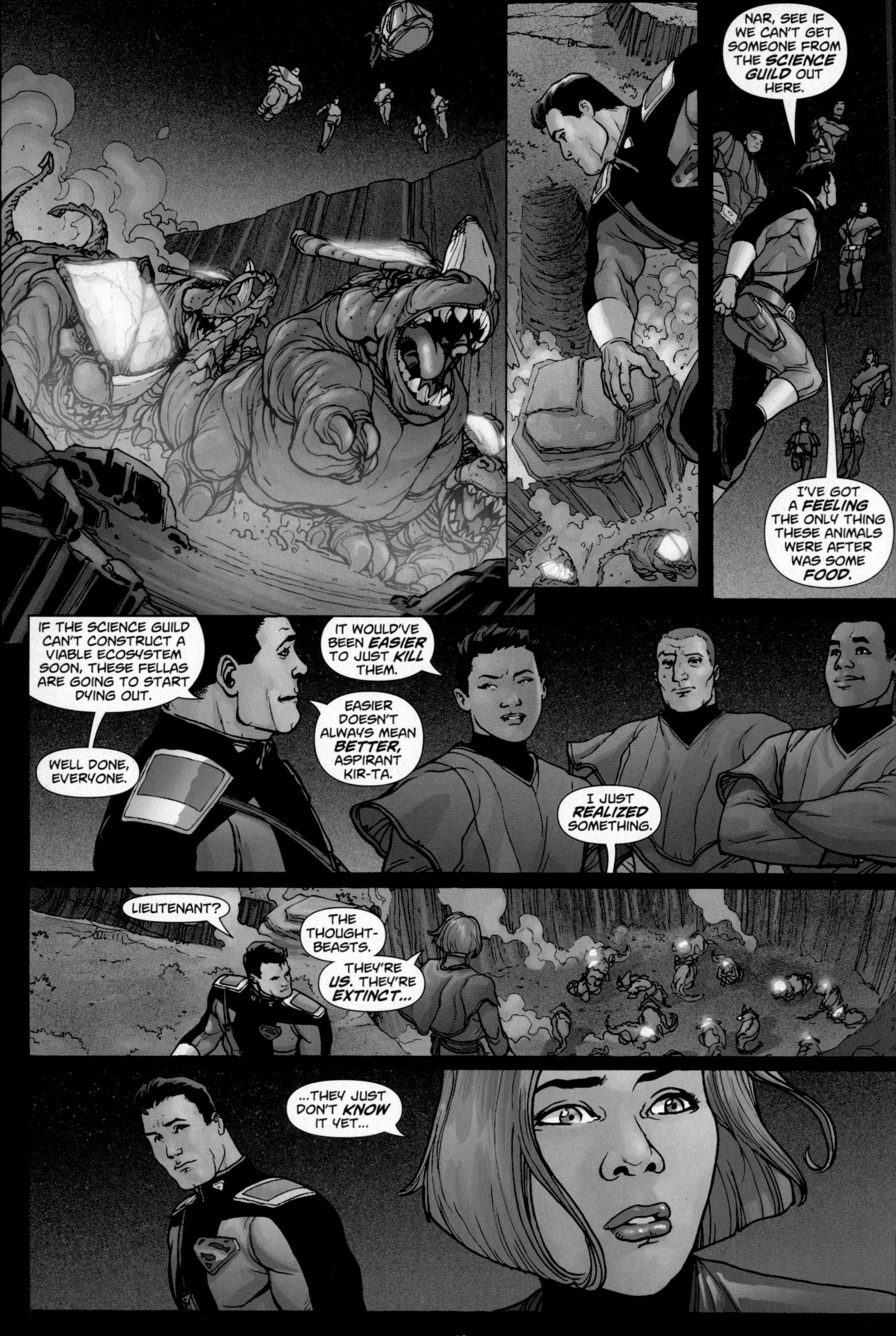
NAR, SEE IF WE CAN'T GET SOMEONE FROM THE SCIENCE GUILD OUT HERE.
I'VE GOT A FEELING THE ONLY THING THESE ANIMALS WERE AFTER WAS SOME FOOD.
IF THE SCIENCE GUILD CAN'T CONSTRUCT A VIABLE ECOSYSTEM SOON, THESE FELLAS ARE GOING TO START DYING OUT.
WELL DONE, EVERYONE.
IT WOULD'VE BEEN EASIER TO JUST KILL THEM.
EASIER DOESN'T ALWAYS MEAN BETTER, ASPIRANT KIR-TA.
I JUST REALIZED SOMETHING.
LIEUTENANT?
THE THOUGHT-BEASTS.
THEY'RE US. THEY'RE EXTINCT...
...THEY JUST DON'T KNOW IT YET...

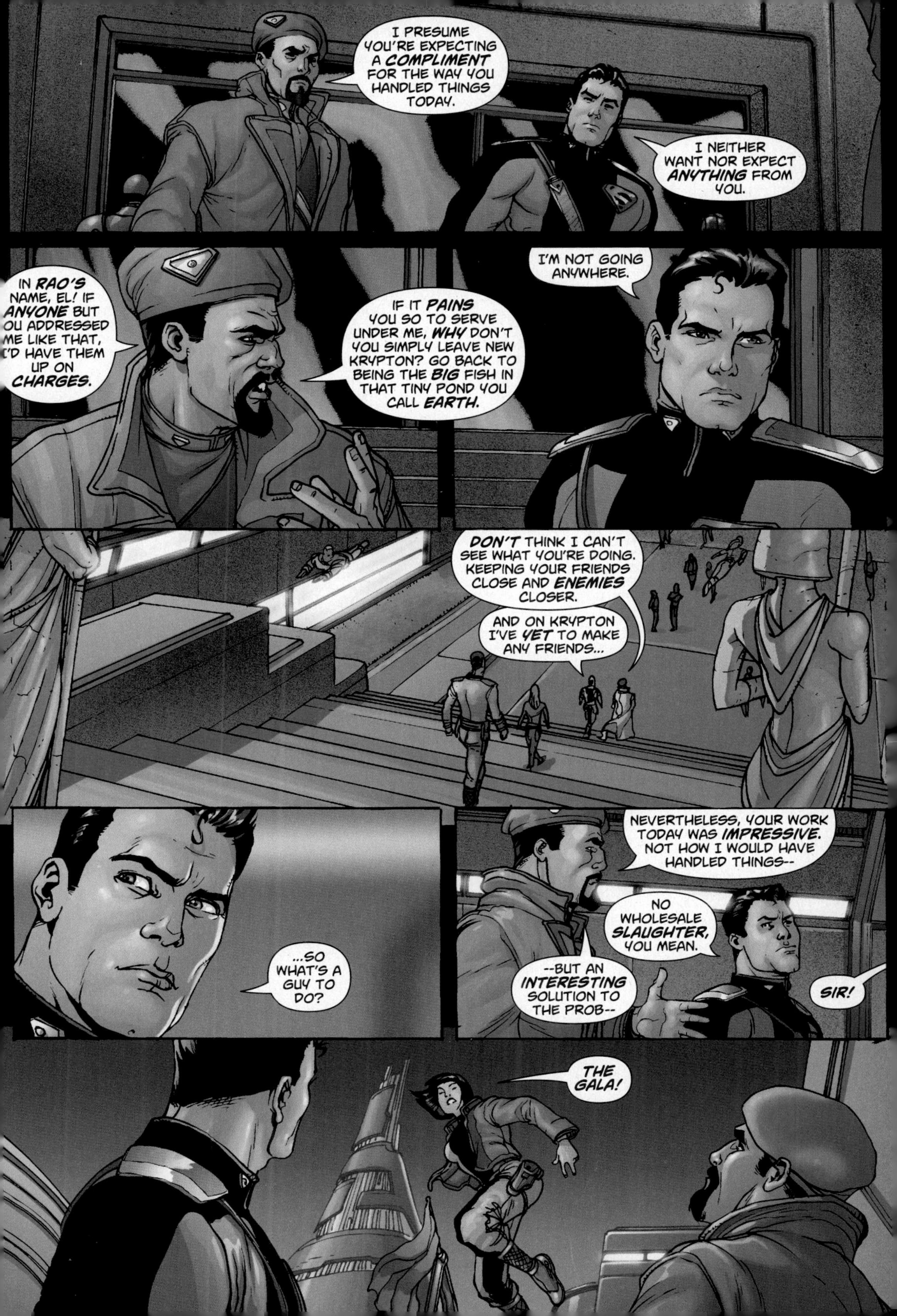
I PRESUME YOU'RE EXPECTING A **COMPLIMENT** FOR THE WAY YOU HANDLED THINGS TODAY.
I NEITHER WANT NOR EXPECT **ANYTHING** FROM YOU.
IN **RAO'S** NAME, EL! IF **ANYONE** BUT YOU ADDRESSED ME LIKE THAT, I'D HAVE THEM UP ON **CHARGES**.
IF IT **PAINS** YOU SO TO SERVE UNDER ME, **WHY** DON'T YOU SIMPLY LEAVE NEW KRYPTON? GO BACK TO BEING THE **BIG** FISH IN THAT TINY POND YOU CALL **EARTH**.
I'M NOT GOING ANYWHERE.
DON'T THINK I CAN'T SEE WHAT YOU'RE DOING. KEEPING YOUR FRIENDS CLOSE AND **ENEMIES** CLOSER.
AND ON KRYPTON I'VE **YET** TO MAKE ANY FRIENDS...
...SO WHAT'S A GUY TO DO?
NEVERTHELESS, YOUR WORK TODAY WAS **IMPRESSIVE**. NOT HOW I WOULD HAVE HANDLED THINGS--
NO WHOLESALE **SLAUGHTER**, YOU MEAN.
--BUT AN **INTERESTING** SOLUTION TO THE PROB--
SIR!
THE GALA!

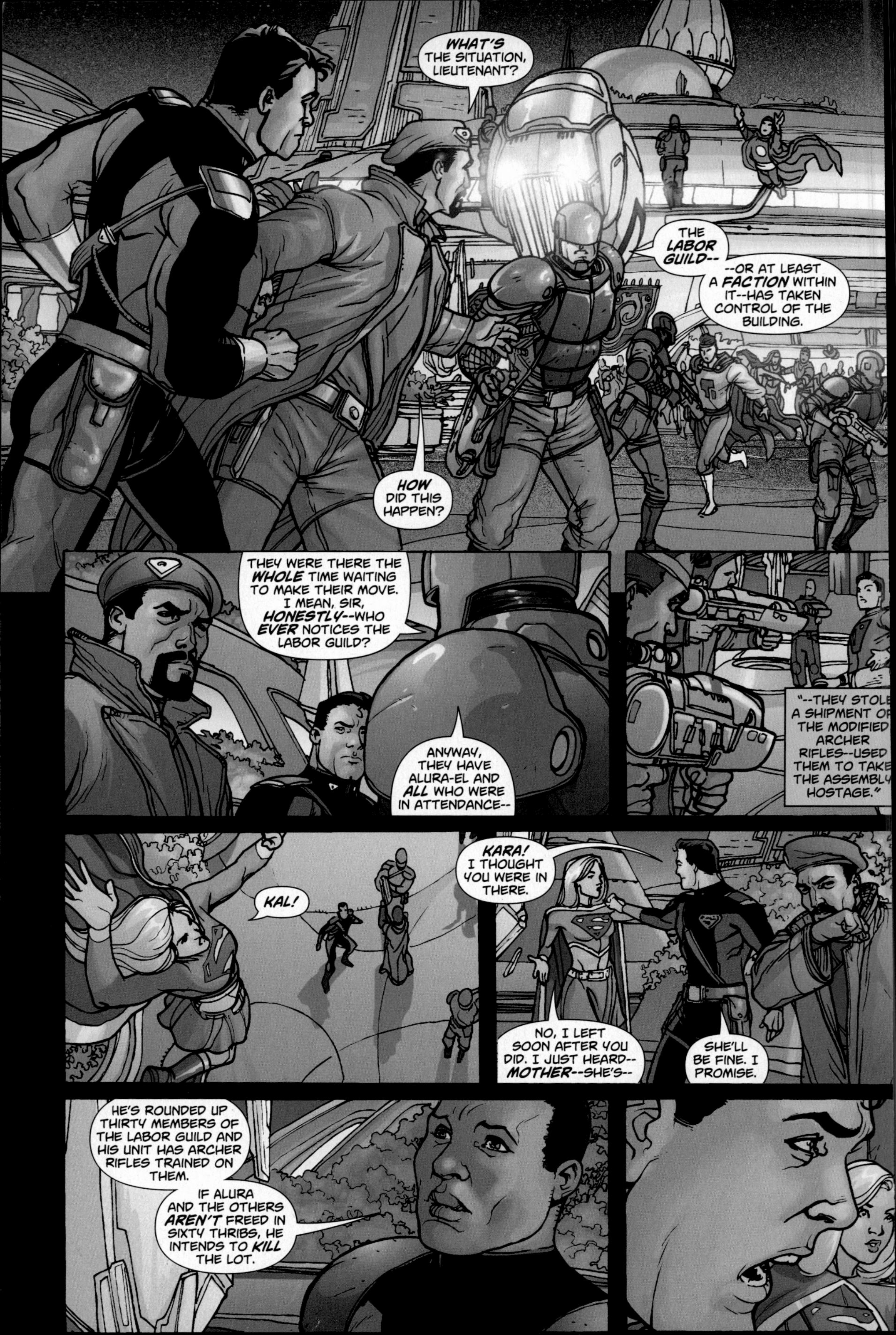
WHAT'S THE SITUATION, LIEUTENANT?
HOW DID THIS HAPPEN?
THE LABOR GUILD--
--OR AT LEAST A FACTION WITHIN IT--HAS TAKEN CONTROL OF THE BUILDING.
THEY WERE THERE THE WHOLE TIME WAITING TO MAKE THEIR MOVE. I MEAN, SIR, HONESTLY--WHO EVER NOTICES THE LABOR GUILD?
ANYWAY, THEY HAVE ALURA-EL AND ALL WHO WERE IN ATTENDANCE--
"--THEY STOLE A SHIPMENT OF THE MODIFIED ARCHER RIFLES--USED THEM TO TAKE THE ASSEMBLY HOSTAGE."
KAL!
KARA! I THOUGHT YOU WERE IN THERE.
NO, I LEFT SOON AFTER YOU DID. I JUST HEARD-- MOTHER--SHE'S--
SHE'LL BE FINE. I PROMISE.
HE'S ROUNDED UP THIRTY MEMBERS OF THE LABOR GUILD AND HIS UNIT HAS ARCHER RIFLES TRAINED ON THEM.
IF ALURA AND THE OTHERS AREN'T FREED IN SIXTY THRIBS, HE INTENDS TO KILL THE LOT.

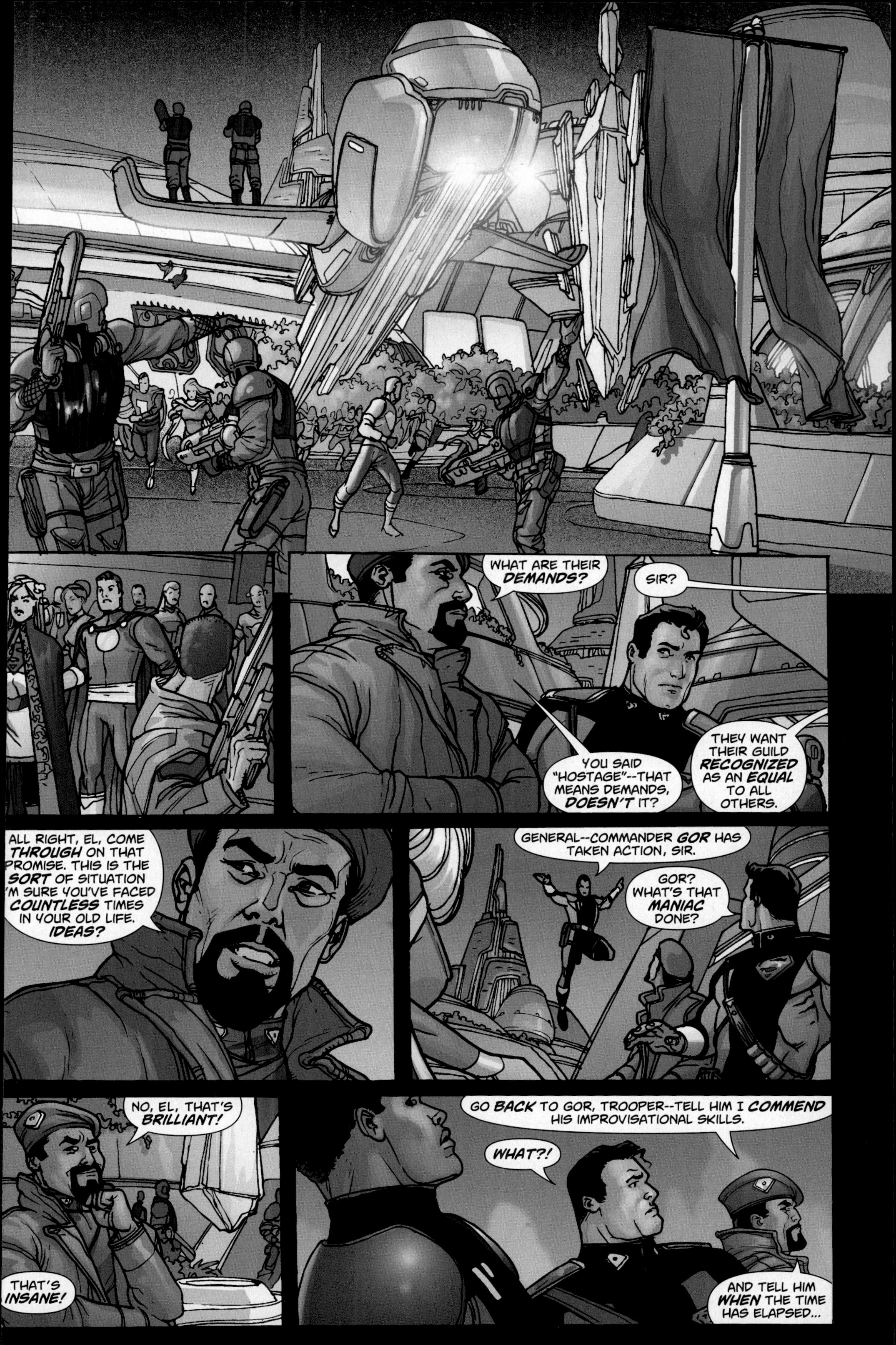
WHAT ARE THEIR DEMANDS?
SIR?
YOU SAID "HOSTAGE"--THAT MEANS DEMANDS, DOESN'T IT?
THEY WANT THEIR GUILD RECOGNIZED AS AN EQUAL TO ALL OTHERS.
ALL RIGHT, EL, COME THROUGH ON THAT PROMISE. THIS IS THE SORT OF SITUATION I'M SURE YOU'VE FACED COUNTLESS TIMES IN YOUR OLD LIFE. IDEAS?
GENERAL--COMMANDER GOR HAS TAKEN ACTION, SIR.
GOR? WHAT'S THAT MANIAC DONE?
NO, EL, THAT'S BRILLIANT!
THAT'S INSANE!
GO BACK TO GOR, TROOPER--TELL HIM I COMMEND HIS IMPROVISATIONAL SKILLS.
WHAT?!
AND TELL HIM WHEN THE TIME HAS ELAPSED...

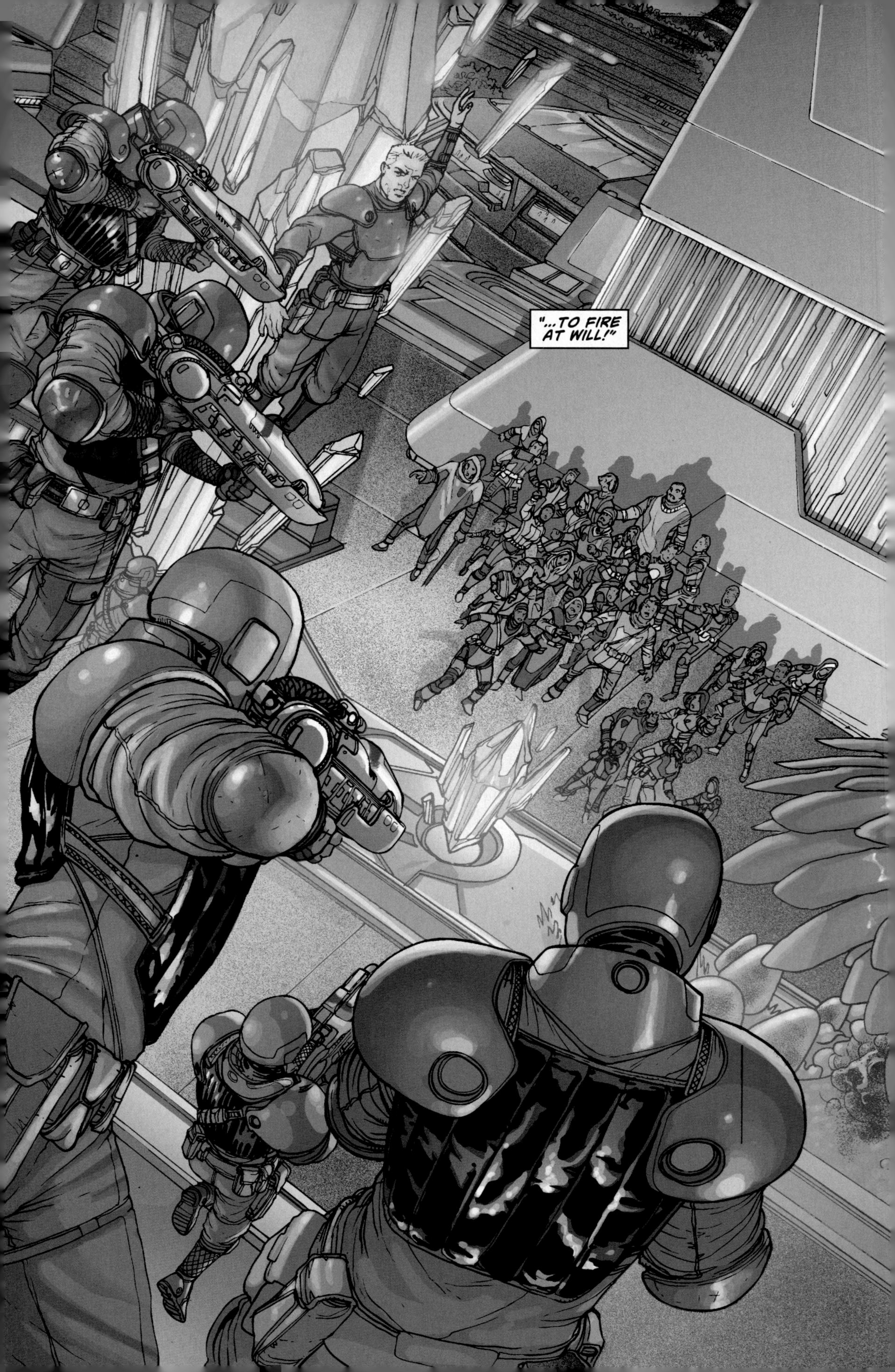
"...TO FIRE AT WILL!"

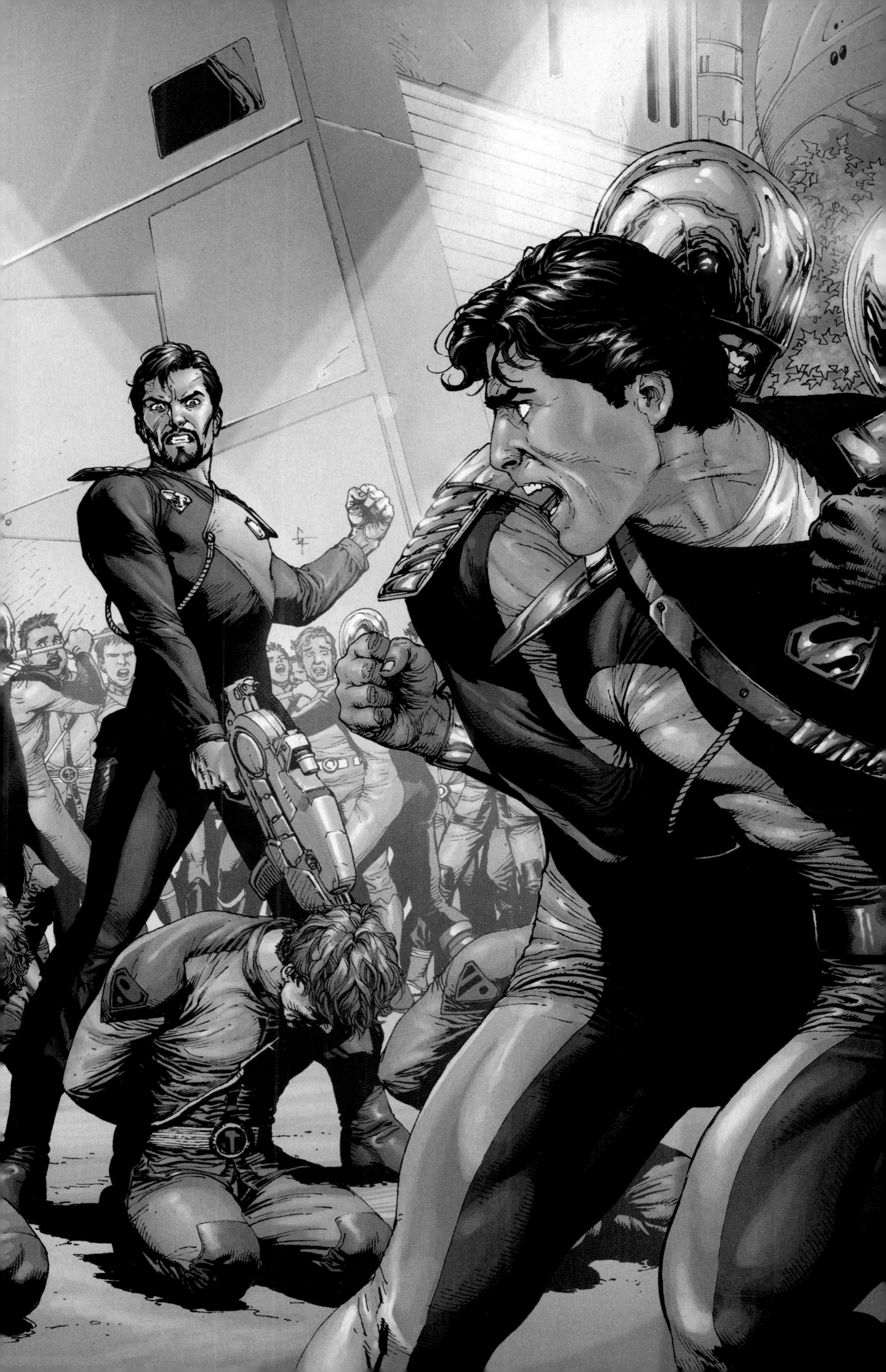

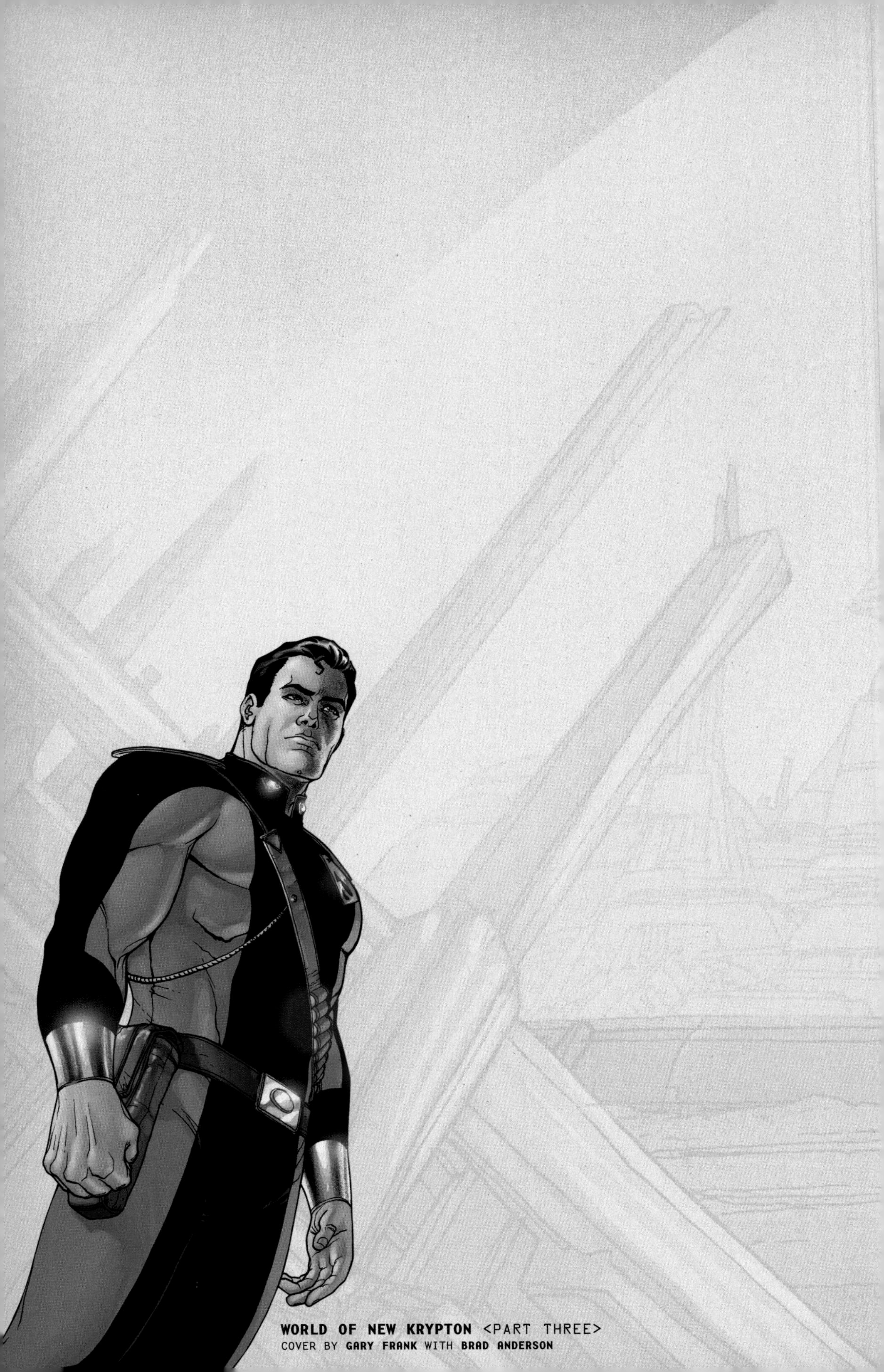

WORLD OF NEW KRYPTON <PART THREE>
COVER BY **GARY FRANK** WITH **BRAD ANDERSON**

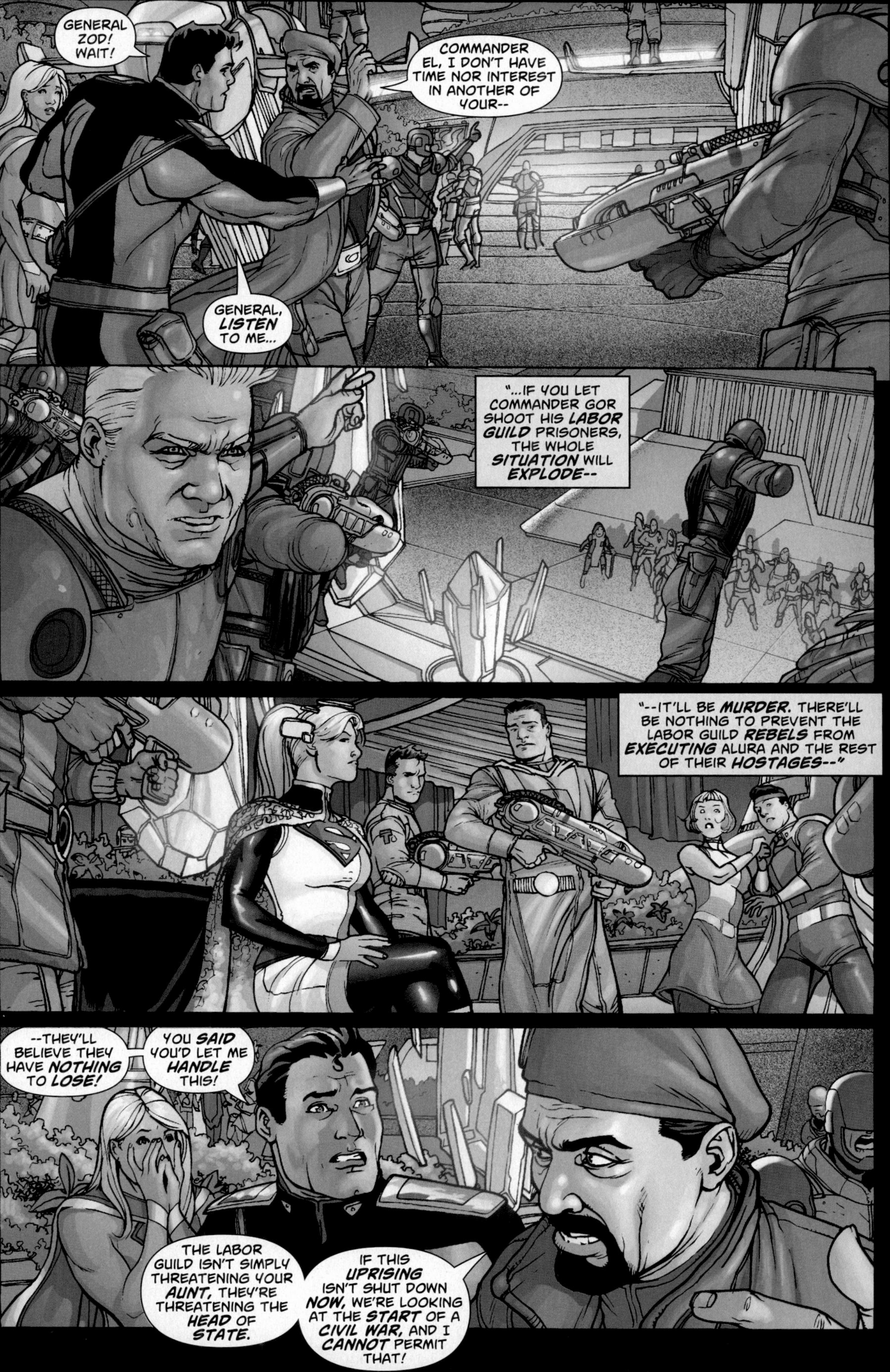
GENERAL ZOD! WAIT!
COMMANDER EL, I DON'T HAVE TIME NOR INTEREST IN ANOTHER OF YOUR--
GENERAL, LISTEN TO ME...
"...IF YOU LET COMMANDER GOR SHOOT HIS LABOR GUILD PRISONERS, THE WHOLE SITUATION WILL EXPLODE--
"--IT'LL BE MURDER. THERE'LL BE NOTHING TO PREVENT THE LABOR GUILD REBELS FROM EXECUTING ALURA AND THE REST OF THEIR HOSTAGES--"
--THEY'LL BELIEVE THEY HAVE NOTHING TO LOSE!
YOU SAID YOU'D LET ME HANDLE THIS!
THE LABOR GUILD ISN'T SIMPLY THREATENING YOUR AUNT, THEY'RE THREATENING THE HEAD OF STATE.
IF THIS UPRISING ISN'T SHUT DOWN NOW, WE'RE LOOKING AT THE START OF A CIVIL WAR, AND I CANNOT PERMIT THAT!

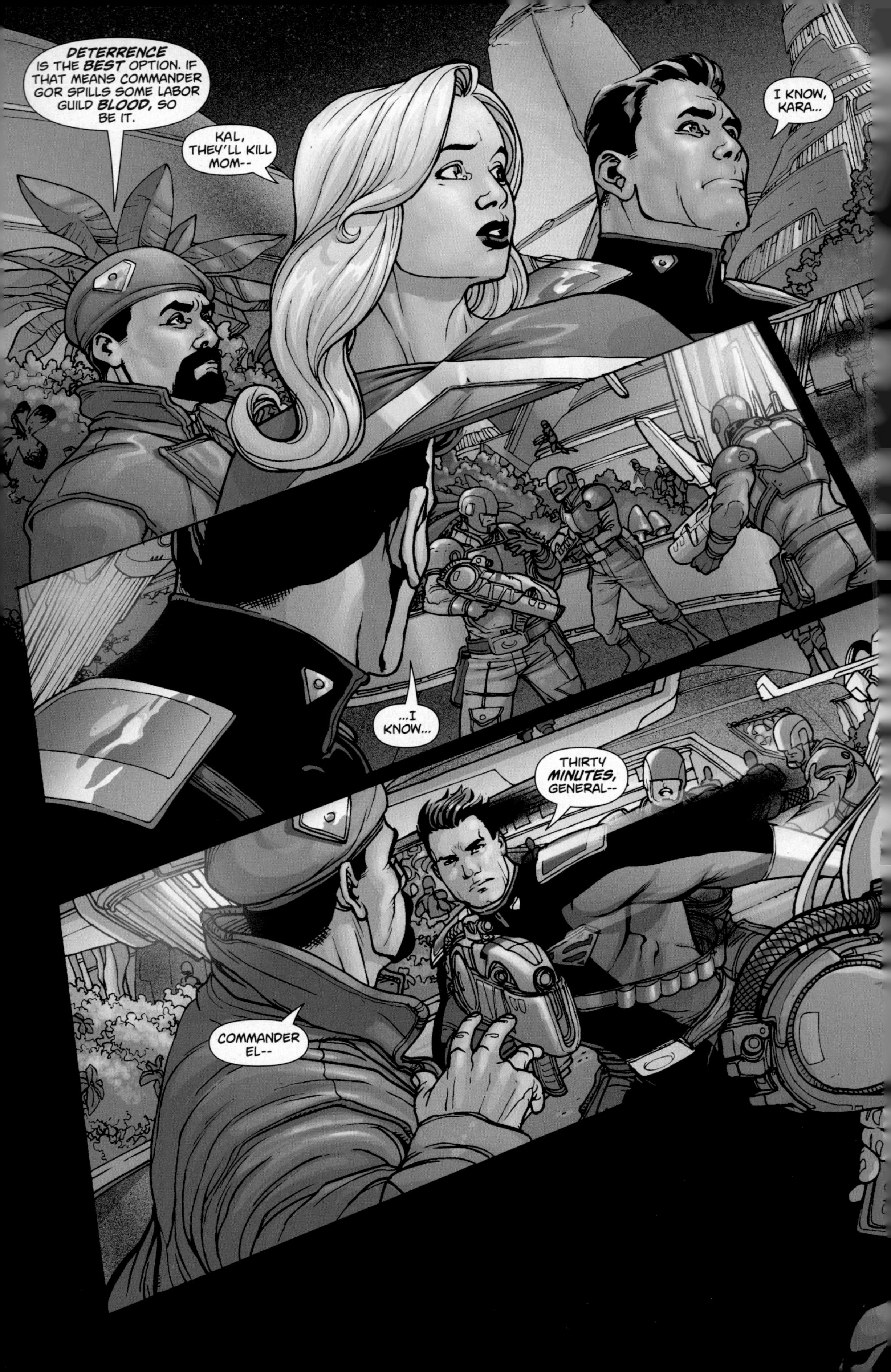
DETERRENCE IS THE BEST OPTION. IF THAT MEANS COMMANDER GOR SPILLS SOME LABOR GUILD BLOOD, SO BE IT.
KAL, THEY'LL KILL MOM--
I KNOW, KARA...
...I KNOW...
THIRTY MINUTES, GENERAL--
COMMANDER EL--

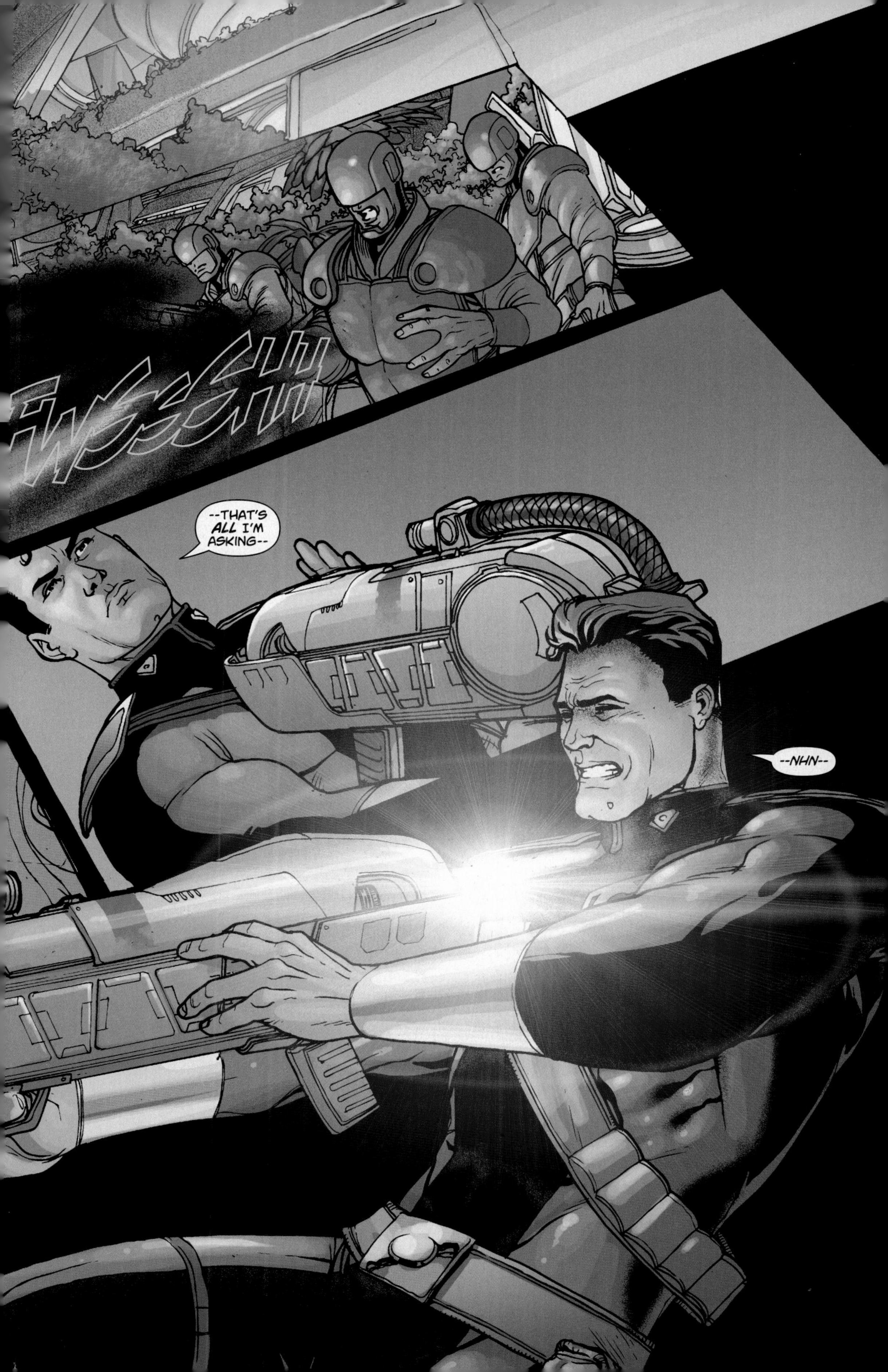
FWSSSHH
--THAT'S ALL I'M ASKING--
--NHN--

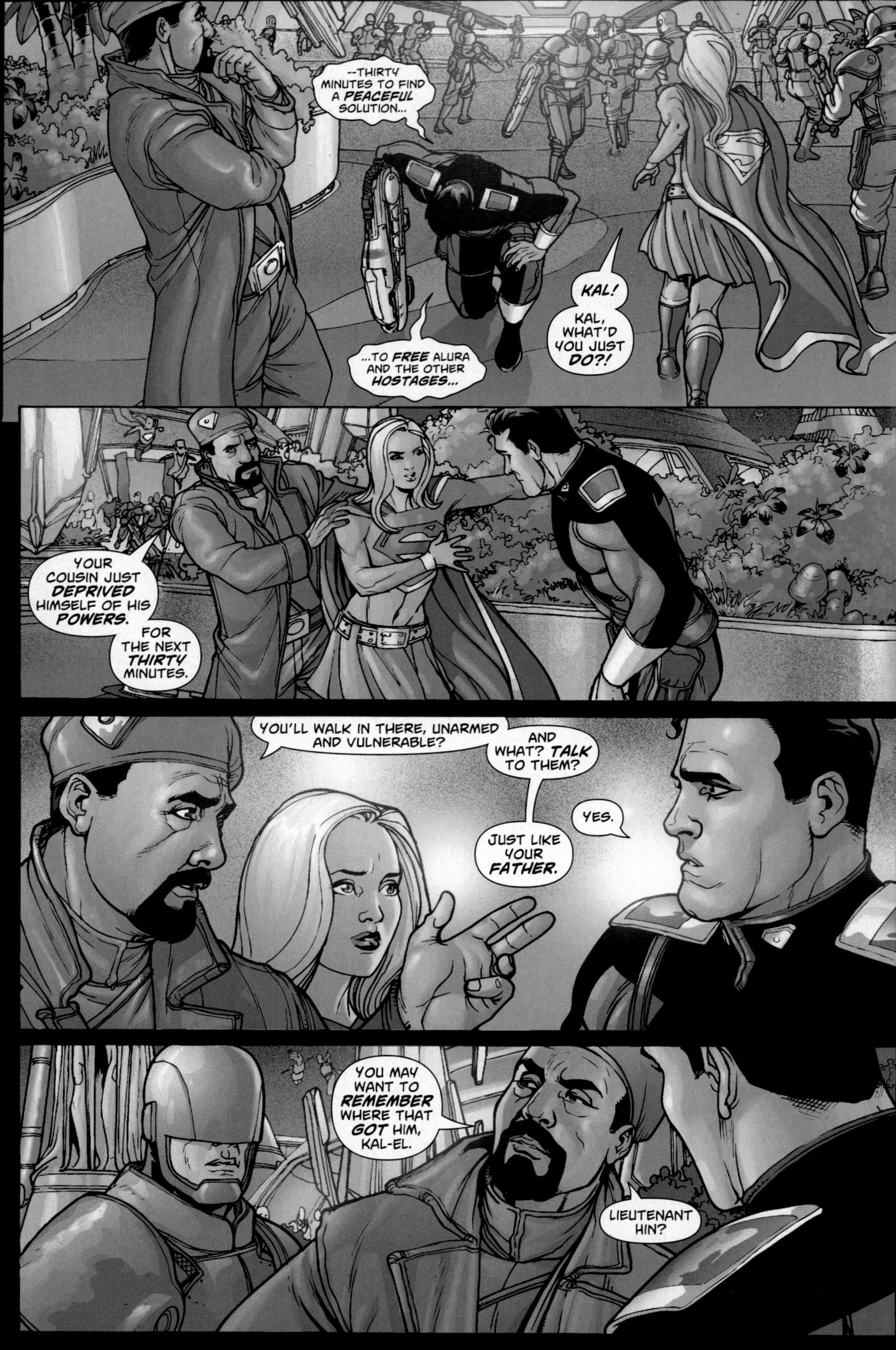

--THIRTY MINUTES TO FIND A PEACEFUL SOLUTION...
...TO FREE ALURA AND THE OTHER HOSTAGES...
KAL!
KAL, WHAT'D YOU JUST DO?!
YOUR COUSIN JUST DEPRIVED HIMSELF OF HIS POWERS.
FOR THE NEXT THIRTY MINUTES.
YOU'LL WALK IN THERE, UNARMED AND VULNERABLE?
AND WHAT? TALK TO THEM?
YES.
JUST LIKE YOUR FATHER.
YOU MAY WANT TO REMEMBER WHERE THAT GOT HIM, KAL-EL.
LIEUTENANT HIN?

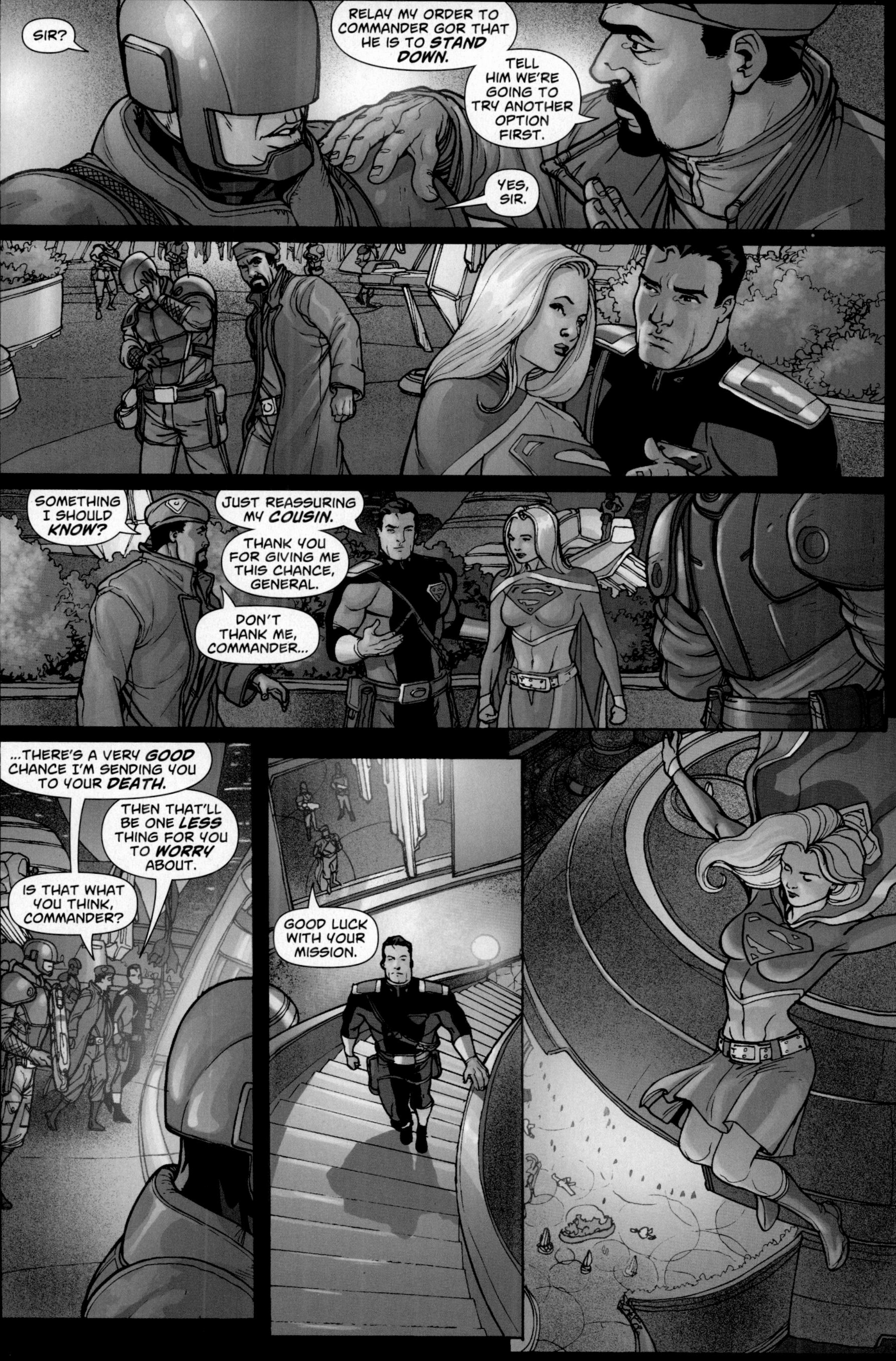
SIR?
RELAY MY ORDER TO COMMANDER GOR THAT HE IS TO STAND DOWN.
TELL HIM WE'RE GOING TO TRY ANOTHER OPTION FIRST.
YES, SIR.
SOMETHING I SHOULD KNOW?
JUST REASSURING MY COUSIN.
THANK YOU FOR GIVING ME THIS CHANCE, GENERAL.
DON'T THANK ME, COMMANDER...
...THERE'S A VERY GOOD CHANCE I'M SENDING YOU TO YOUR DEATH.
THEN THAT'LL BE ONE LESS THING FOR YOU TO WORRY ABOUT.
IS THAT WHAT YOU THINK, COMMANDER?
GOOD LUCK WITH YOUR MISSION.

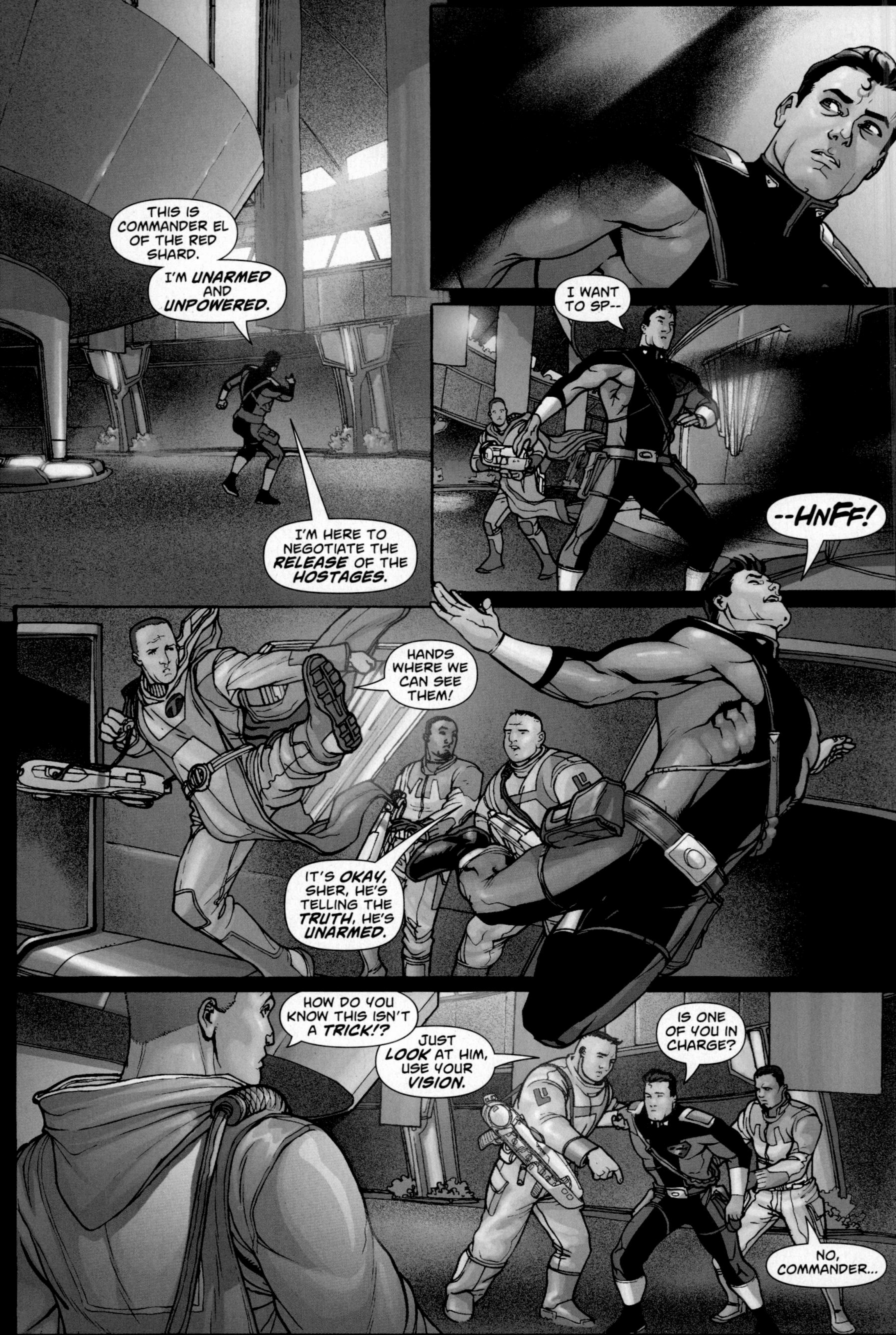

THIS IS COMMANDER EL OF THE RED SHARD.
I'M UNARMED AND UNPOWERED.
I'M HERE TO NEGOTIATE THE RELEASE OF THE HOSTAGES.
I WANT TO SP--
--HNFF!
HANDS WHERE WE CAN SEE THEM!
IT'S OKAY, SHER, HE'S TELLING THE TRUTH, HE'S UNARMED.
HOW DO YOU KNOW THIS ISN'T A TRICK!?
JUST LOOK AT HIM, USE YOUR VISION.
IS ONE OF YOU IN CHARGE?
NO, COMMANDER...

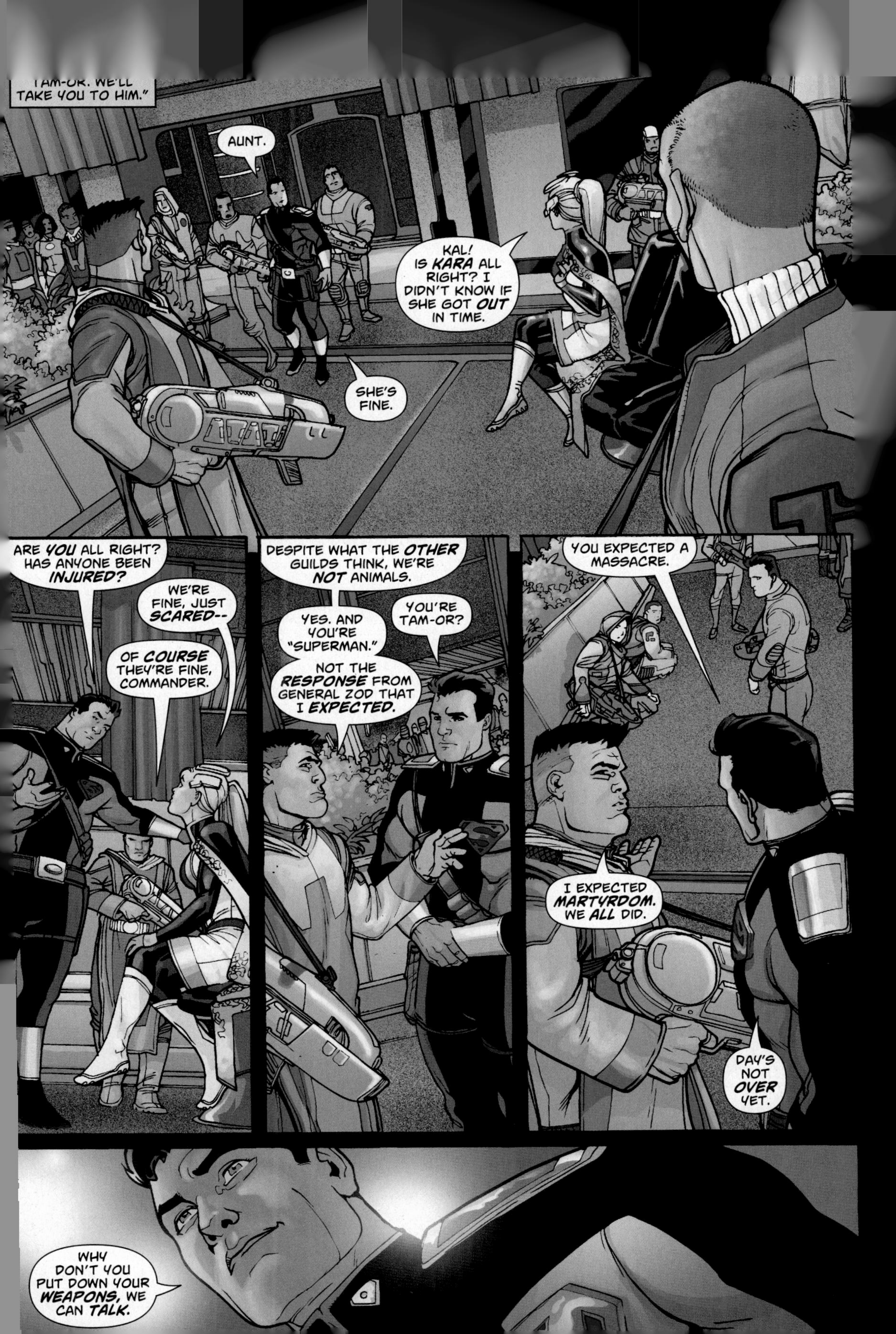
TAM-OR. WE'LL TAKE YOU TO HIM."
AUNT.
KAL! IS KARA ALL RIGHT? I DIDN'T KNOW IF SHE GOT OUT IN TIME.
SHE'S FINE.
ARE YOU ALL RIGHT? HAS ANYONE BEEN INJURED?
WE'RE FINE, JUST SCARED--
OF COURSE THEY'RE FINE, COMMANDER.
DESPITE WHAT THE OTHER GUILDS THINK, WE'RE NOT ANIMALS.
YOU'RE TAM-OR?
YES. AND YOU'RE "SUPERMAN."
NOT THE RESPONSE FROM GENERAL ZOD THAT I EXPECTED.
YOU EXPECTED A MASSACRE.
I EXPECTED MARTYRDOM. WE ALL DID.
DAY'S NOT OVER YET.
WHY DON'T YOU PUT DOWN YOUR WEAPONS, WE CAN TALK.

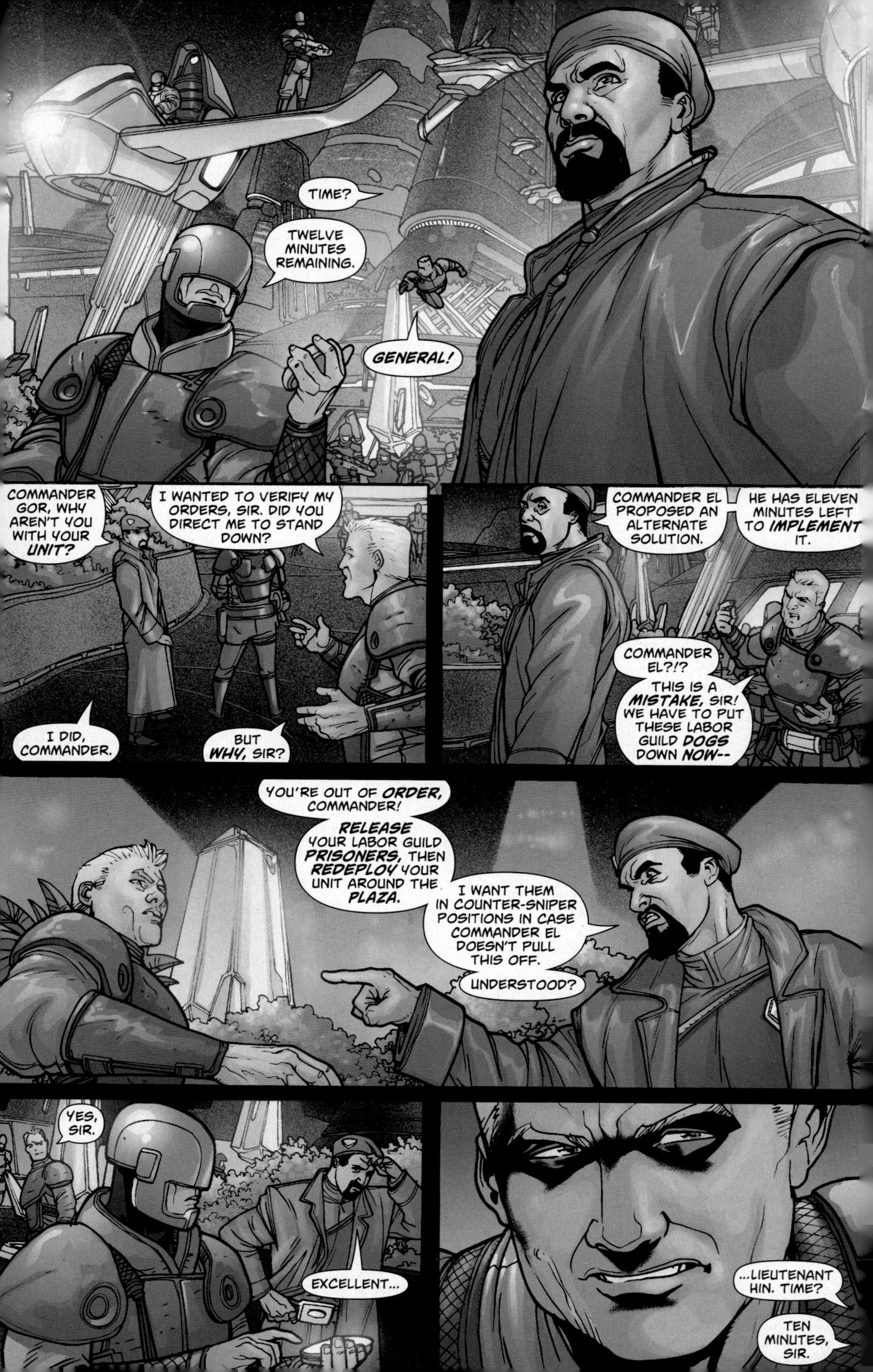
TIME?
TWELVE MINUTES REMAINING.
GENERAL!
COMMANDER GOR, WHY AREN'T YOU WITH YOUR UNIT?
I WANTED TO VERIFY MY ORDERS, SIR. DID YOU DIRECT ME TO STAND DOWN?
I DID, COMMANDER.
BUT WHY, SIR?
COMMANDER EL PROPOSED AN ALTERNATE SOLUTION.
HE HAS ELEVEN MINUTES LEFT TO IMPLEMENT IT.
COMMANDER EL?!? THIS IS A MISTAKE, SIR! WE HAVE TO PUT THESE LABOR GUILD DOGS DOWN NOW--
YOU'RE OUT OF ORDER, COMMANDER!
RELEASE YOUR LABOR GUILD PRISONERS, THEN REDEPLOY YOUR UNIT AROUND THE PLAZA.
I WANT THEM IN COUNTER-SNIPER POSITIONS IN CASE COMMANDER EL DOESN'T PULL THIS OFF.
UNDERSTOOD?
YES, SIR.
EXCELLENT...
...LIEUTENANT HIN. TIME?
TEN MINUTES, SIR.

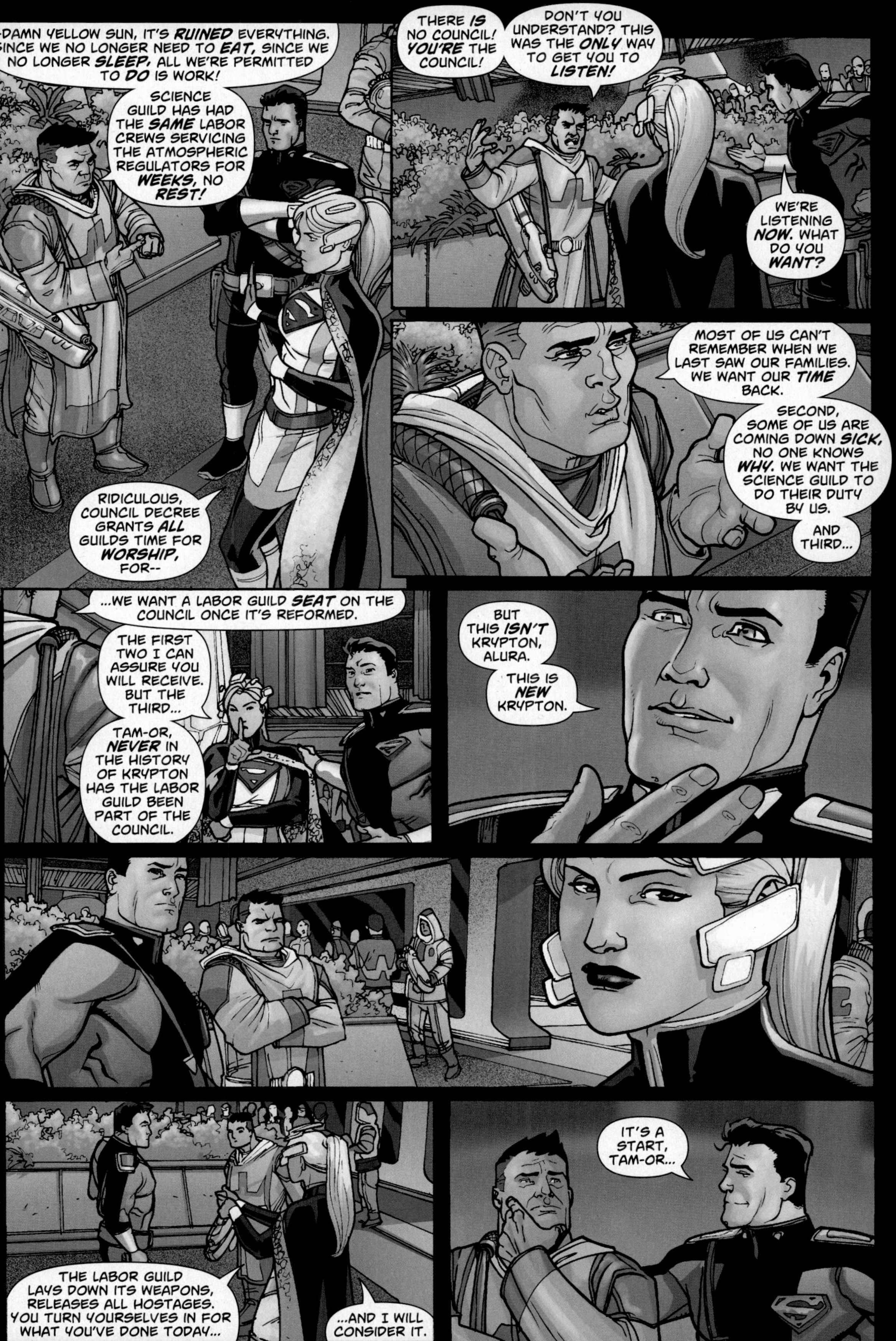
-DAMN YELLOW SUN, IT'S RUINED EVERYTHING. SINCE WE NO LONGER NEED TO EAT, SINCE WE NO LONGER SLEEP, ALL WE'RE PERMITTED TO DO IS WORK!
SCIENCE GUILD HAS HAD THE SAME LABOR CREWS SERVICING THE ATMOSPHERIC REGULATORS FOR WEEKS, NO REST!
RIDICULOUS, COUNCIL DECREE GRANTS ALL GUILDS TIME FOR WORSHIP, FOR--
THERE IS NO COUNCIL! YOU'RE THE COUNCIL!
DON'T YOU UNDERSTAND? THIS WAS THE ONLY WAY TO GET YOU TO LISTEN!
WE'RE LISTENING NOW. WHAT DO YOU WANT?
MOST OF US CAN'T REMEMBER WHEN WE LAST SAW OUR FAMILIES. WE WANT OUR TIME BACK.
SECOND, SOME OF US ARE COMING DOWN SICK, NO ONE KNOWS WHY. WE WANT THE SCIENCE GUILD TO DO THEIR DUTY BY US.
AND THIRD...
...WE WANT A LABOR GUILD SEAT ON THE COUNCIL ONCE IT'S REFORMED.
THE FIRST TWO I CAN ASSURE YOU WILL RECEIVE. BUT THE THIRD...
TAM-OR, NEVER IN THE HISTORY OF KRYPTON HAS THE LABOR GUILD BEEN PART OF THE COUNCIL.
BUT THIS ISN'T KRYPTON, ALURA.
THIS IS NEW KRYPTON.
THE LABOR GUILD LAYS DOWN ITS WEAPONS, RELEASES ALL HOSTAGES. YOU TURN YOURSELVES IN FOR WHAT YOU'VE DONE TODAY...
...AND I WILL CONSIDER IT.
IT'S A START, TAM-OR...

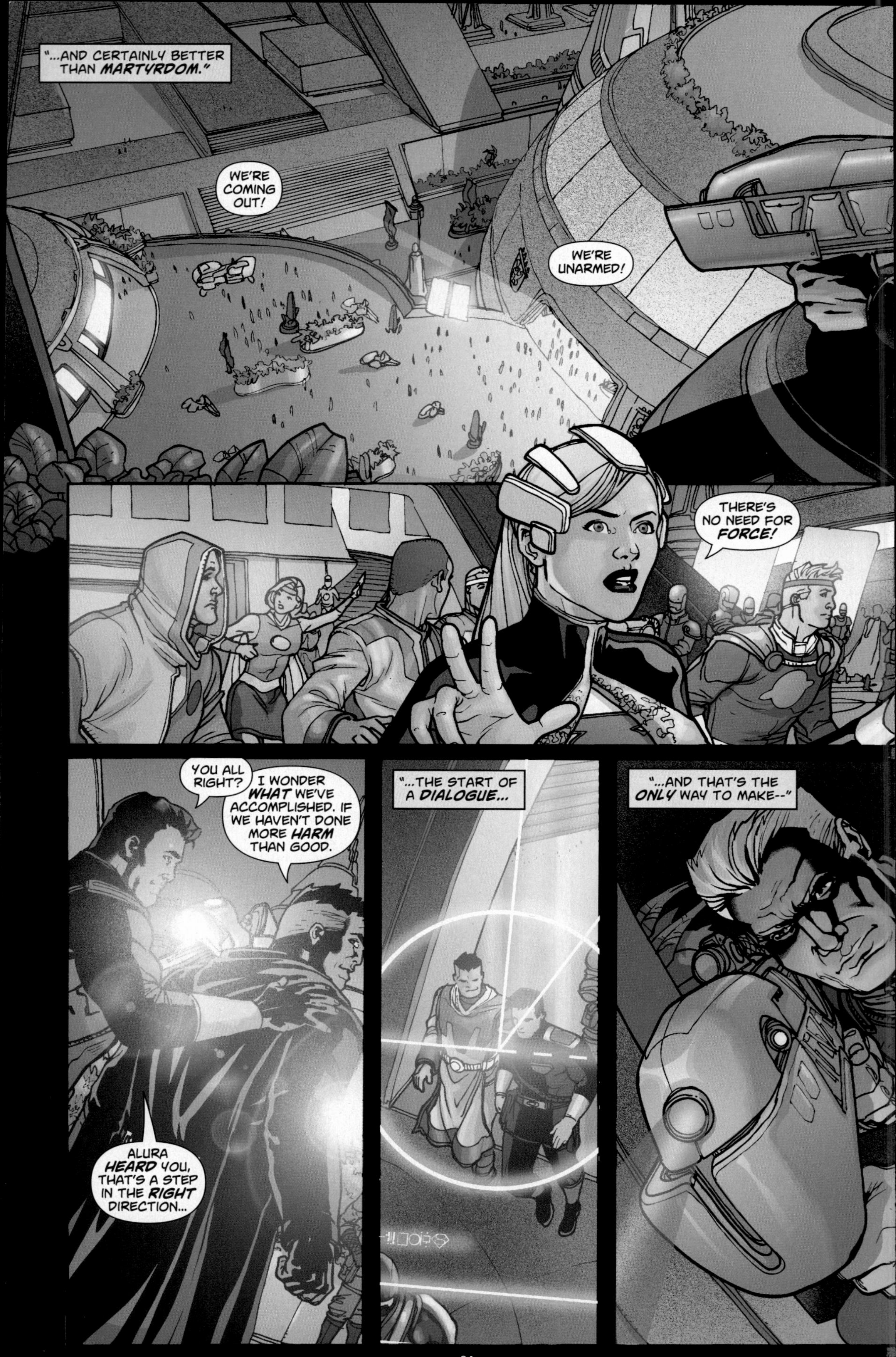
"...AND CERTAINLY BETTER THAN MARTYRDOM."
WE'RE COMING OUT!
WE'RE UNARMED!
THERE'S NO NEED FOR FORCE!
YOU ALL RIGHT?
I WONDER WHAT WE'VE ACCOMPLISHED. IF WE HAVEN'T DONE MORE HARM THAN GOOD.
ALURA HEARD YOU, THAT'S A STEP IN THE RIGHT DIRECTION...
"...THE START OF A DIALOGUE...
"...AND THAT'S THE ONLY WAY TO MAKE--"

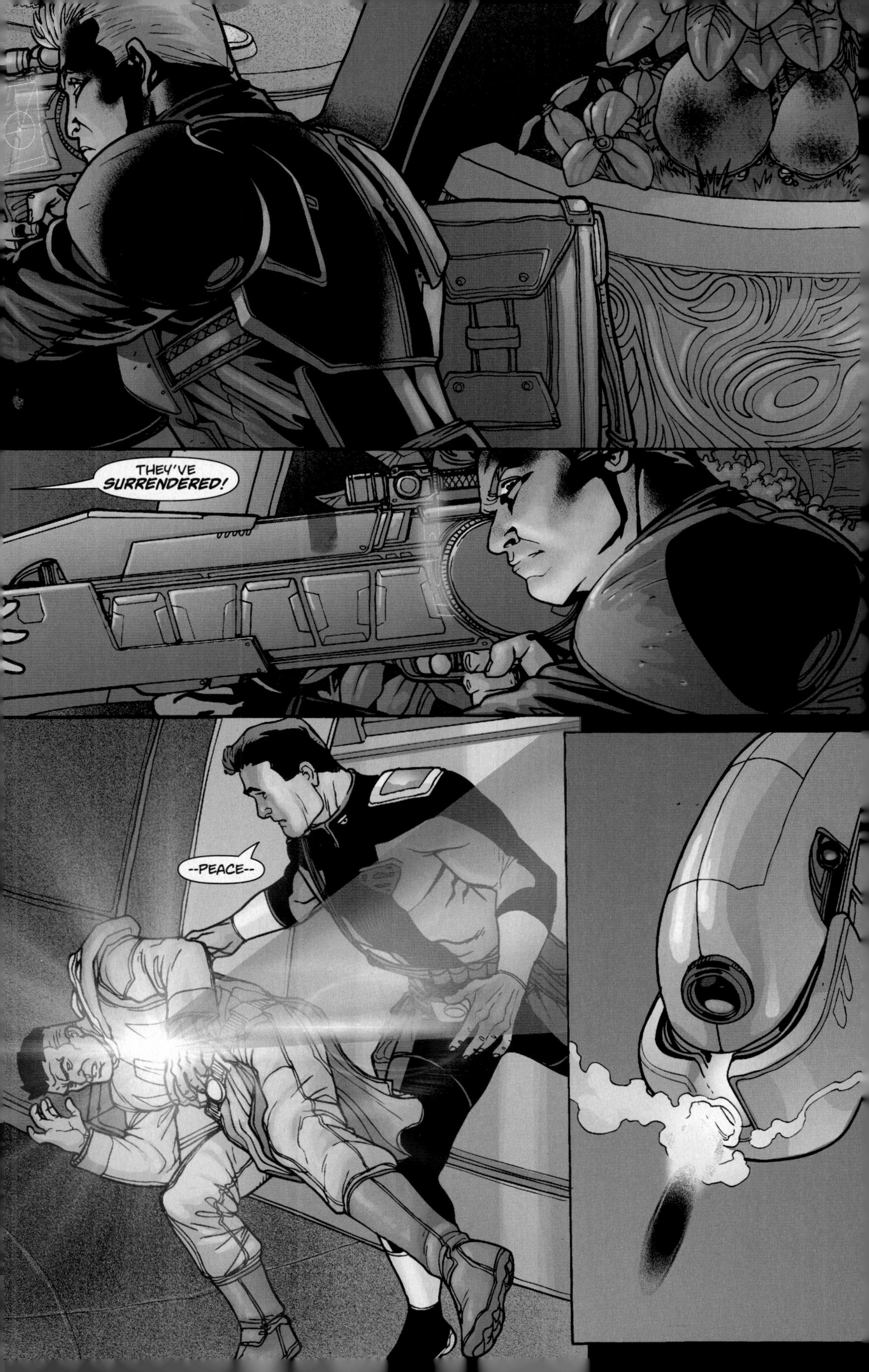
THEY'VE SURRENDERED!
--PEACE--

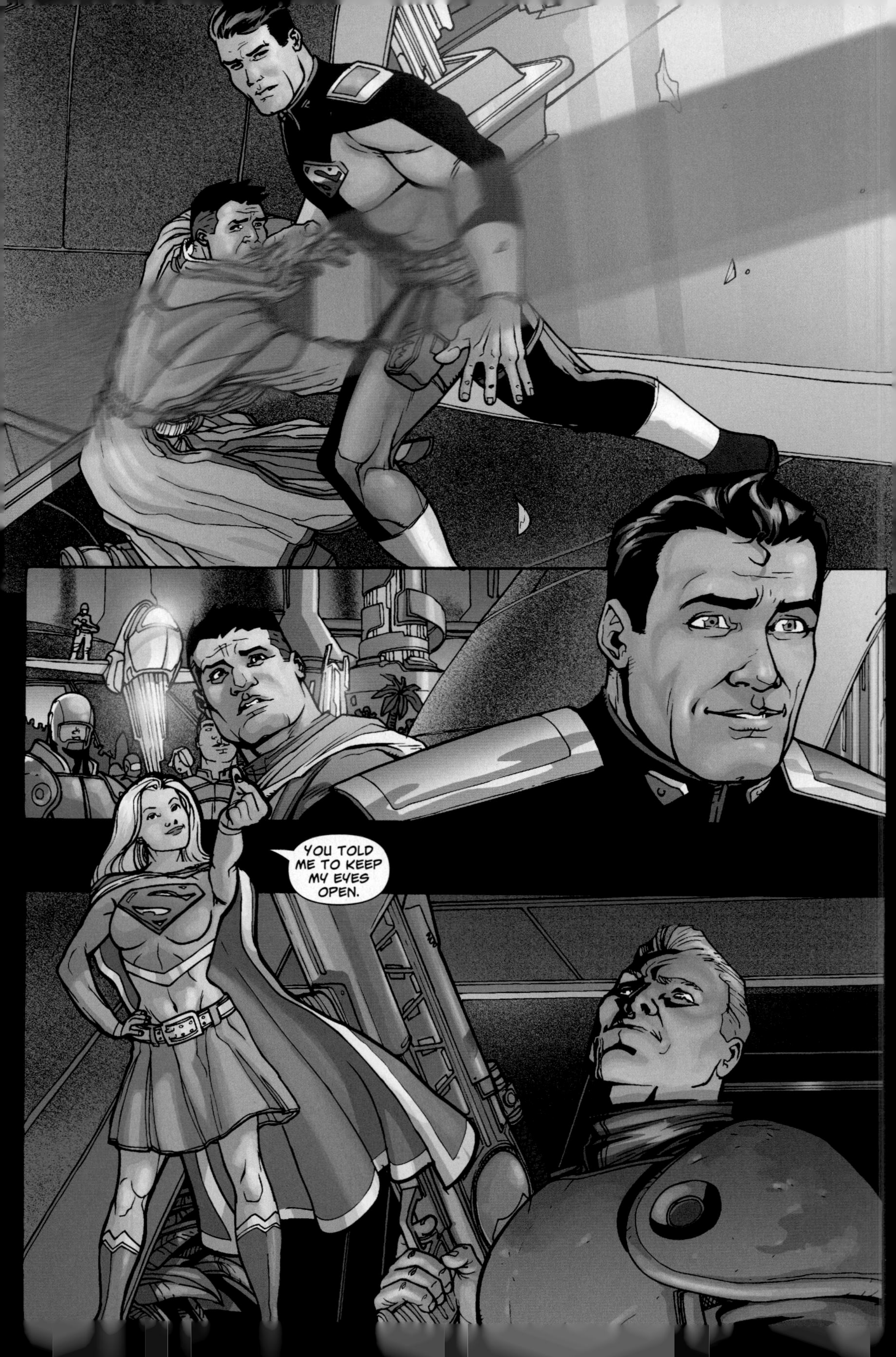
YOU TOLD ME TO KEEP MY EYES OPEN.

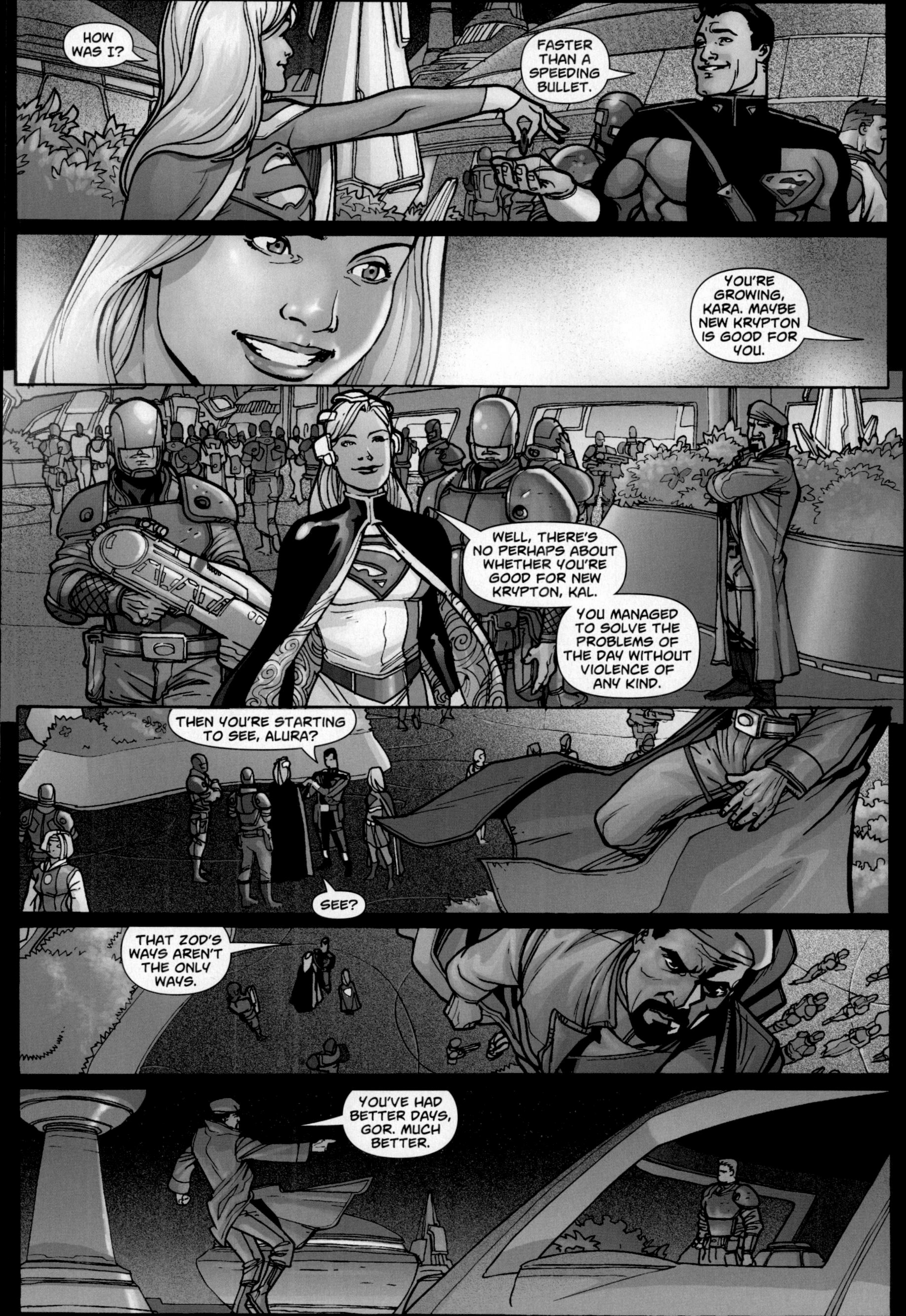
HOW WAS I?
FASTER THAN A SPEEDING BULLET.
YOU'RE GROWING, KARA. MAYBE NEW KRYPTON IS GOOD FOR YOU.
WELL, THERE'S NO PERHAPS ABOUT WHETHER YOU'RE GOOD FOR NEW KRYPTON, KAL.
YOU MANAGED TO SOLVE THE PROBLEMS OF THE DAY WITHOUT VIOLENCE OF ANY KIND.
THEN YOU'RE STARTING TO SEE, ALURA?
SEE?
THAT ZOD'S WAYS AREN'T THE ONLY WAYS.
YOU'VE HAD BETTER DAYS, GOR. MUCH BETTER.

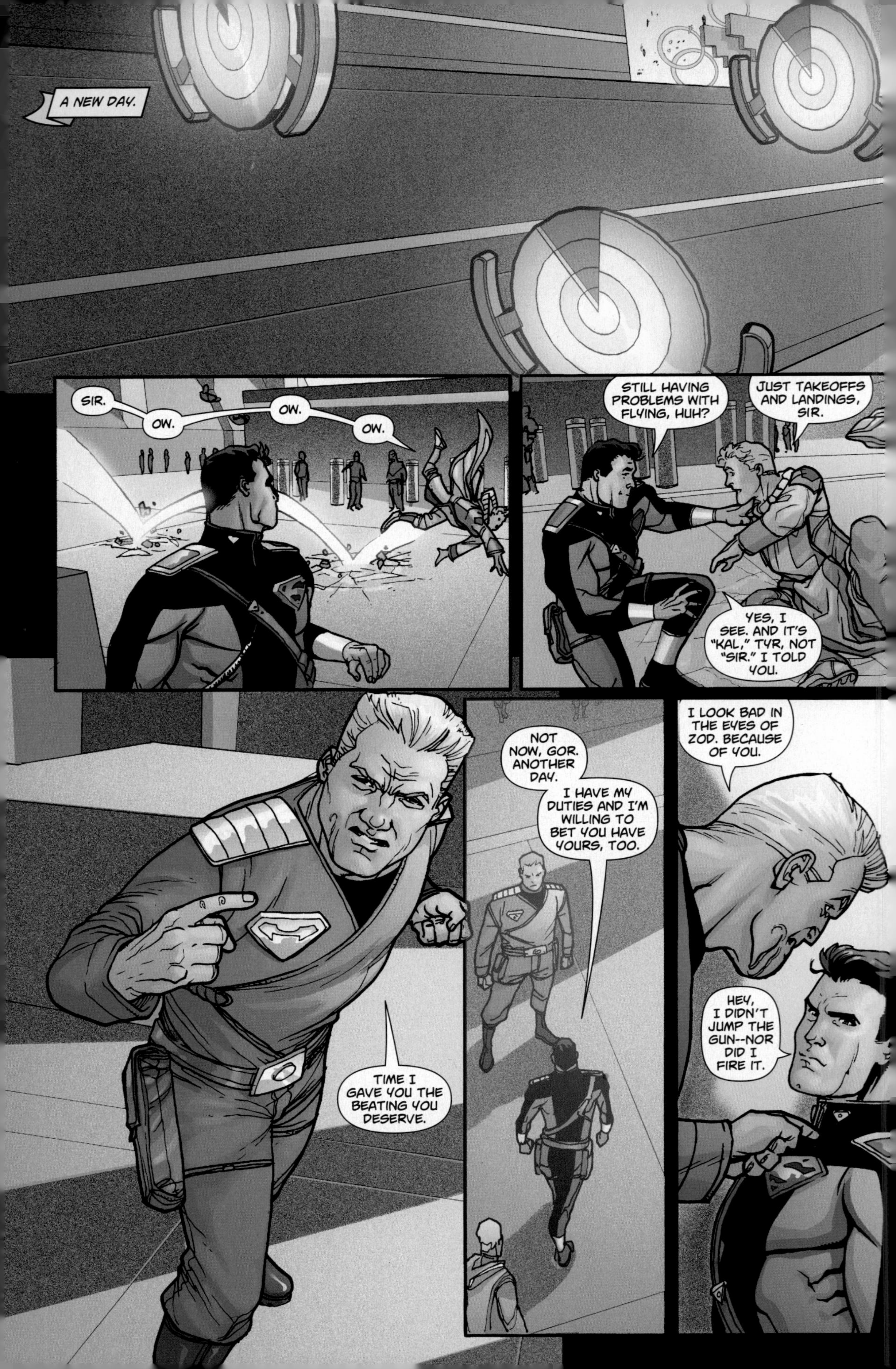

A NEW DAY.
SIR.
OW.
OW.
OW.
STILL HAVING PROBLEMS WITH FLYING, HUH?
JUST TAKEOFFS AND LANDINGS, SIR.
YES, I SEE. AND IT'S "KAL," TYR, NOT "SIR." I TOLD YOU.
TIME I GAVE YOU THE BEATING YOU DESERVE.
NOT NOW, GOR. ANOTHER DAY.
I HAVE MY DUTIES AND I'M WILLING TO BET YOU HAVE YOURS, TOO.
I LOOK BAD IN THE EYES OF ZOD. BECAUSE OF YOU.
HEY, I DIDN'T JUMP THE GUN--NOR DID I FIRE IT.

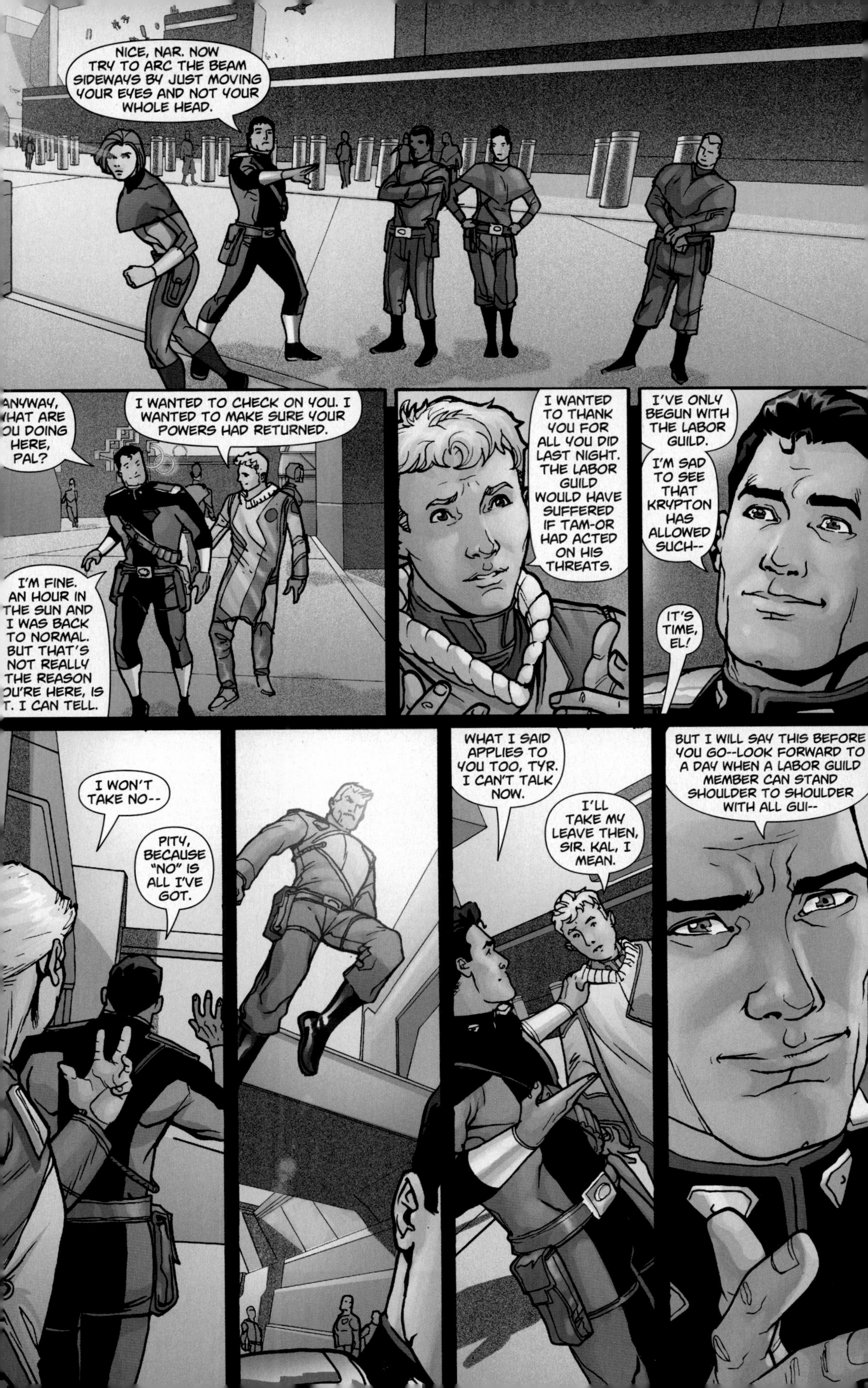
NICE, NAR. NOW TRY TO ARC THE BEAM SIDEWAYS BY JUST MOVING YOUR EYES AND NOT YOUR WHOLE HEAD.
ANYWAY, WHAT ARE OU DOING HERE, PAL?
I WANTED TO CHECK ON YOU. I WANTED TO MAKE SURE YOUR POWERS HAD RETURNED.
I'M FINE. AN HOUR IN THE SUN AND I WAS BACK TO NORMAL. BUT THAT'S NOT REALLY THE REASON OU'RE HERE, IS T. I CAN TELL.
I WANTED TO THANK YOU FOR ALL YOU DID LAST NIGHT. THE LABOR GUILD WOULD HAVE SUFFERED IF TAM-OR HAD ACTED ON HIS THREATS.
I'VE ONLY BEGUN WITH THE LABOR GUILD.
I'M SAD TO SEE THAT KRYPTON HAS ALLOWED SUCH--
IT'S TIME, EL!
I WON'T TAKE NO--
PITY, BECAUSE "NO" IS ALL I'VE GOT.
WHAT I SAID APPLIES TO YOU TOO, TYR. I CAN'T TALK NOW.
I'LL TAKE MY LEAVE THEN, SIR. KAL, I MEAN.
BUT I WILL SAY THIS BEFORE YOU GO--LOOK FORWARD TO A DAY WHEN A LABOR GUILD MEMBER CAN STAND SHOULDER TO SHOULDER WITH ALL GUI--

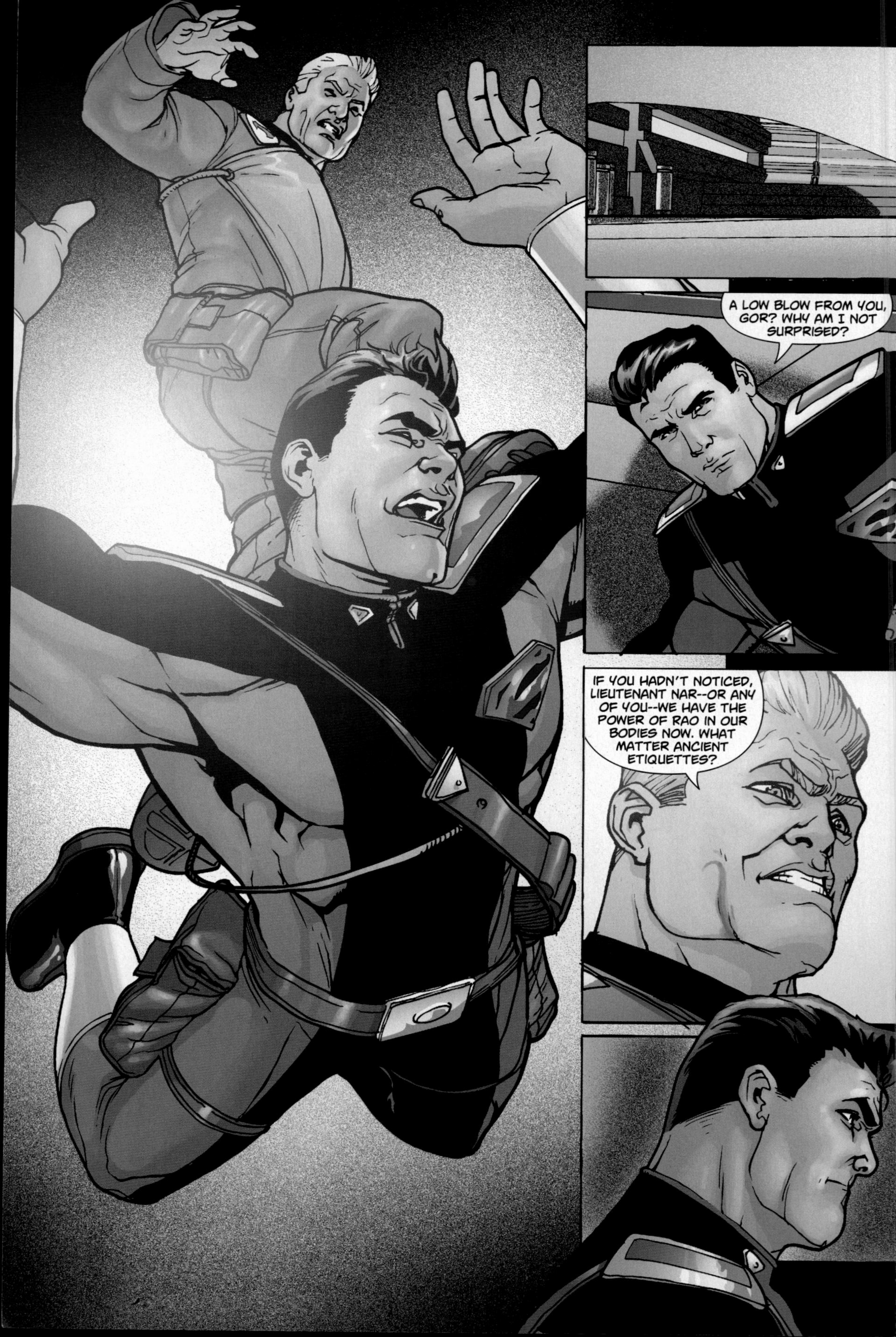
A LOW BLOW FROM YOU, GOR? WHY AM I NOT SURPRISED?
IF YOU HADN'T NOTICED, LIEUTENANT NAR--OR ANY OF YOU--WE HAVE THE POWER OF RAO IN OUR BODIES NOW. WHAT MATTER ANCIENT ETIQUETTES?

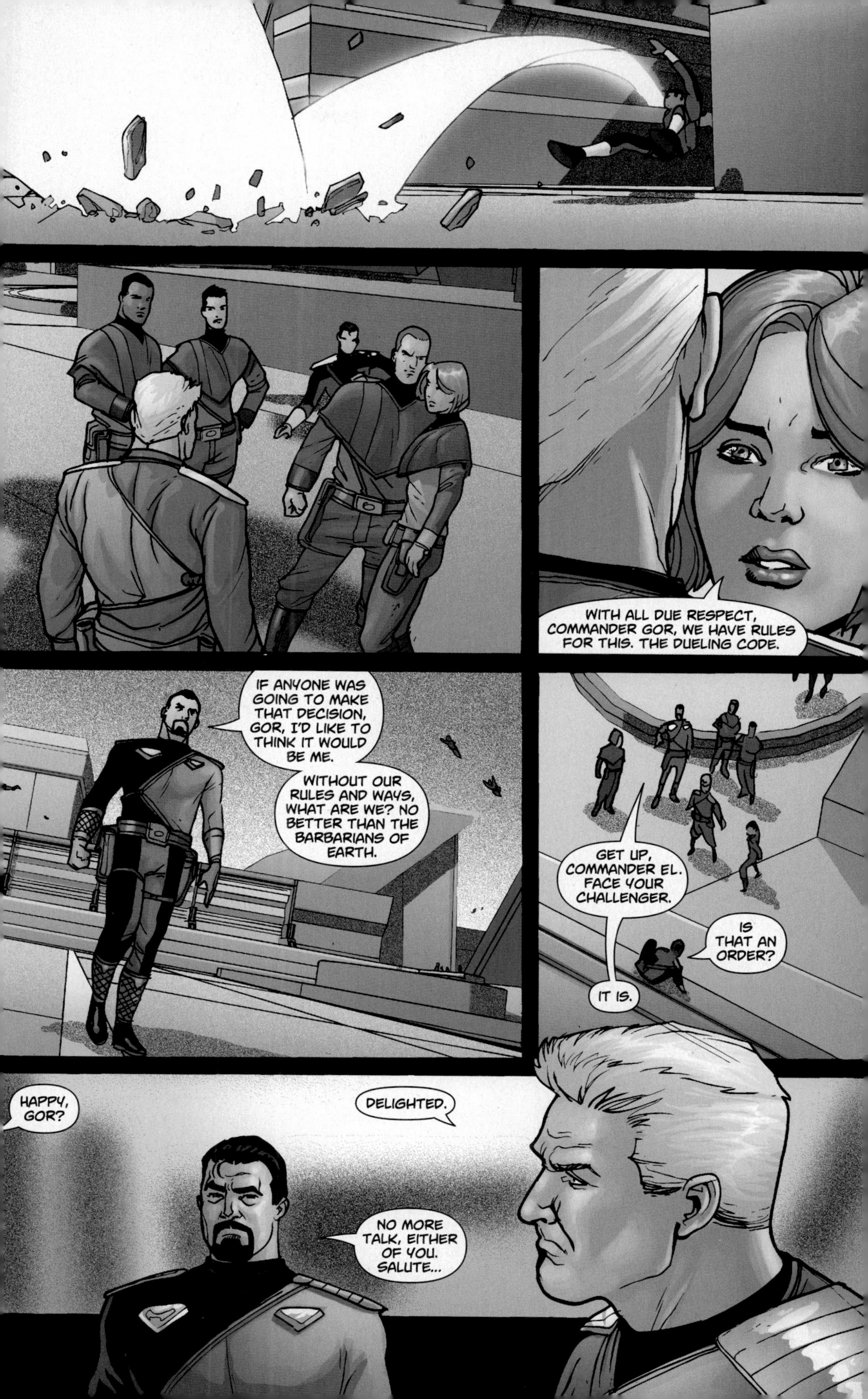
WITH ALL DUE RESPECT, COMMANDER GOR, WE HAVE RULES FOR THIS. THE DUELING CODE.
IF ANYONE WAS GOING TO MAKE THAT DECISION, GOR, I'D LIKE TO THINK IT WOULD BE ME.
WITHOUT OUR RULES AND WAYS, WHAT ARE WE? NO BETTER THAN THE BARBARIANS OF EARTH.
GET UP, COMMANDER EL. FACE YOUR CHALLENGER.
IS THAT AN ORDER?
IT IS.
HAPPY, GOR?
DELIGHTED.
NO MORE TALK, EITHER OF YOU. SALUTE...

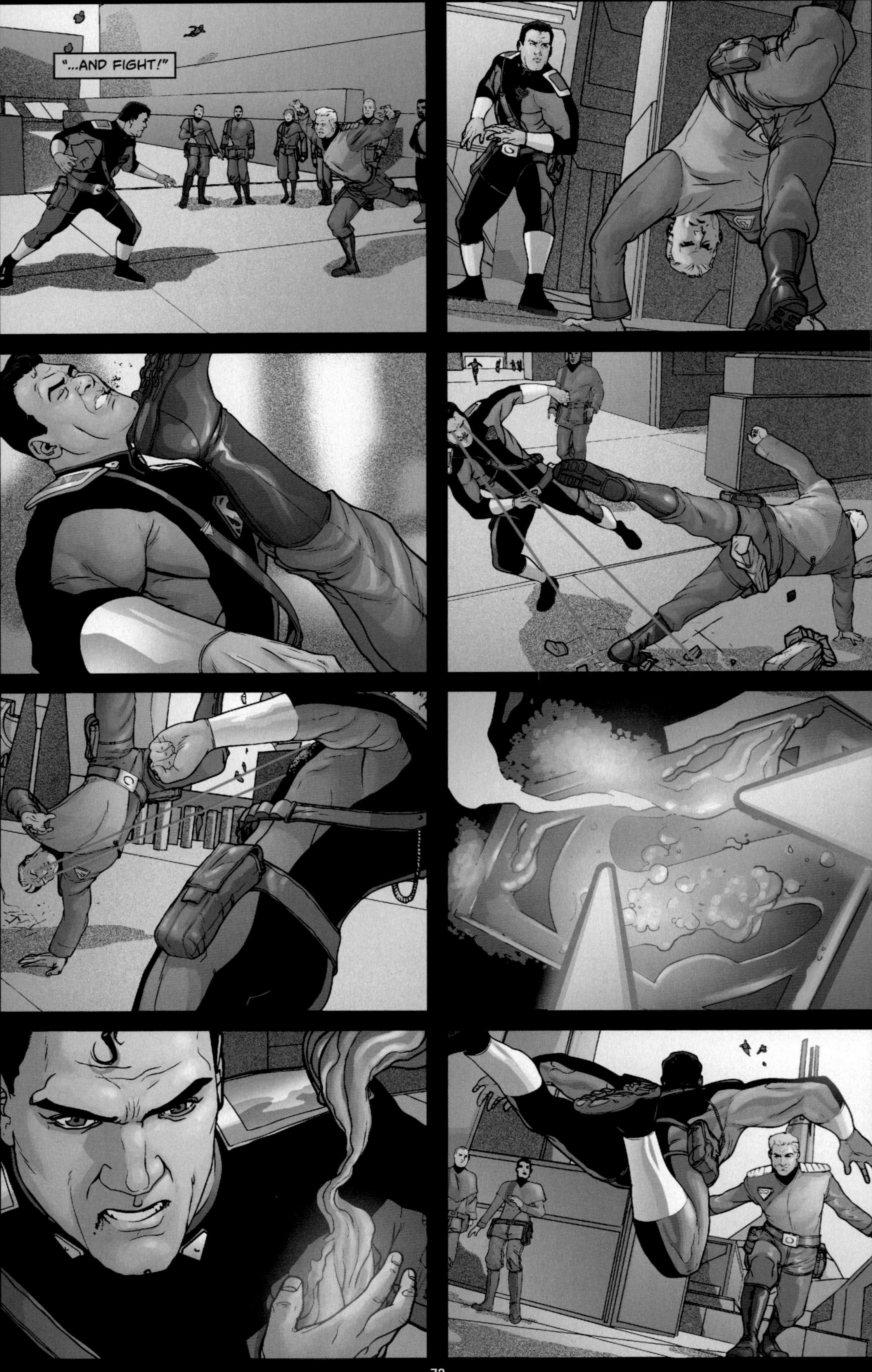
"...AND FIGHT!"

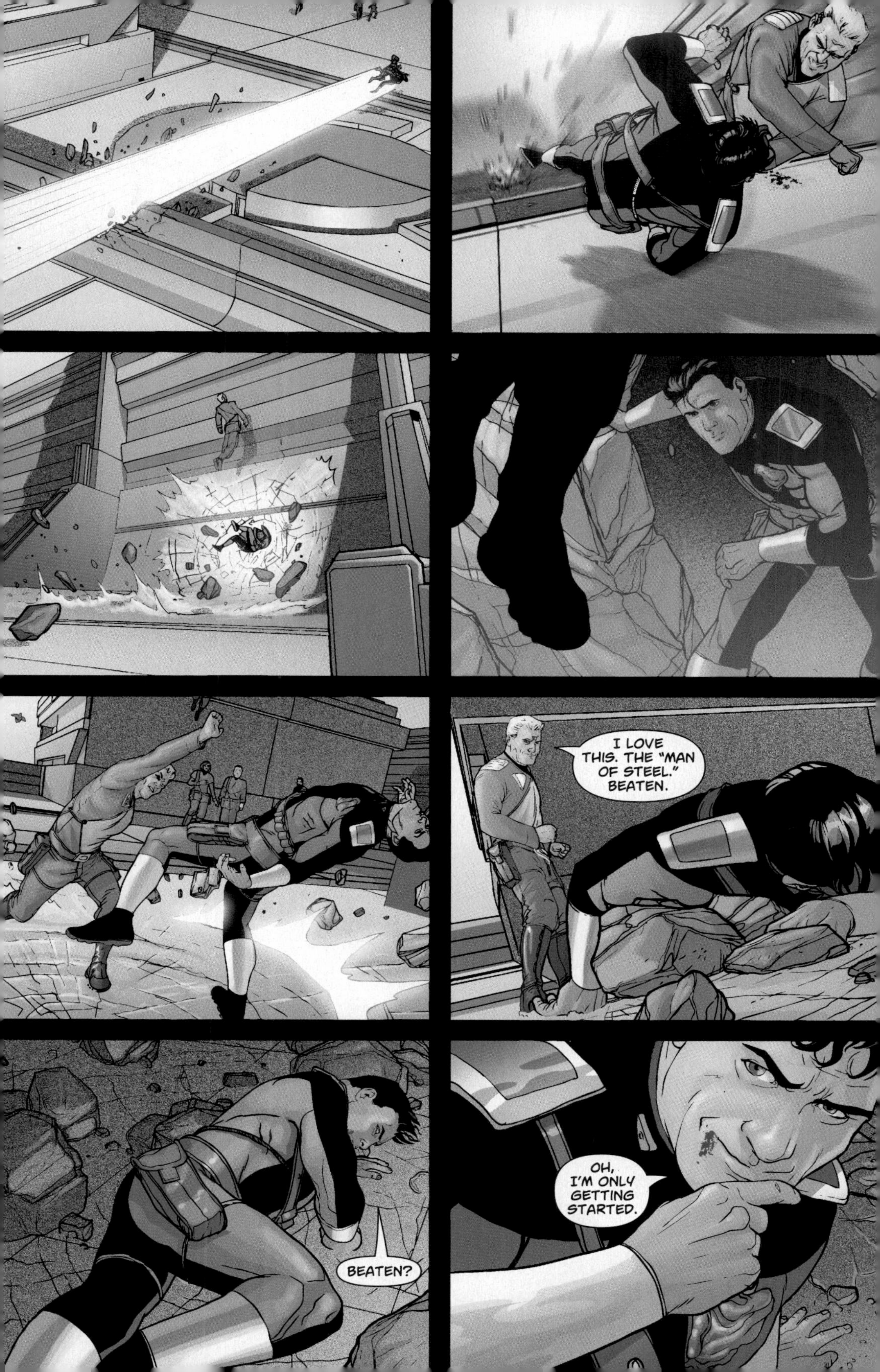
I LOVE THIS. THE "MAN OF STEEL." BEATEN.
BEATEN?
OH, I'M ONLY GETTING STARTED.

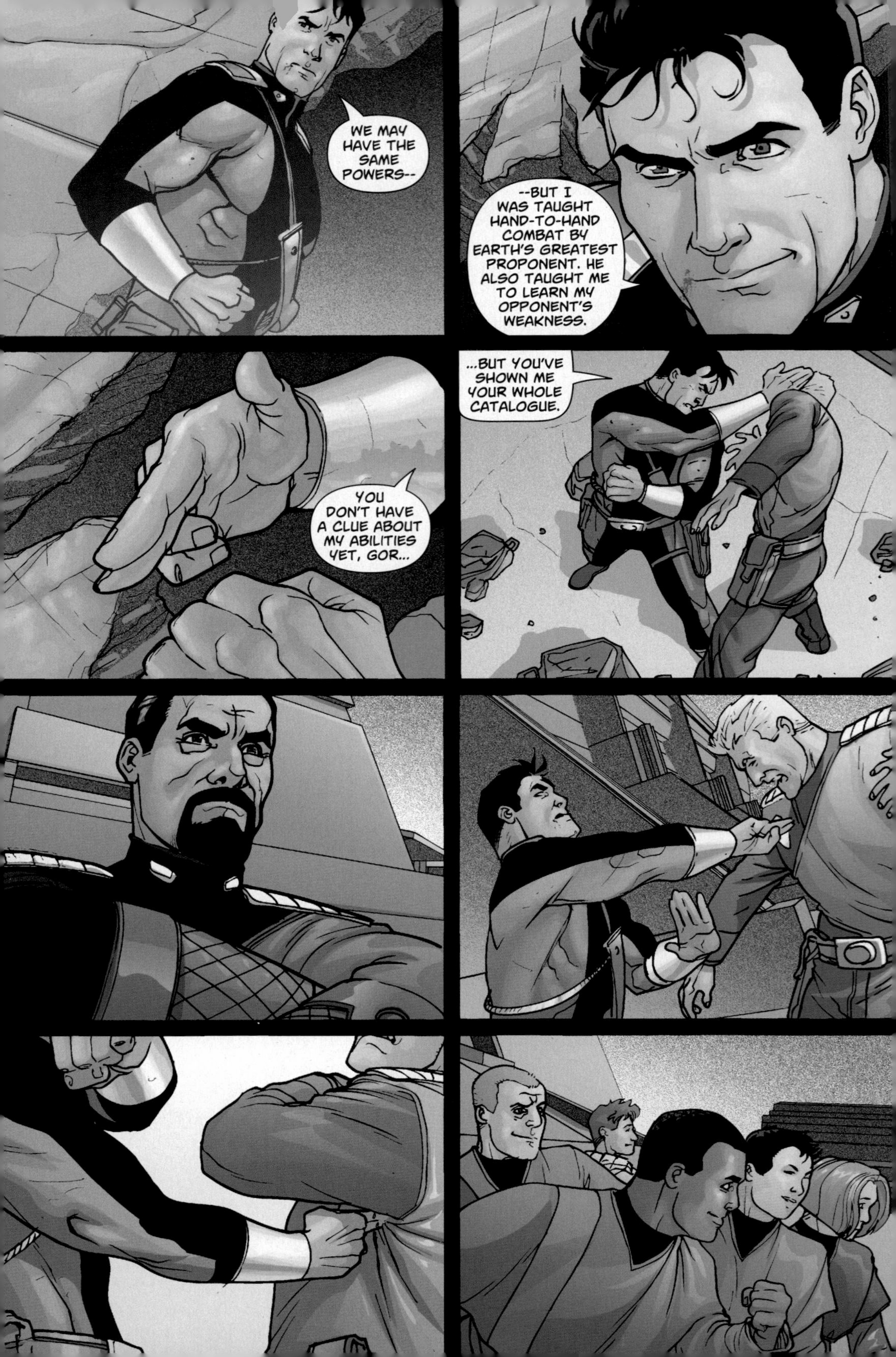
WE MAY HAVE THE SAME POWERS--
--BUT I WAS TAUGHT HAND-TO-HAND COMBAT BY EARTH'S GREATEST PROPONENT. HE ALSO TAUGHT ME TO LEARN MY OPPONENT'S WEAKNESS.
YOU DON'T HAVE A CLUE ABOUT MY ABILITIES YET, GOR...
...BUT YOU'VE SHOWN ME YOUR WHOLE CATALOGUE.

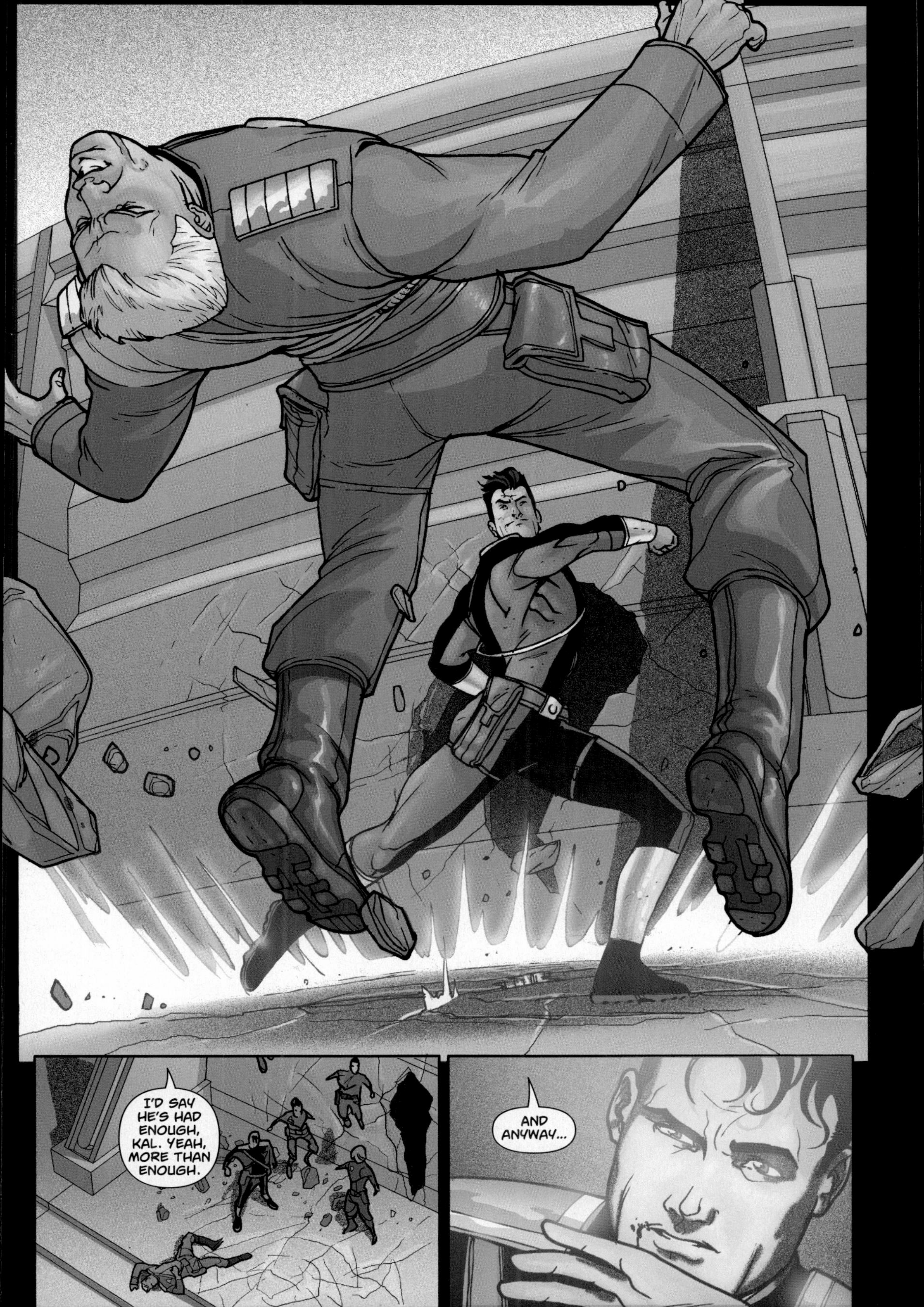
I'D SAY HE'S HAD ENOUGH, KAL. YEAH, MORE THAN ENOUGH.
AND ANYWAY...

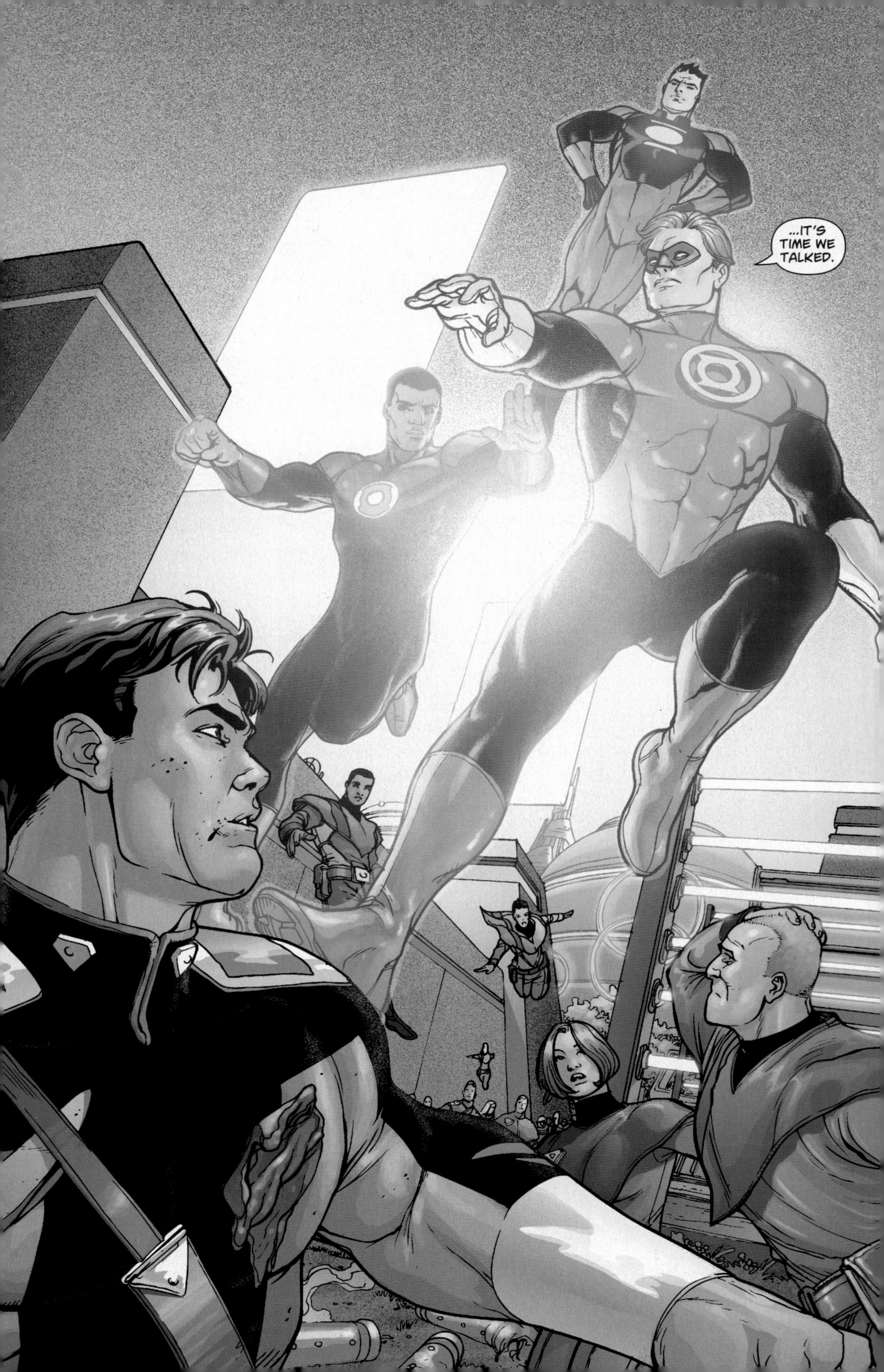
...IT'S TIME WE TALKED.

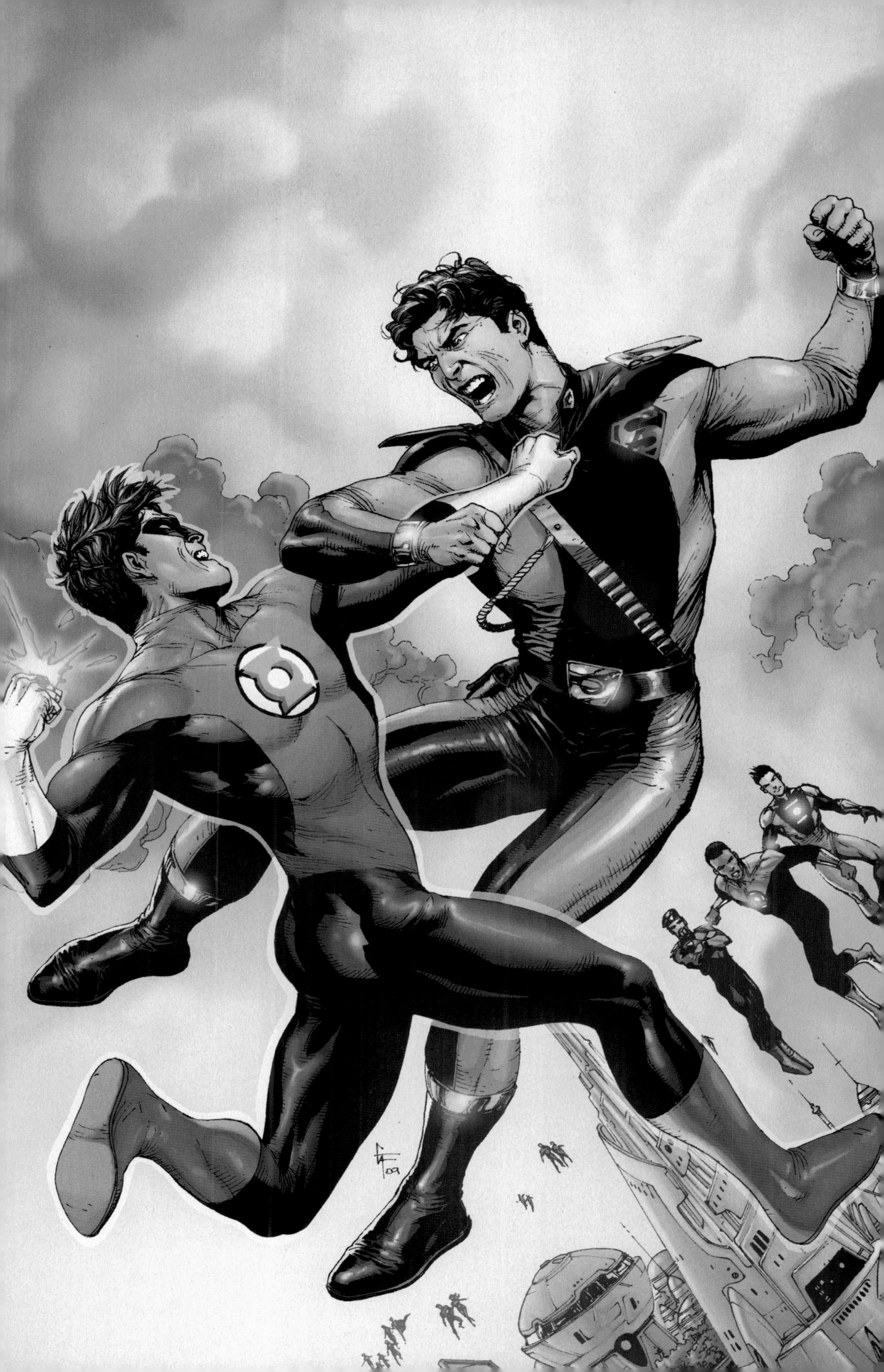

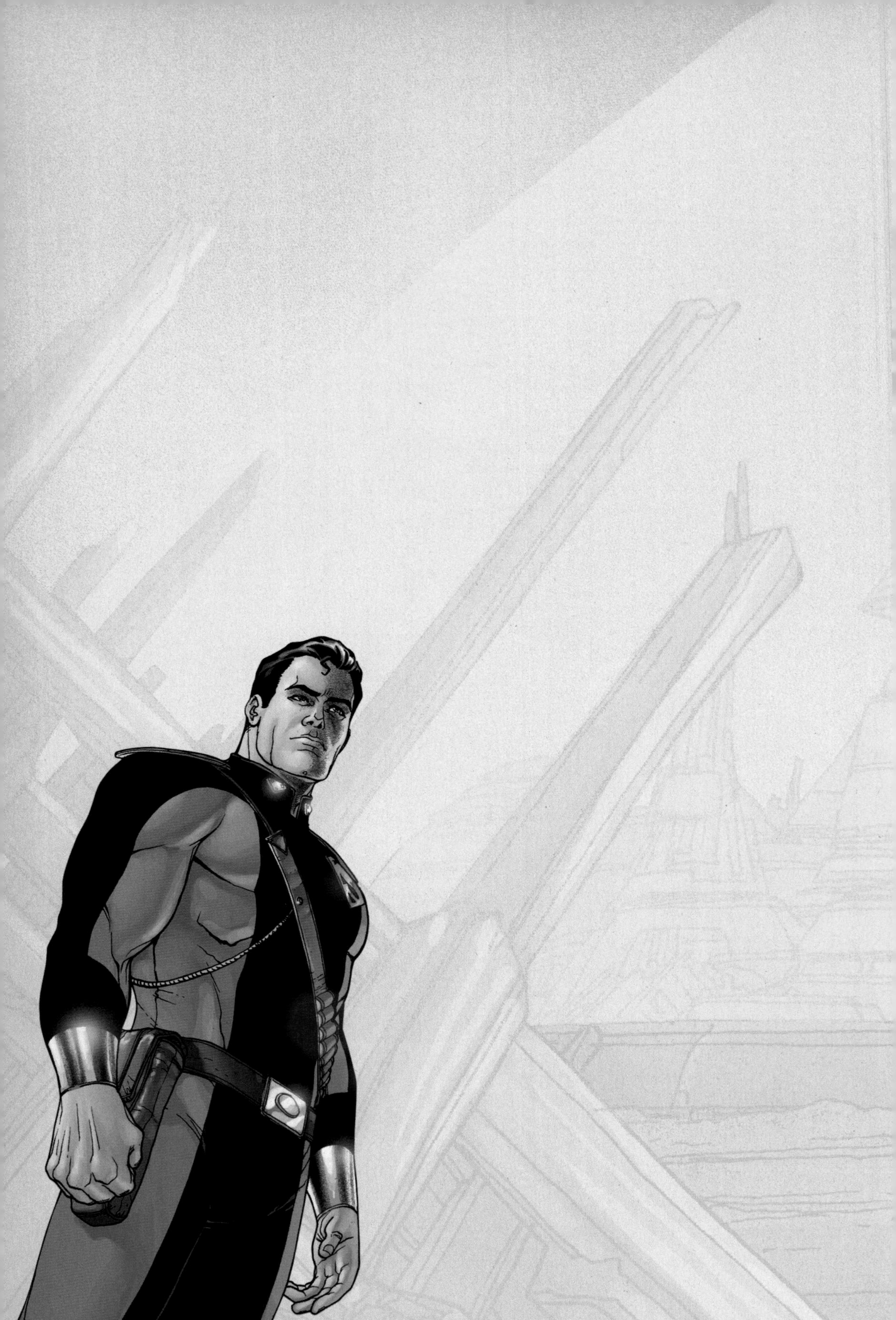

WORLD OF NEW KRYPTON <PART FOUR>

COVER BY **GARY FRANK** WITH **BRAD ANDERSON**

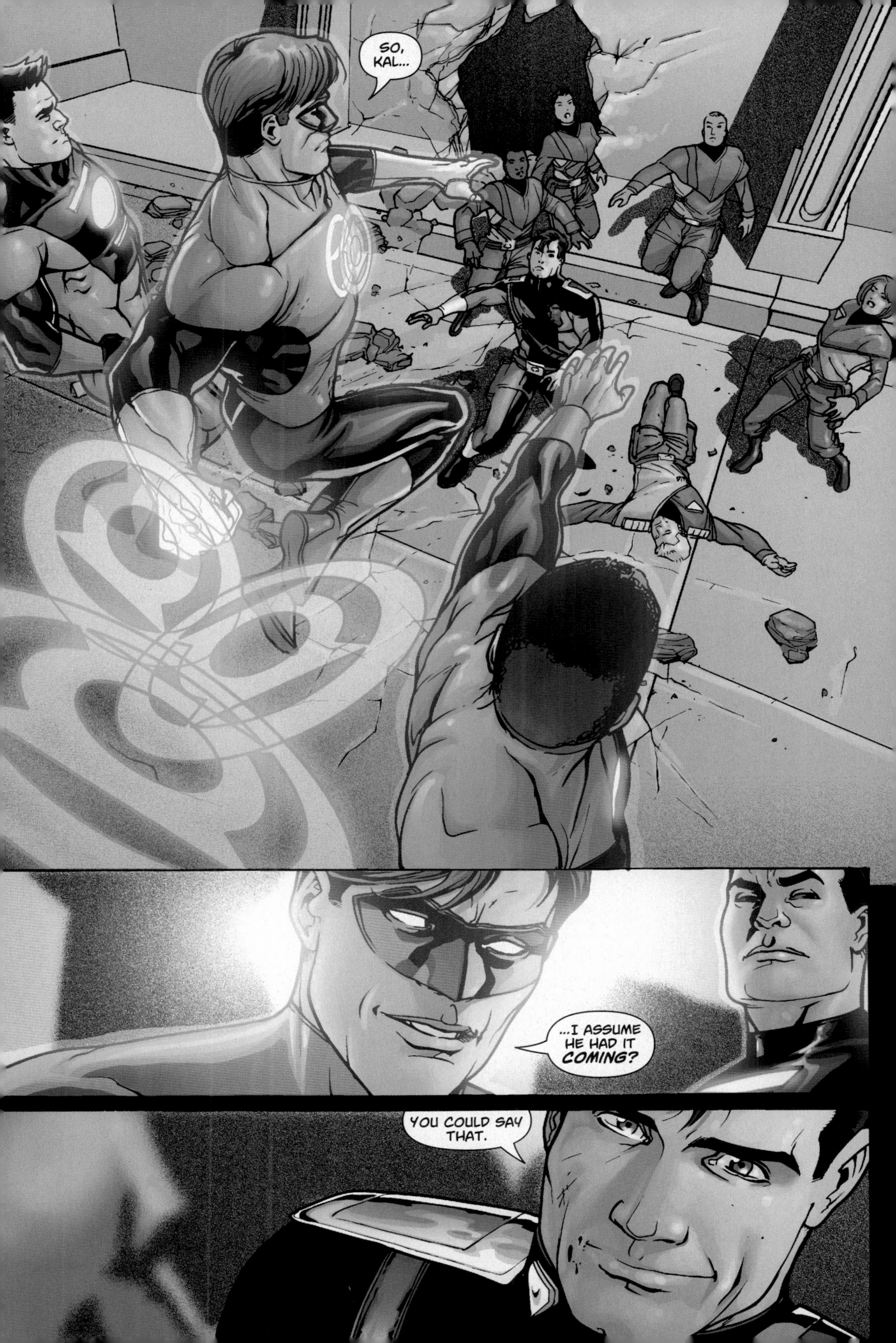
SO, KAL...
...I ASSUME HE HAD IT *COMING?*
YOU COULD SAY THAT.

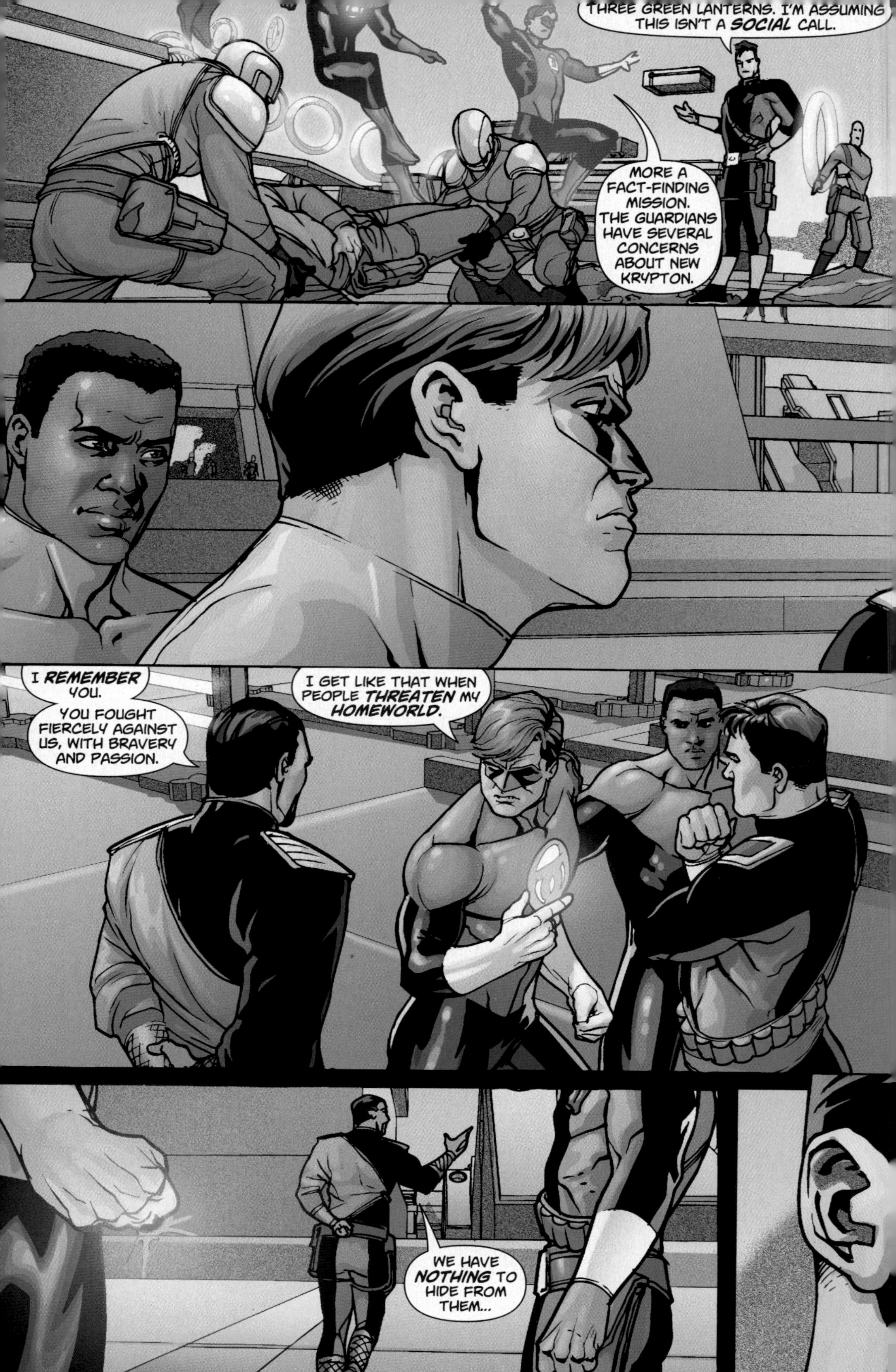
THREE GREEN LANTERNS. I'M ASSUMING THIS ISN'T A SOCIAL CALL.
MORE A FACT-FINDING MISSION. THE GUARDIANS HAVE SEVERAL CONCERNS ABOUT NEW KRYPTON.
I REMEMBER YOU.
YOU FOUGHT FIERCELY AGAINST US, WITH BRAVERY AND PASSION.
I GET LIKE THAT WHEN PEOPLE THREATEN MY HOMEWORLD.
WE HAVE NOTHING TO HIDE FROM THEM...

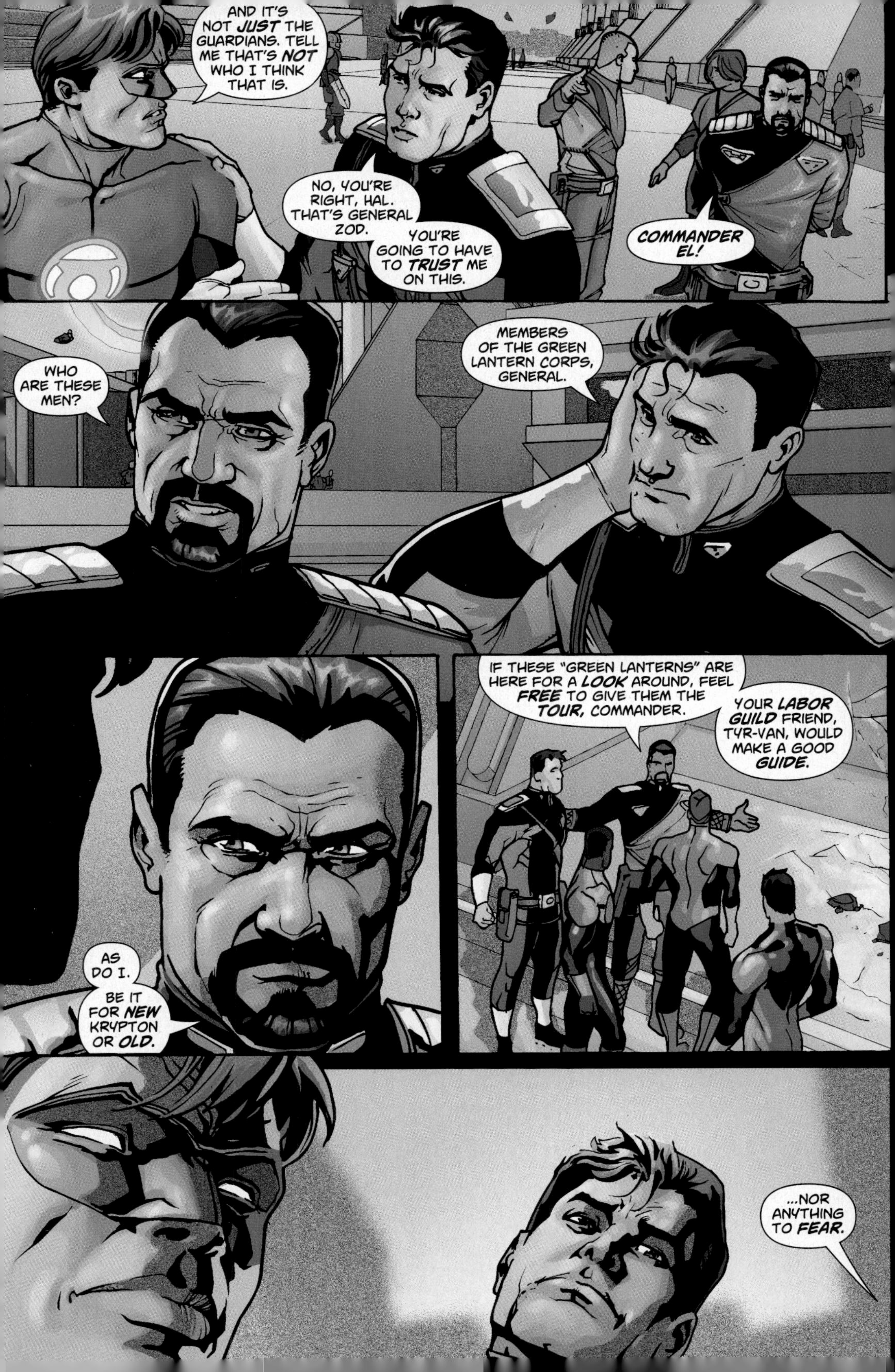
AND IT'S NOT JUST THE GUARDIANS. TELL ME THAT'S NOT WHO I THINK THAT IS.
NO, YOU'RE RIGHT, HAL. THAT'S GENERAL ZOD.
YOU'RE GOING TO HAVE TO TRUST ME ON THIS.
COMMANDER EL!
WHO ARE THESE MEN?
MEMBERS OF THE GREEN LANTERN CORPS, GENERAL.
AS DO I.
BE IT FOR NEW KRYPTON OR OLD.
IF THESE "GREEN LANTERNS" ARE HERE FOR A LOOK AROUND, FEEL FREE TO GIVE THEM THE TOUR, COMMANDER.
YOUR LABOR GUILD FRIEND, TYR-VAN, WOULD MAKE A GOOD GUIDE.
...NOR ANYTHING TO FEAR.

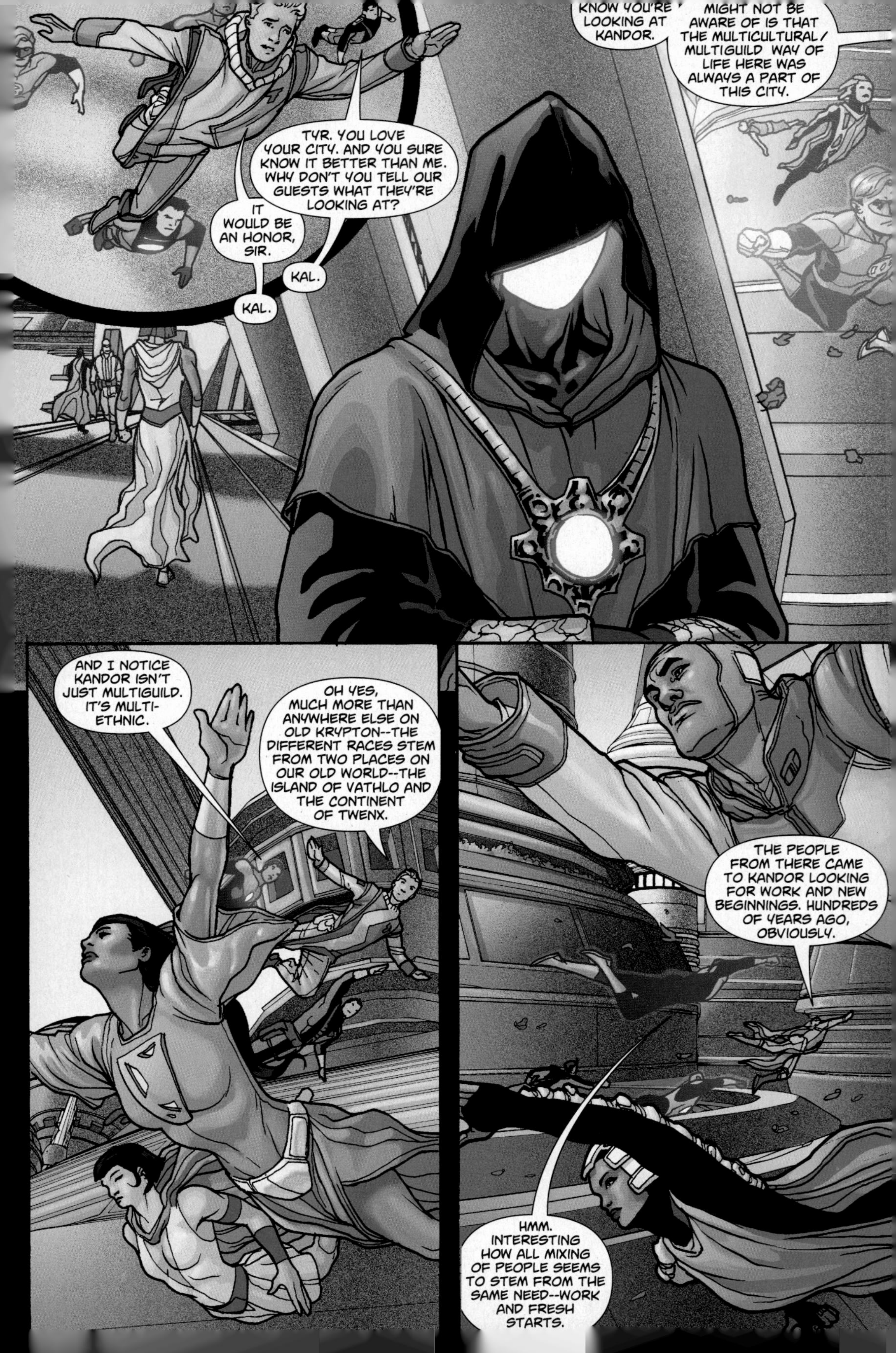
KNOW YOU'RE LOOKING AT KANDOR.
MIGHT NOT BE AWARE OF IS THAT THE MULTICULTURAL/ MULTIGUILD WAY OF LIFE HERE WAS ALWAYS A PART OF THIS CITY.
TYR. YOU LOVE YOUR CITY. AND YOU SURE KNOW IT BETTER THAN ME. WHY DON'T YOU TELL OUR GUESTS WHAT THEY'RE LOOKING AT?
KAL.
IT WOULD BE AN HONOR, SIR.
KAL.
AND I NOTICE KANDOR ISN'T JUST MULTIGUILD. IT'S MULTI-ETHNIC.
OH YES, MUCH MORE THAN ANYWHERE ELSE ON OLD KRYPTON--THE DIFFERENT RACES STEM FROM TWO PLACES ON OUR OLD WORLD--THE ISLAND OF VATHLO AND THE CONTINENT OF TWENX.
THE PEOPLE FROM THERE CAME TO KANDOR LOOKING FOR WORK AND NEW BEGINNINGS. HUNDREDS OF YEARS AGO, OBVIOUSLY.
HMM. INTERESTING HOW ALL MIXING OF PEOPLE SEEMS TO STEM FROM THE SAME NEED--WORK AND FRESH STARTS.

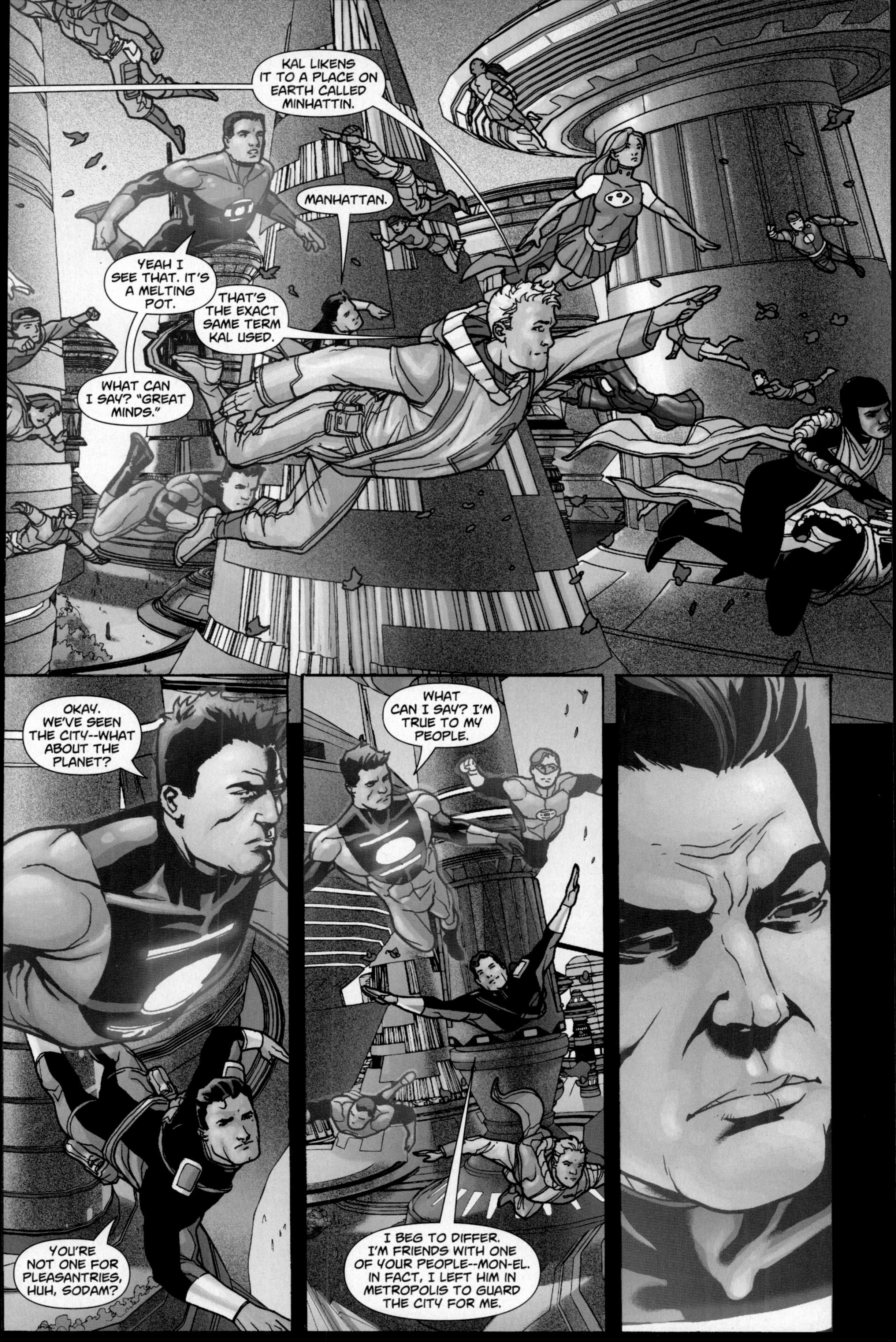
KAL LIKENS IT TO A PLACE ON EARTH CALLED MINHATTIN.
MANHATTAN.
YEAH I SEE THAT. IT'S A MELTING POT.
THAT'S THE EXACT SAME TERM KAL USED.
WHAT CAN I SAY? "GREAT MINDS."
OKAY. WE'VE SEEN THE CITY--WHAT ABOUT THE PLANET?
YOU'RE NOT ONE FOR PLEASANTRIES, HUH, SODAM?
WHAT CAN I SAY? I'M TRUE TO MY PEOPLE.
I BEG TO DIFFER. I'M FRIENDS WITH ONE OF YOUR PEOPLE--MON-EL. IN FACT, I LEFT HIM IN METROPOLIS TO GUARD THE CITY FOR ME.

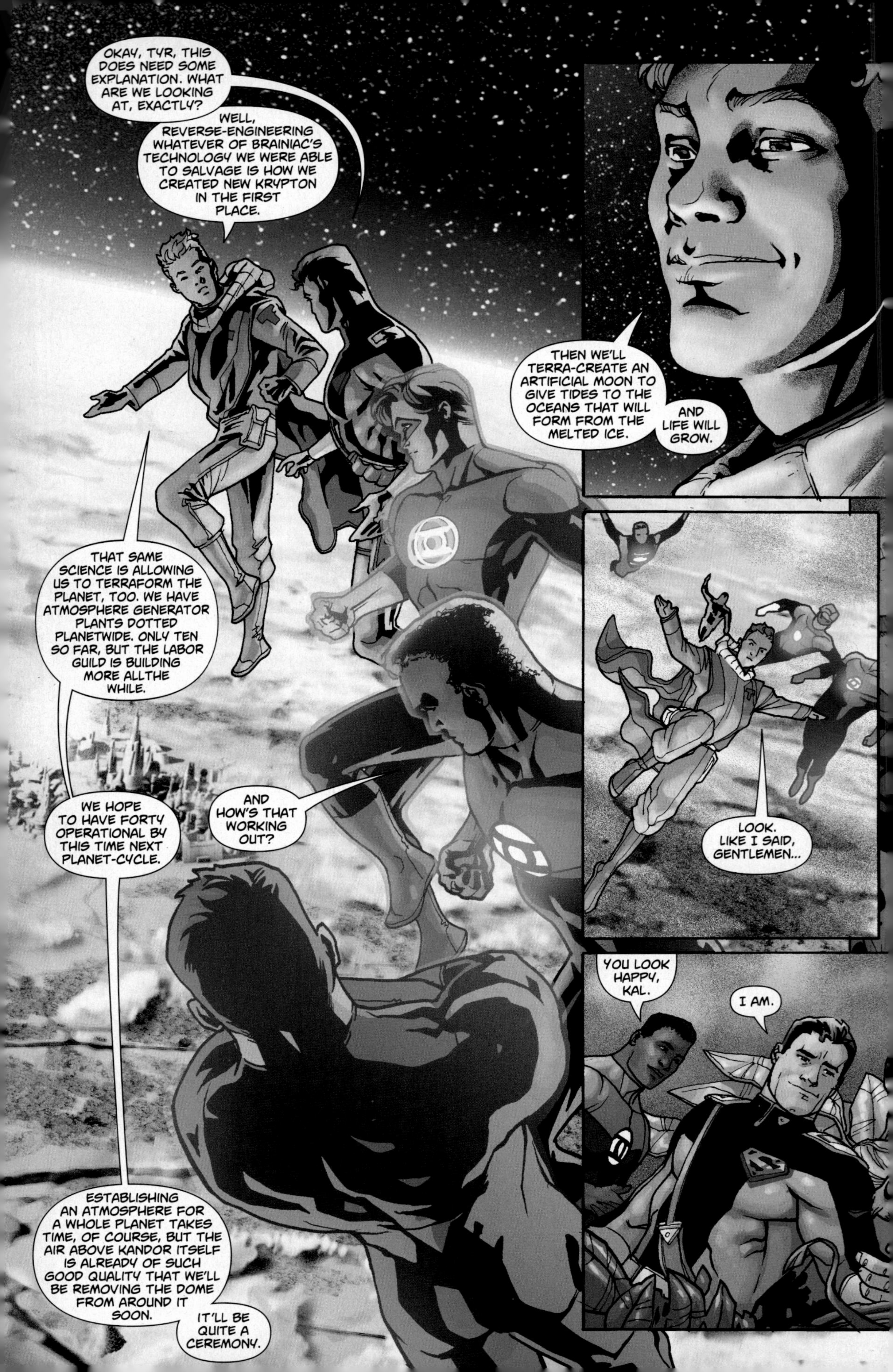
OKAY, TYR, THIS DOES NEED SOME EXPLANATION. WHAT ARE WE LOOKING AT, EXACTLY?
WELL, REVERSE-ENGINEERING WHATEVER OF BRAINIAC'S TECHNOLOGY WE WERE ABLE TO SALVAGE IS HOW WE CREATED NEW KRYPTON IN THE FIRST PLACE.
THAT SAME SCIENCE IS ALLOWING US TO TERRAFORM THE PLANET, TOO. WE HAVE ATMOSPHERE GENERATOR PLANTS DOTTED PLANETWIDE. ONLY TEN SO FAR, BUT THE LABOR GUILD IS BUILDING MORE ALLTHE WHILE.
WE HOPE TO HAVE FORTY OPERATIONAL BY THIS TIME NEXT PLANET-CYCLE.
AND HOW'S THAT WORKING OUT?
ESTABLISHING AN ATMOSPHERE FOR A WHOLE PLANET TAKES TIME, OF COURSE, BUT THE AIR ABOVE KANDOR ITSELF IS ALREADY OF SUCH GOOD QUALITY THAT WE'LL BE REMOVING THE DOME FROM AROUND IT SOON.
IT'LL BE QUITE A CEREMONY.
THEN WE'LL TERRA-CREATE AN ARTIFICIAL MOON TO GIVE TIDES TO THE OCEANS THAT WILL FORM FROM THE MELTED ICE.
AND LIFE WILL GROW.
LOOK. LIKE I SAID, GENTLEMEN...
YOU LOOK HAPPY, KAL.
I AM.

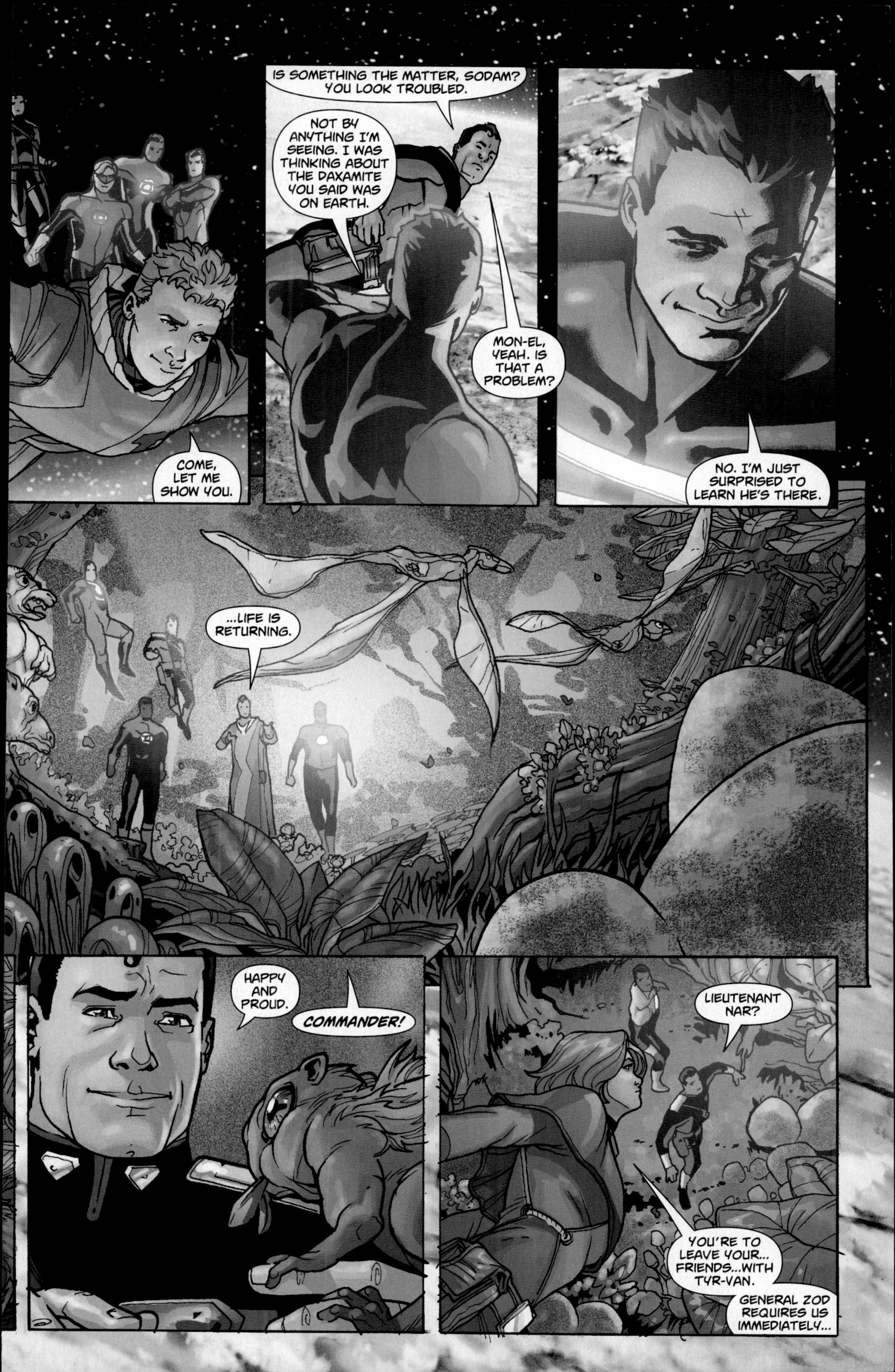
COME, LET ME SHOW YOU.
IS SOMETHING THE MATTER, SODAM? YOU LOOK TROUBLED.
NOT BY ANYTHING I'M SEEING. I WAS THINKING ABOUT THE DAXAMITE YOU SAID WAS ON EARTH.
MON-EL, YEAH. IS THAT A PROBLEM?
NO. I'M JUST SURPRISED TO LEARN HE'S THERE.
...LIFE IS RETURNING.
HAPPY AND PROUD.
COMMANDER!
LIEUTENANT NAR?
YOU'RE TO LEAVE YOUR... FRIENDS...WITH TYR-VAN.
GENERAL ZOD REQUIRES US IMMEDIATELY...

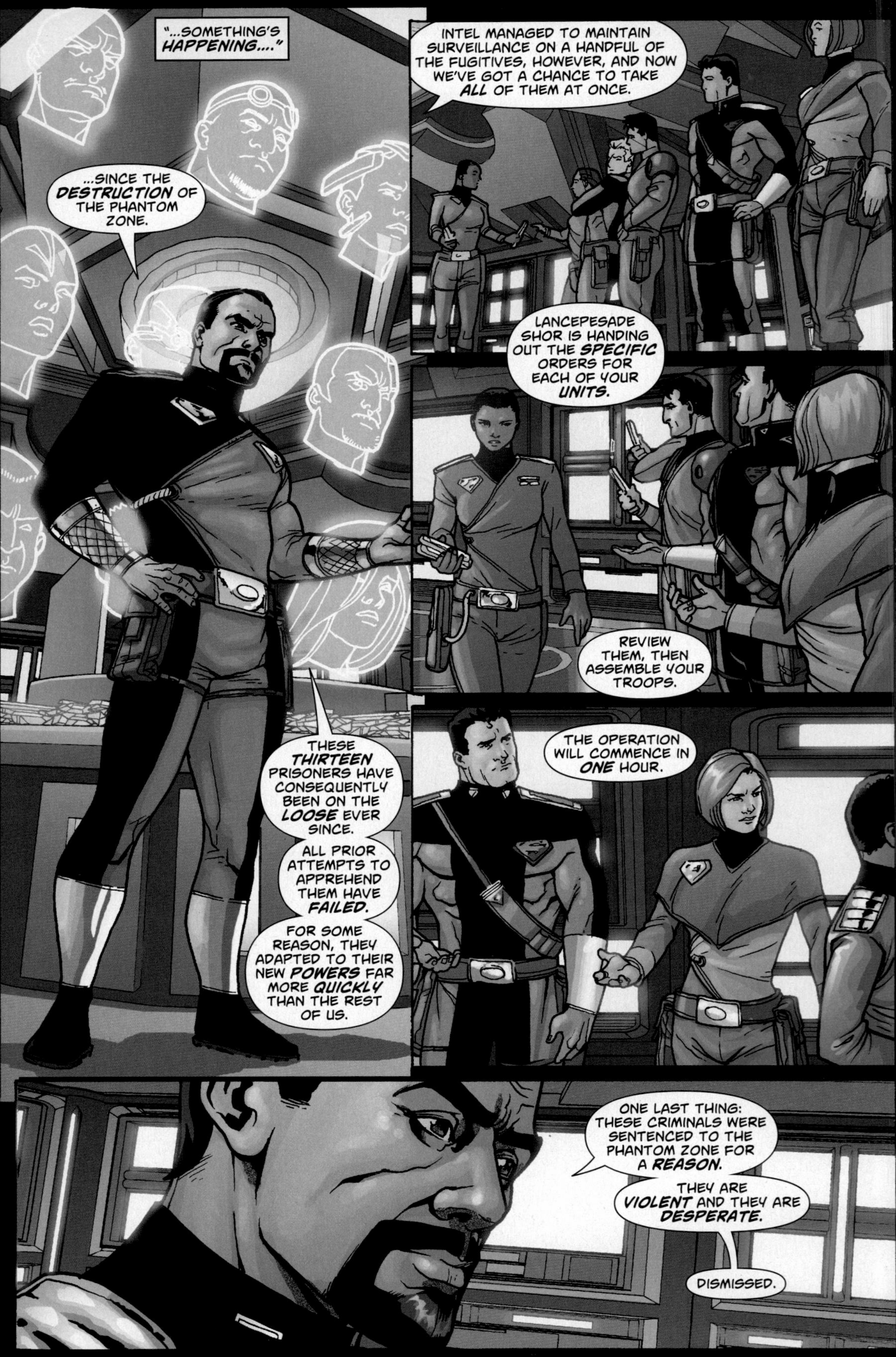
"...SOMETHING'S HAPPENING...."
...SINCE THE DESTRUCTION OF THE PHANTOM ZONE.
THESE THIRTEEN PRISONERS HAVE CONSEQUENTLY BEEN ON THE LOOSE EVER SINCE.
ALL PRIOR ATTEMPTS TO APPREHEND THEM HAVE FAILED.
FOR SOME REASON, THEY ADAPTED TO THEIR NEW POWERS FAR MORE QUICKLY THAN THE REST OF US.
INTEL MANAGED TO MAINTAIN SURVEILLANCE ON A HANDFUL OF THE FUGITIVES, HOWEVER, AND NOW WE'VE GOT A CHANCE TO TAKE ALL OF THEM AT ONCE.
LANCEPESADE SHOR IS HANDING OUT THE SPECIFIC ORDERS FOR EACH OF YOUR UNITS.
REVIEW THEM, THEN ASSEMBLE YOUR TROOPS.
THE OPERATION WILL COMMENCE IN ONE HOUR.
ONE LAST THING: THESE CRIMINALS WERE SENTENCED TO THE PHANTOM ZONE FOR A REASON.
THEY ARE VIOLENT AND THEY ARE DESPERATE.
DISMISSED.

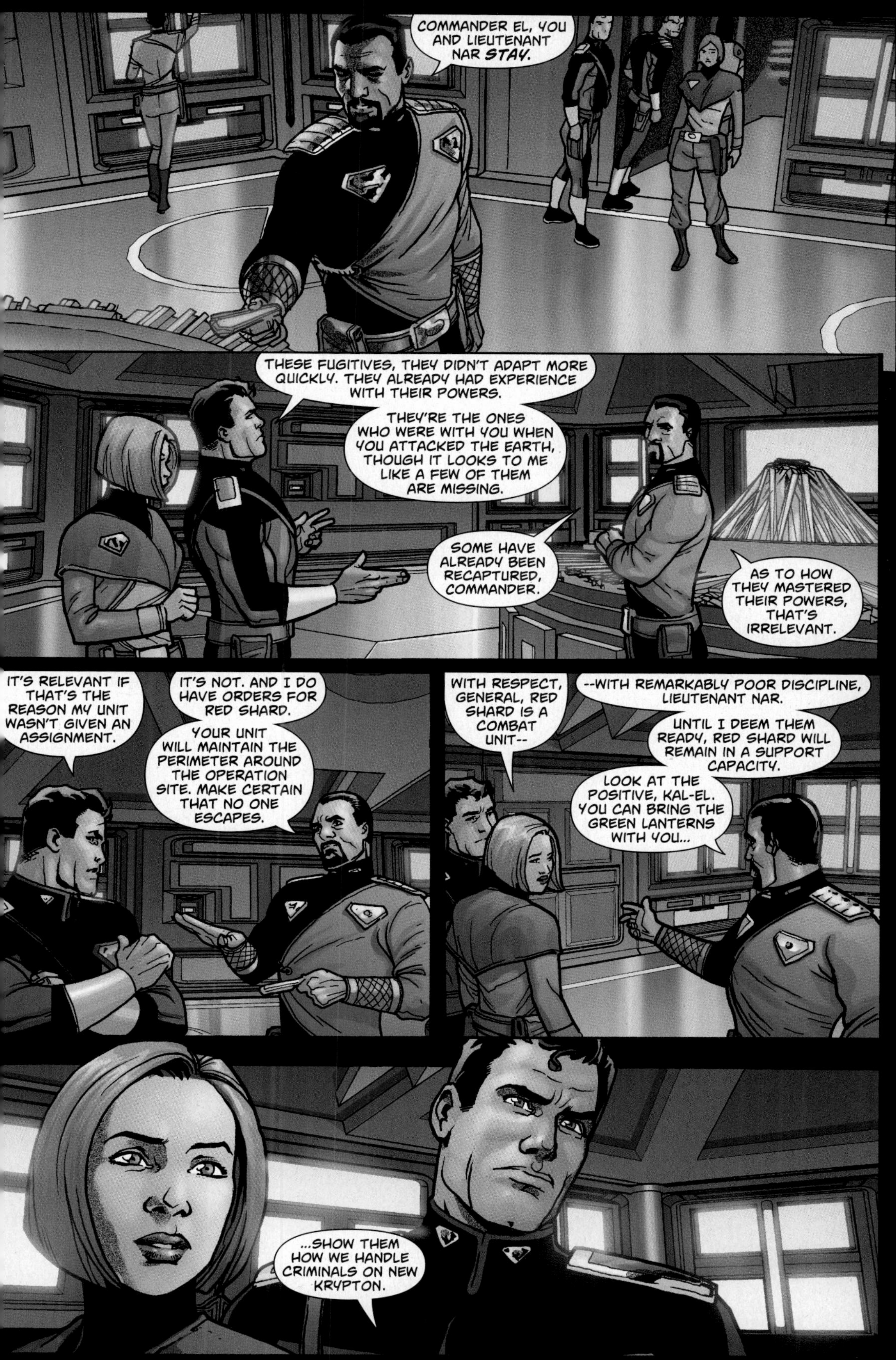
COMMANDER EL, YOU AND LIEUTENANT NAR STAY.
THESE FUGITIVES, THEY DIDN'T ADAPT MORE QUICKLY. THEY ALREADY HAD EXPERIENCE WITH THEIR POWERS.
THEY'RE THE ONES WHO WERE WITH YOU WHEN YOU ATTACKED THE EARTH, THOUGH IT LOOKS TO ME LIKE A FEW OF THEM ARE MISSING.
SOME HAVE ALREADY BEEN RECAPTURED, COMMANDER.
AS TO HOW THEY MASTERED THEIR POWERS, THAT'S IRRELEVANT.
IT'S RELEVANT IF THAT'S THE REASON MY UNIT WASN'T GIVEN AN ASSIGNMENT.
IT'S NOT. AND I DO HAVE ORDERS FOR RED SHARD.
YOUR UNIT WILL MAINTAIN THE PERIMETER AROUND THE OPERATION SITE. MAKE CERTAIN THAT NO ONE ESCAPES.
WITH RESPECT, GENERAL, RED SHARD IS A COMBAT UNIT--
--WITH REMARKABLY POOR DISCIPLINE, LIEUTENANT NAR.
UNTIL I DEEM THEM READY, RED SHARD WILL REMAIN IN A SUPPORT CAPACITY.
LOOK AT THE POSITIVE, KAL-EL. YOU CAN BRING THE GREEN LANTERNS WITH YOU...
...SHOW THEM HOW WE HANDLE CRIMINALS ON NEW KRYPTON.

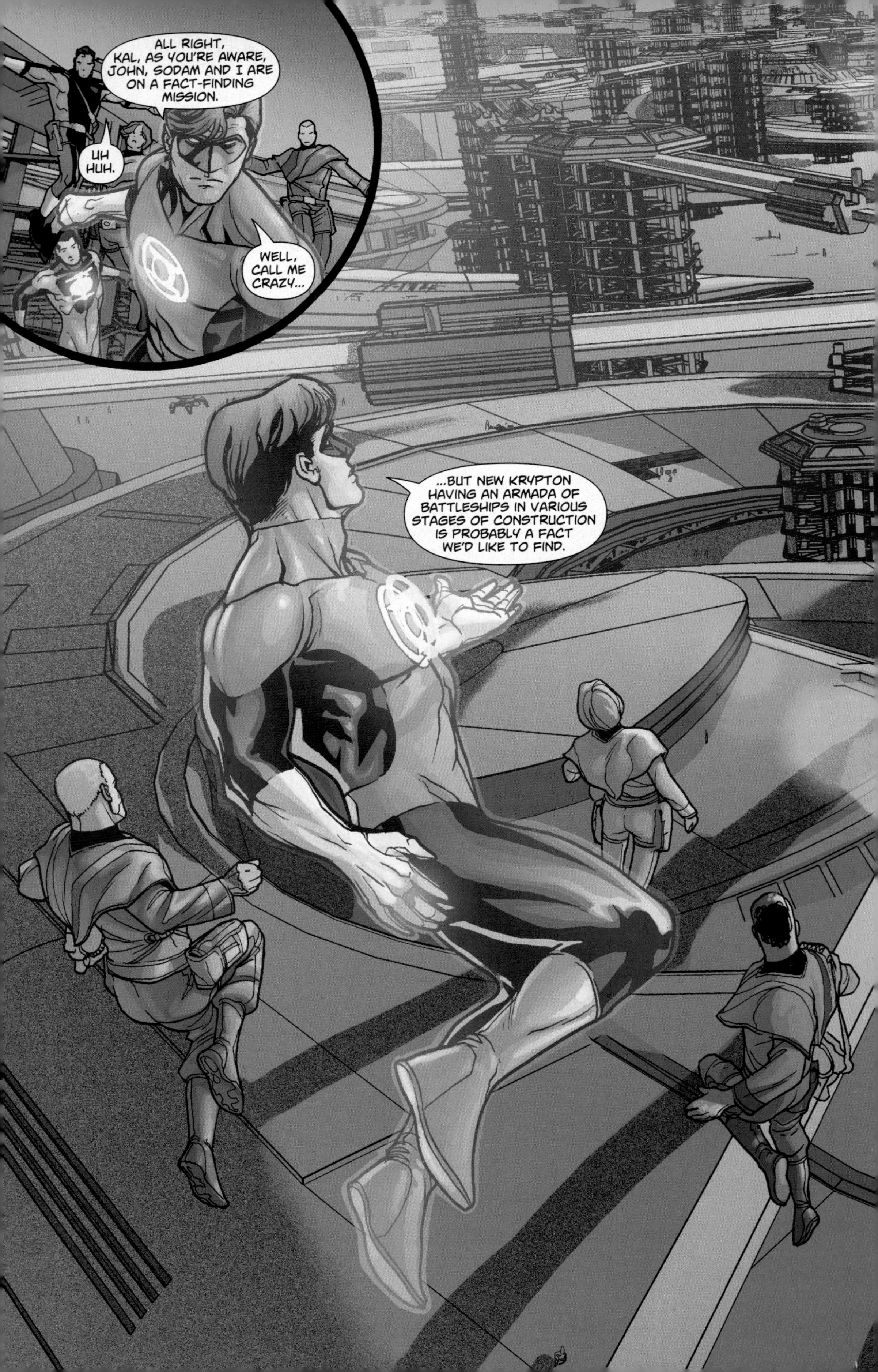
ALL RIGHT, KAL, AS YOU'RE AWARE, JOHN, SODAM AND I ARE ON A FACT-FINDING MISSION.
UH HUH.
WELL, CALL ME CRAZY...
...BUT NEW KRYPTON HAVING AN ARMADA OF BATTLESHIPS IN VARIOUS STAGES OF CONSTRUCTION IS PROBABLY A FACT WE'D LIKE TO FIND.

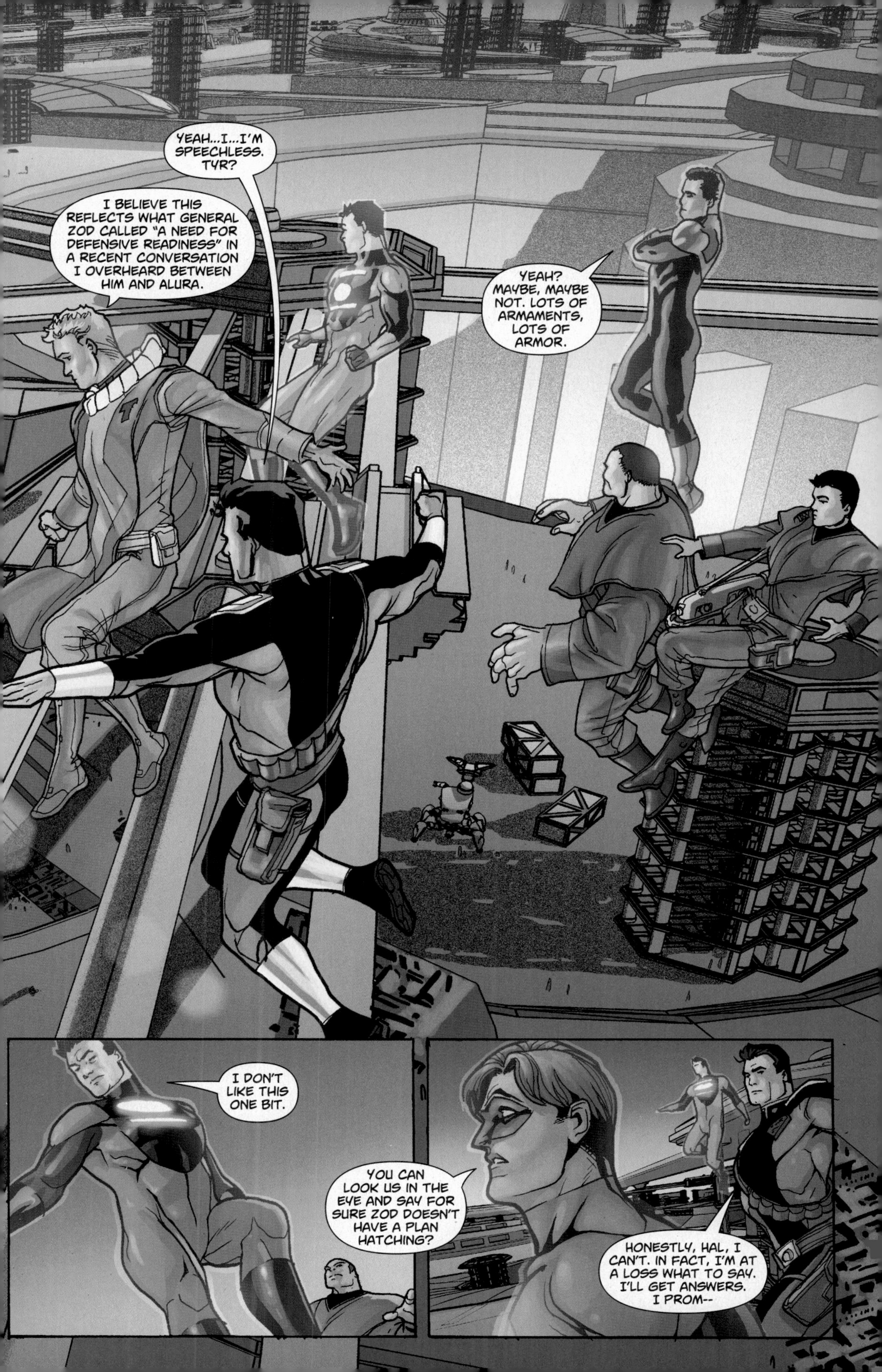
I BELIEVE THIS REFLECTS WHAT GENERAL ZOD CALLED "A NEED FOR DEFENSIVE READINESS" IN A RECENT CONVERSATION I OVERHEARD BETWEEN HIM AND ALURA.
YEAH...I...I'M SPEECHLESS. TYR?
YEAH? MAYBE, MAYBE NOT. LOTS OF ARMAMENTS, LOTS OF ARMOR.
I DON'T LIKE THIS ONE BIT.
YOU CAN LOOK US IN THE EYE AND SAY FOR SURE ZOD DOESN'T HAVE A PLAN HATCHING?
HONESTLY, HAL, I CAN'T. IN FACT, I'M AT A LOSS WHAT TO SAY. I'LL GET ANSWERS. I PROM--

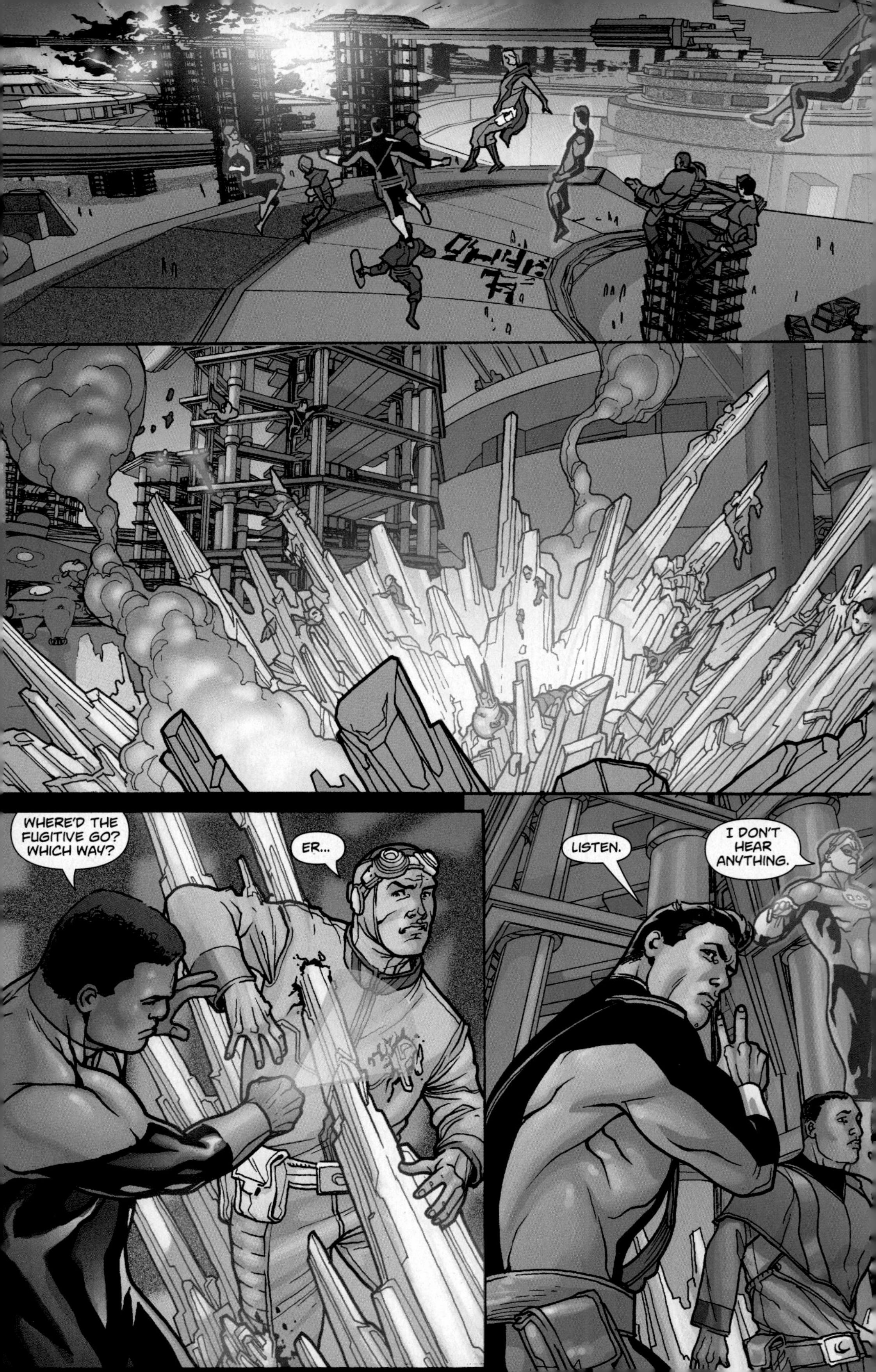

WHERE'D THE FUGITIVE GO? WHICH WAY?
ER...
LISTEN.
I DON'T HEAR ANYTHING.

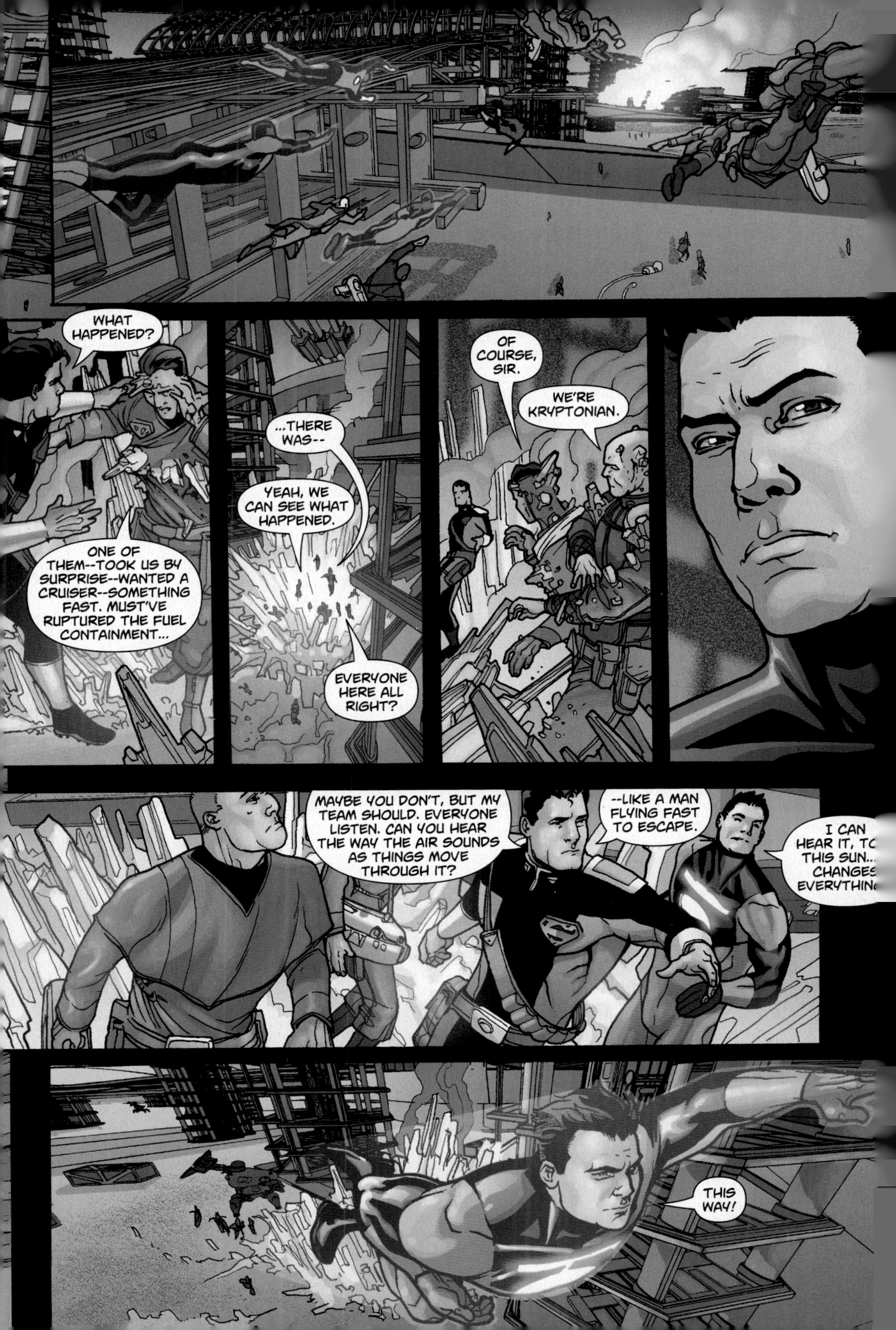

WHAT HAPPENED?
...THERE WAS--
ONE OF THEM--TOOK US BY SURPRISE--WANTED A CRUISER--SOMETHING FAST. MUST'VE RUPTURED THE FUEL CONTAINMENT...
YEAH, WE CAN SEE WHAT HAPPENED.
EVERYONE HERE ALL RIGHT?
OF COURSE, SIR.
WE'RE KRYPTONIAN.
MAYBE YOU DON'T, BUT MY TEAM SHOULD. EVERYONE LISTEN. CAN YOU HEAR THE WAY THE AIR SOUNDS AS THINGS MOVE THROUGH IT?
--LIKE A MAN FLYING FAST TO ESCAPE.
I CAN HEAR IT, TO THIS SUN... CHANGES EVERYTHIN
THIS WAY!

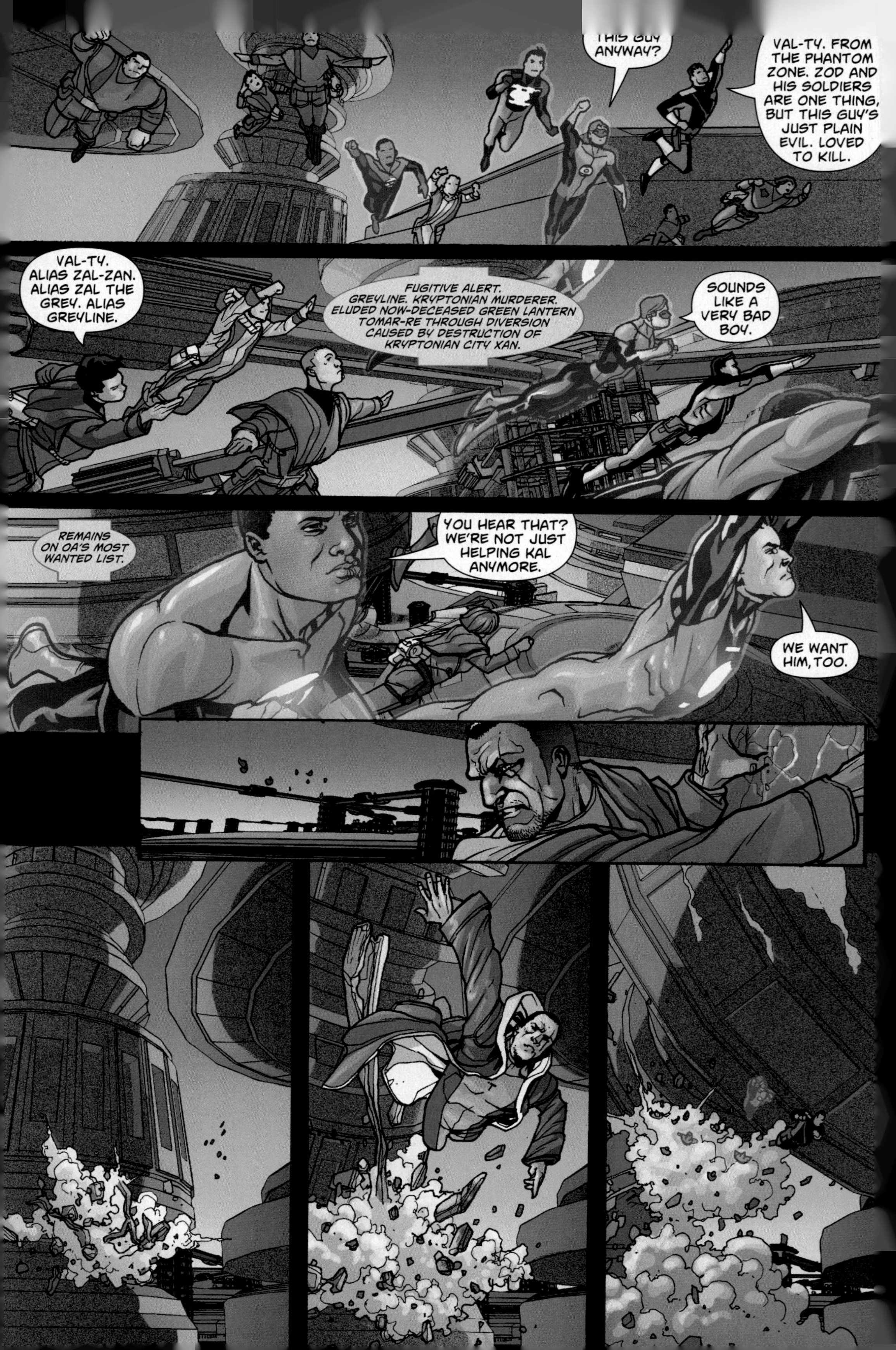

THIS GUY ANYWAY?
VAL-TY. FROM THE PHANTOM ZONE. ZOD AND HIS SOLDIERS ARE ONE THING, BUT THIS GUY'S JUST PLAIN EVIL. LOVED TO KILL.
VAL-TY. ALIAS ZAL-ZAN. ALIAS ZAL THE GREY. ALIAS GREYLINE.
FUGITIVE ALERT. GREYLINE. KRYPTONIAN MURDERER. ELUDED NOW-DECEASED GREEN LANTERN TOMAR-RE THROUGH DIVERSION CAUSED BY DESTRUCTION OF KRYPTONIAN CITY XAN.
SOUNDS LIKE A VERY BAD BOY.
REMAINS ON OA'S MOST WANTED LIST.
YOU HEAR THAT? WE'RE NOT JUST HELPING KAL ANYMORE.
WE WANT HIM, TOO.

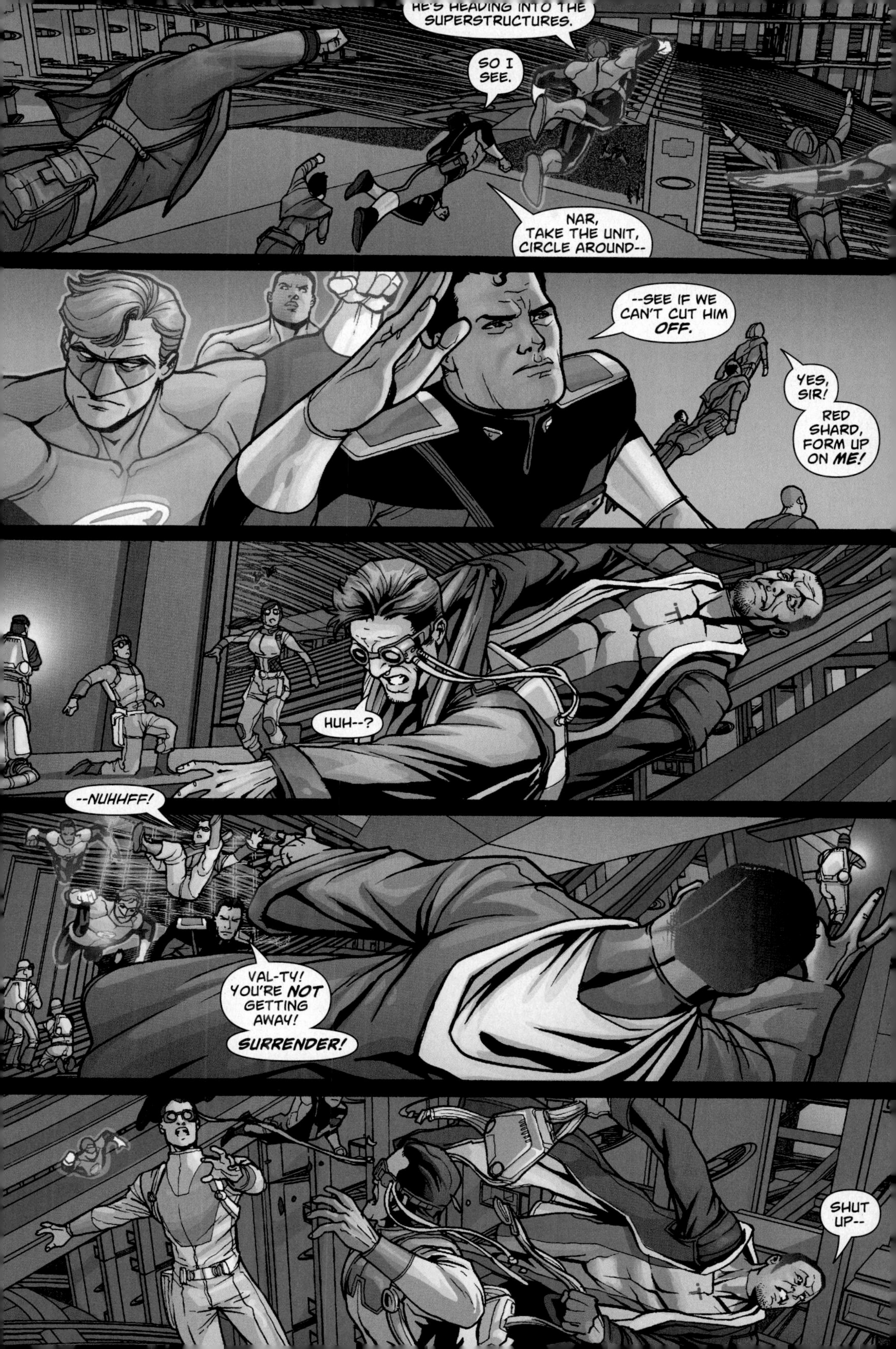
HE'S HEADING INTO THE SUPERSTRUCTURES.
SO I SEE.
NAR, TAKE THE UNIT, CIRCLE AROUND--
--SEE IF WE CAN'T CUT HIM OFF.
YES, SIR!
RED SHARD, FORM UP ON ME!
HUH--?
--NUHHFF!
VAL-TY! YOU'RE NOT GETTING AWAY!
SURRENDER!
SHUT UP--

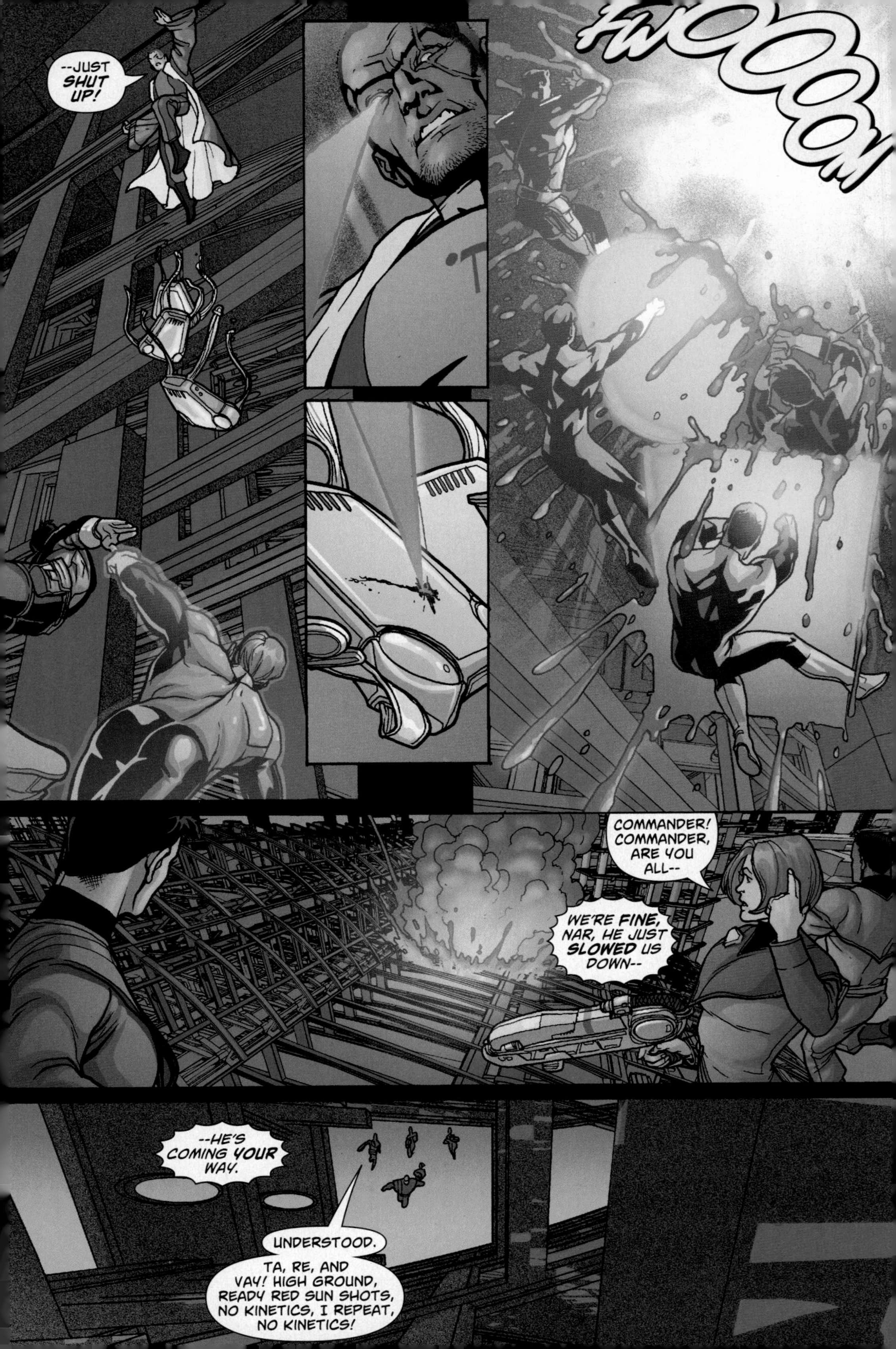
--JUST SHUT UP!
FWOOOOOM
COMMANDER! COMMANDER, ARE YOU ALL--
WE'RE FINE, NAR, HE JUST SLOWED US DOWN--
--HE'S COMING YOUR WAY.
UNDERSTOOD.
TA, RE, AND VAY! HIGH GROUND, READY RED SUN SHOTS, NO KINETICS, I REPEAT, NO KINETICS!

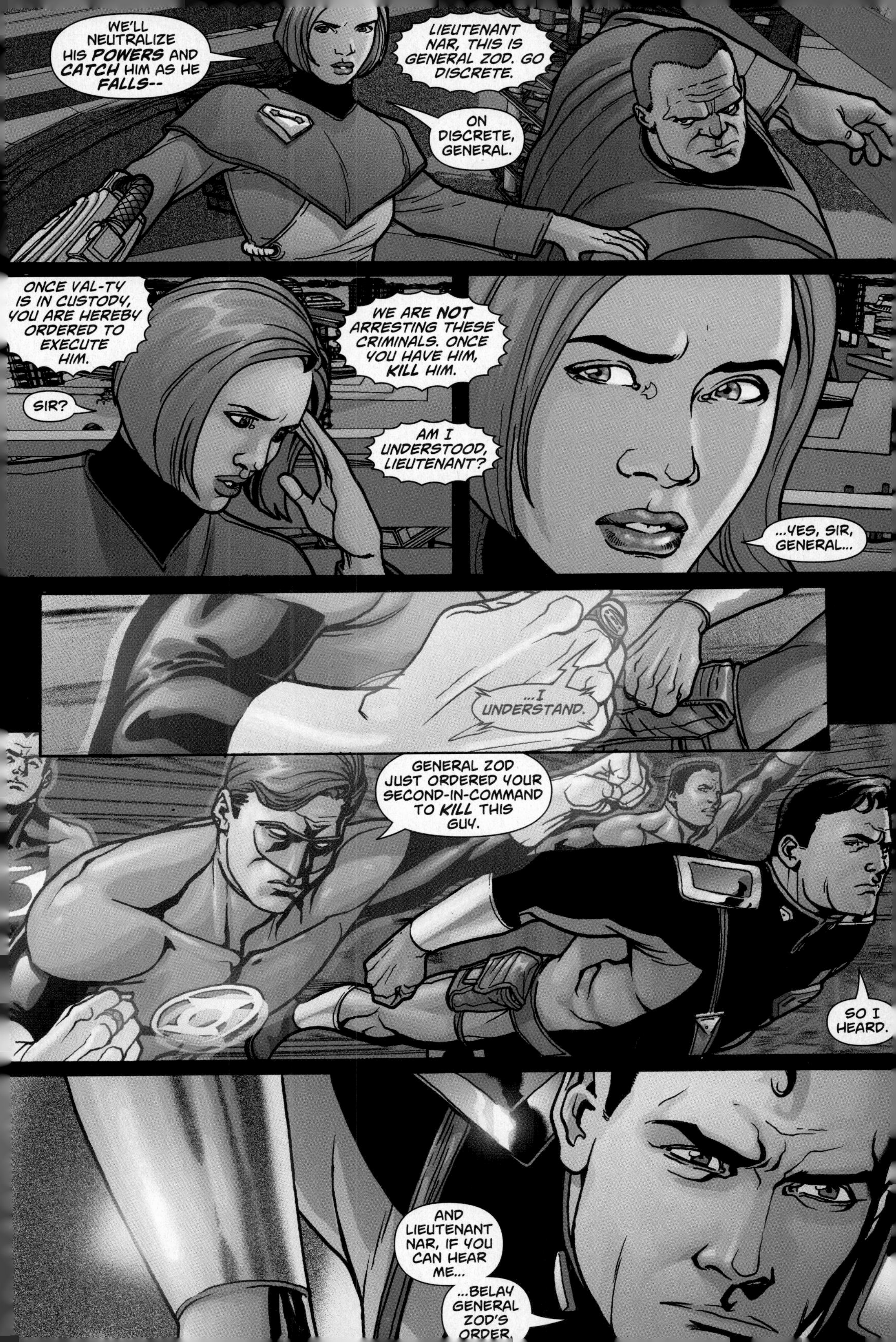
WE'LL NEUTRALIZE HIS POWERS AND CATCH HIM AS HE FALLS--
LIEUTENANT NAR, THIS IS GENERAL ZOD. GO DISCRETE.
ON DISCRETE, GENERAL.
ONCE VAL-TY IS IN CUSTODY, YOU ARE HEREBY ORDERED TO EXECUTE HIM.
SIR?
WE ARE NOT ARRESTING THESE CRIMINALS. ONCE YOU HAVE HIM, KILL HIM.
AM I UNDERSTOOD, LIEUTENANT?
...YES, SIR, GENERAL...
...I UNDERSTAND.
GENERAL ZOD JUST ORDERED YOUR SECOND-IN-COMMAND TO KILL THIS GUY.
SO I HEARD.
AND LIEUTENANT NAR, IF YOU CAN HEAR ME...
...BELAY GENERAL ZOD'S ORDER.

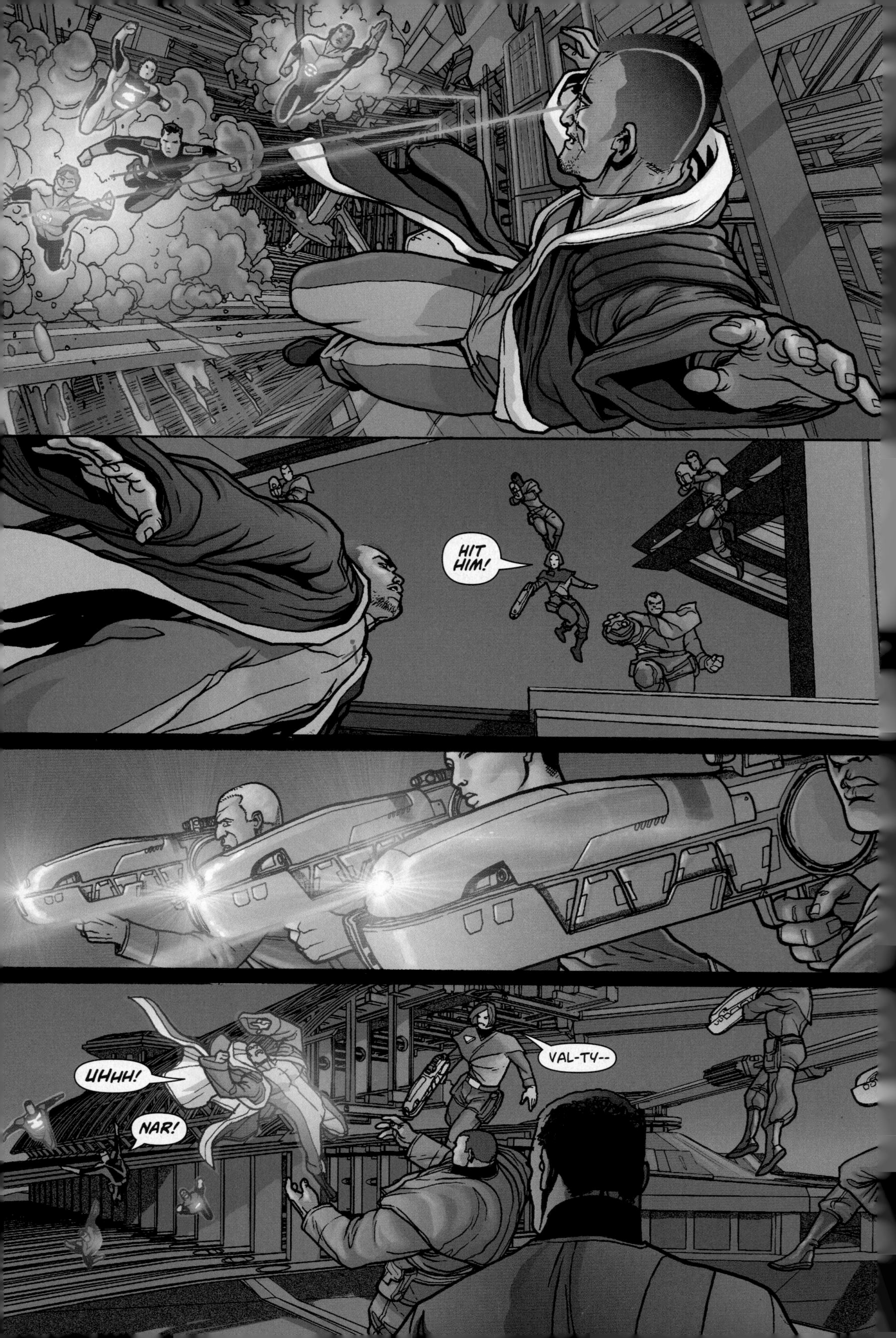
HIT HIM!
VAL-TY--
UHHH!
NAR!

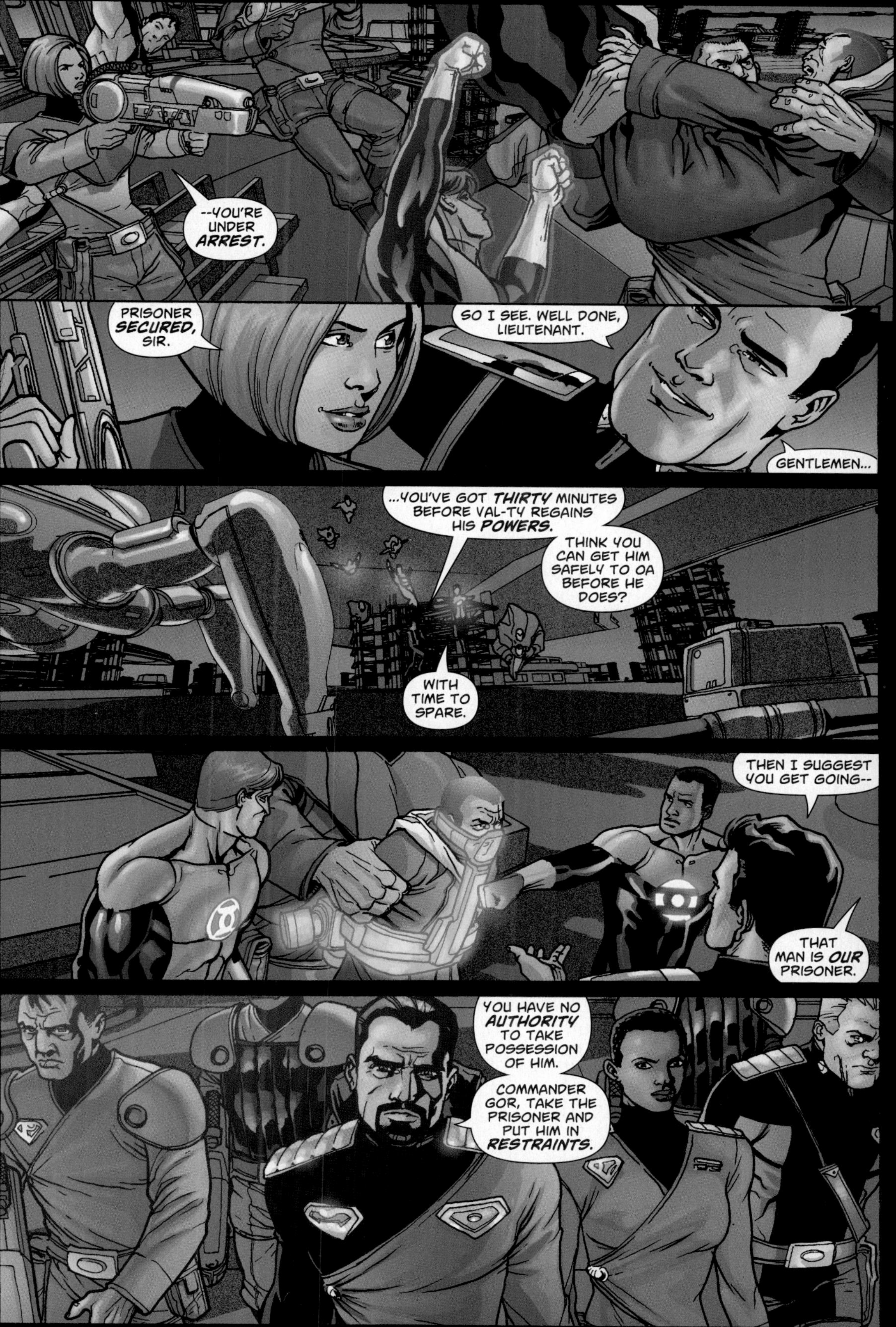
--YOU'RE UNDER ARREST.
PRISONER SECURED, SIR.
SO I SEE. WELL DONE, LIEUTENANT.
GENTLEMEN...
...YOU'VE GOT THIRTY MINUTES BEFORE VAL-TY REGAINS HIS POWERS.
THINK YOU CAN GET HIM SAFELY TO OA BEFORE HE DOES?
WITH TIME TO SPARE.
THEN I SUGGEST YOU GET GOING--
THAT MAN IS OUR PRISONER.
YOU HAVE NO AUTHORITY TO TAKE POSSESSION OF HIM.
COMMANDER GOR, TAKE THE PRISONER AND PUT HIM IN RESTRAINTS.

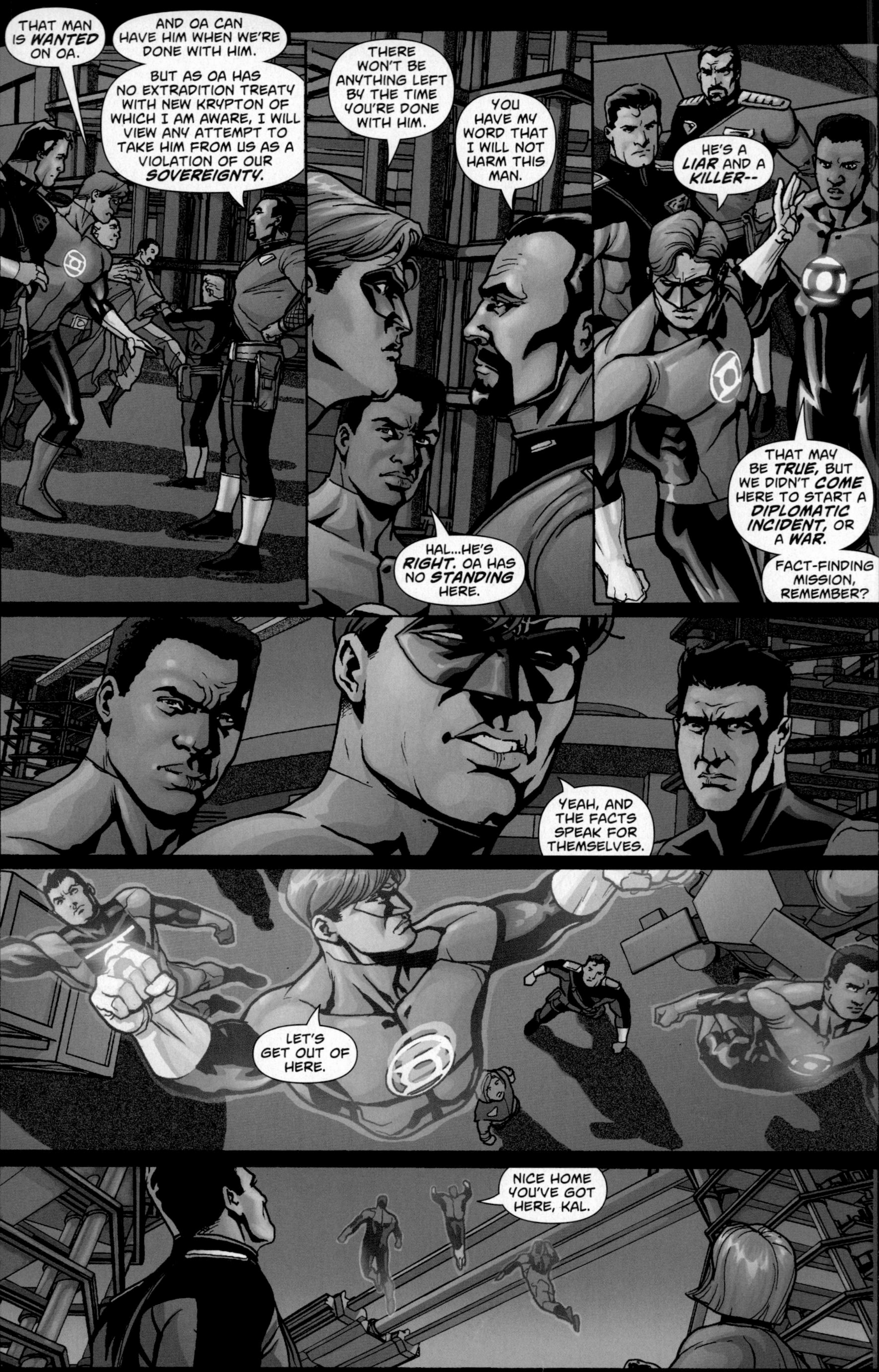
THAT MAN IS WANTED ON OA.
AND OA CAN HAVE HIM WHEN WE'RE DONE WITH HIM.
BUT AS OA HAS NO EXTRADITION TREATY WITH NEW KRYPTON OF WHICH I AM AWARE, I WILL VIEW ANY ATTEMPT TO TAKE HIM FROM US AS A VIOLATION OF OUR SOVEREIGNTY.
THERE WON'T BE ANYTHING LEFT BY THE TIME YOU'RE DONE WITH HIM.
YOU HAVE MY WORD THAT I WILL NOT HARM THIS MAN.
HAL...HE'S RIGHT. OA HAS NO STANDING HERE.
HE'S A LIAR AND A KILLER--
THAT MAY BE TRUE, BUT WE DIDN'T COME HERE TO START A DIPLOMATIC INCIDENT, OR A WAR.
FACT-FINDING MISSION, REMEMBER?
YEAH, AND THE FACTS SPEAK FOR THEMSELVES.
LET'S GET OUT OF HERE.
NICE HOME YOU'VE GOT HERE, KAL.

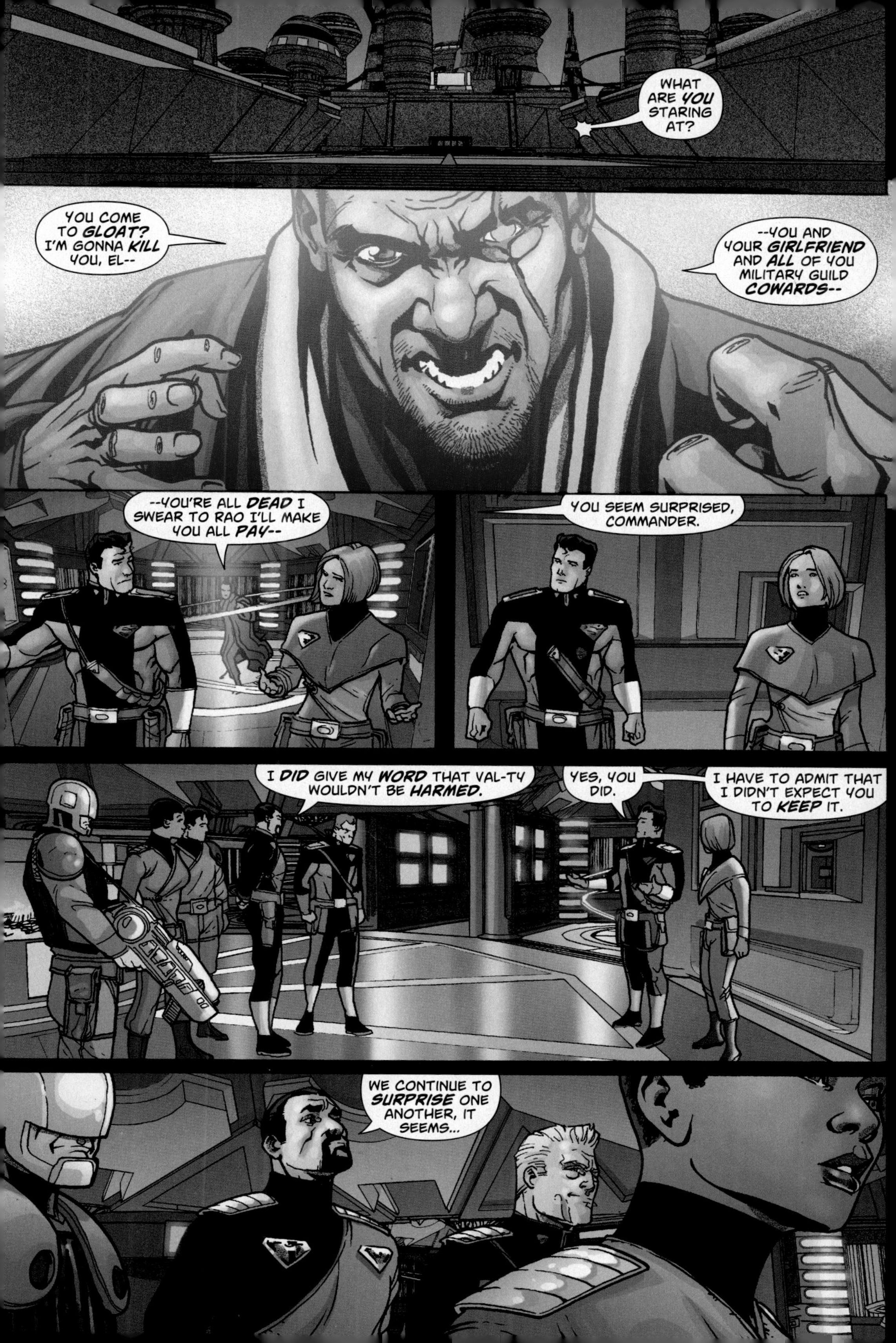

WHAT ARE YOU STARING AT?
YOU COME TO GLOAT? I'M GONNA KILL YOU, EL--
--YOU AND YOUR GIRLFRIEND AND ALL OF YOU MILITARY GUILD COWARDS--
--YOU'RE ALL DEAD I SWEAR TO RAO I'LL MAKE YOU ALL PAY--
YOU SEEM SURPRISED, COMMANDER.
I DID GIVE MY WORD THAT VAL-TY WOULDN'T BE HARMED.
YES, YOU DID.
I HAVE TO ADMIT THAT I DIDN'T EXPECT YOU TO KEEP IT.
WE CONTINUE TO SURPRISE ONE ANOTHER, IT SEEMS...

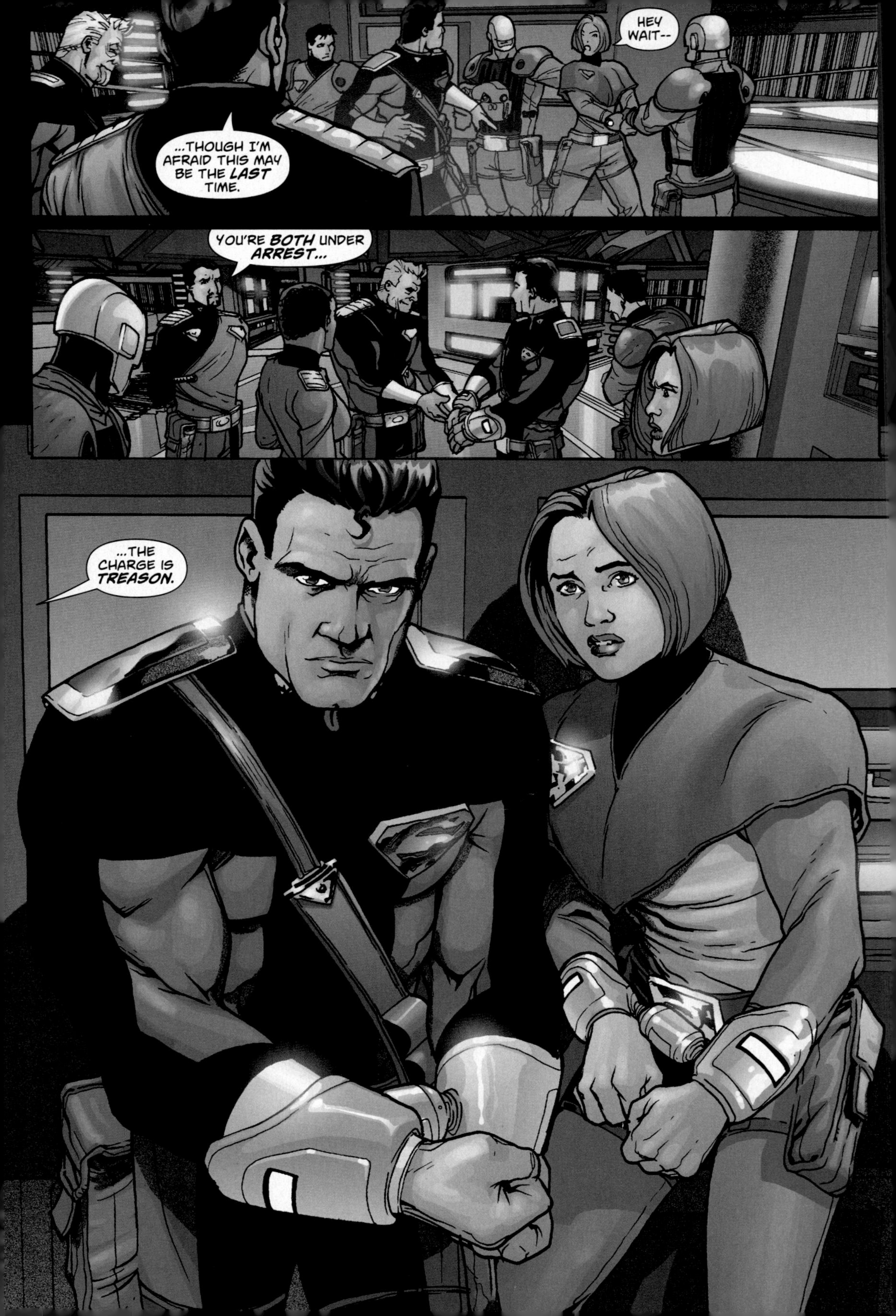

...THOUGH I'M AFRAID THIS MAY BE THE LAST TIME.
HEY WAIT--
YOU'RE BOTH UNDER ARREST...
...THE CHARGE IS TREASON.

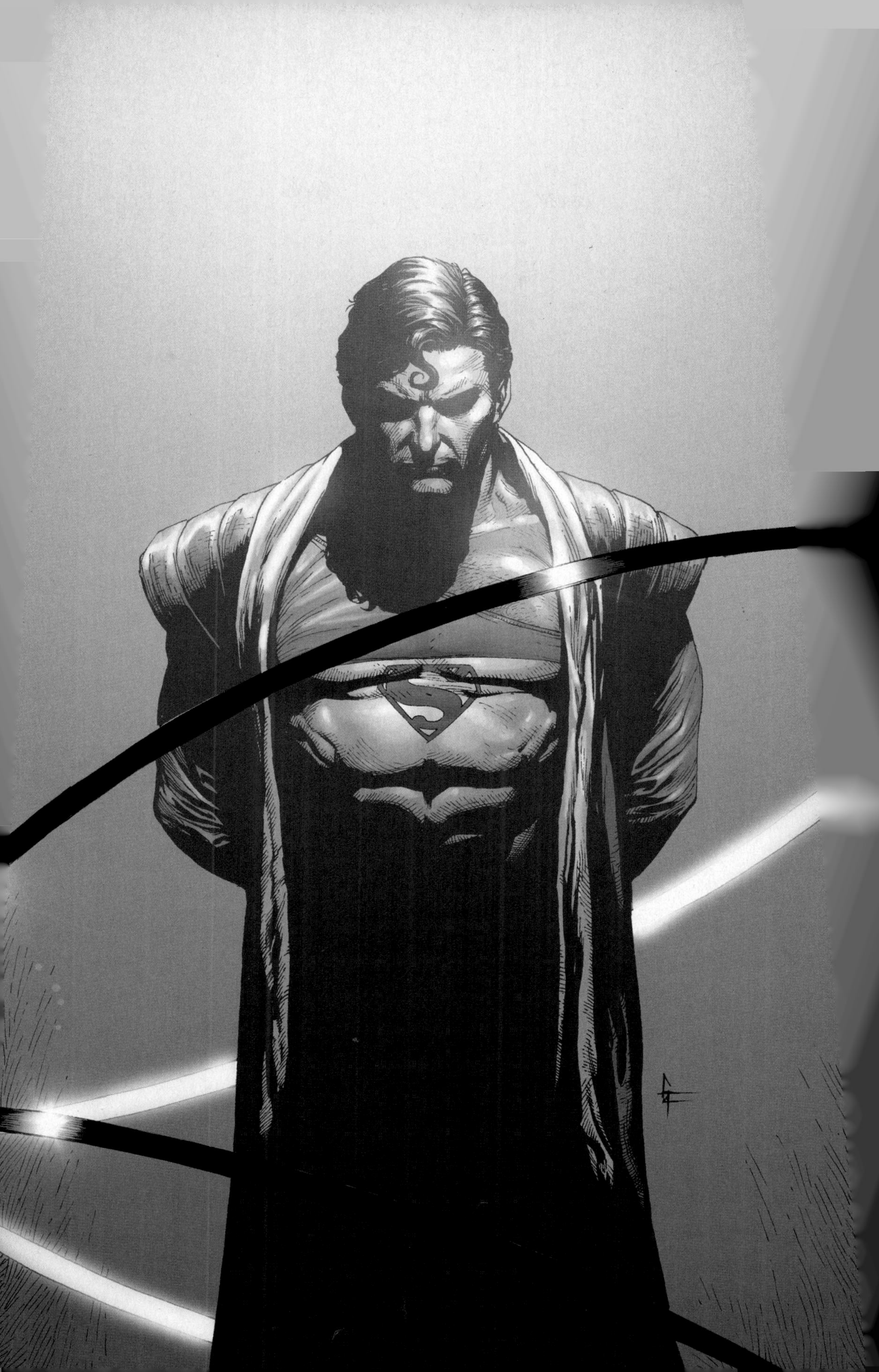

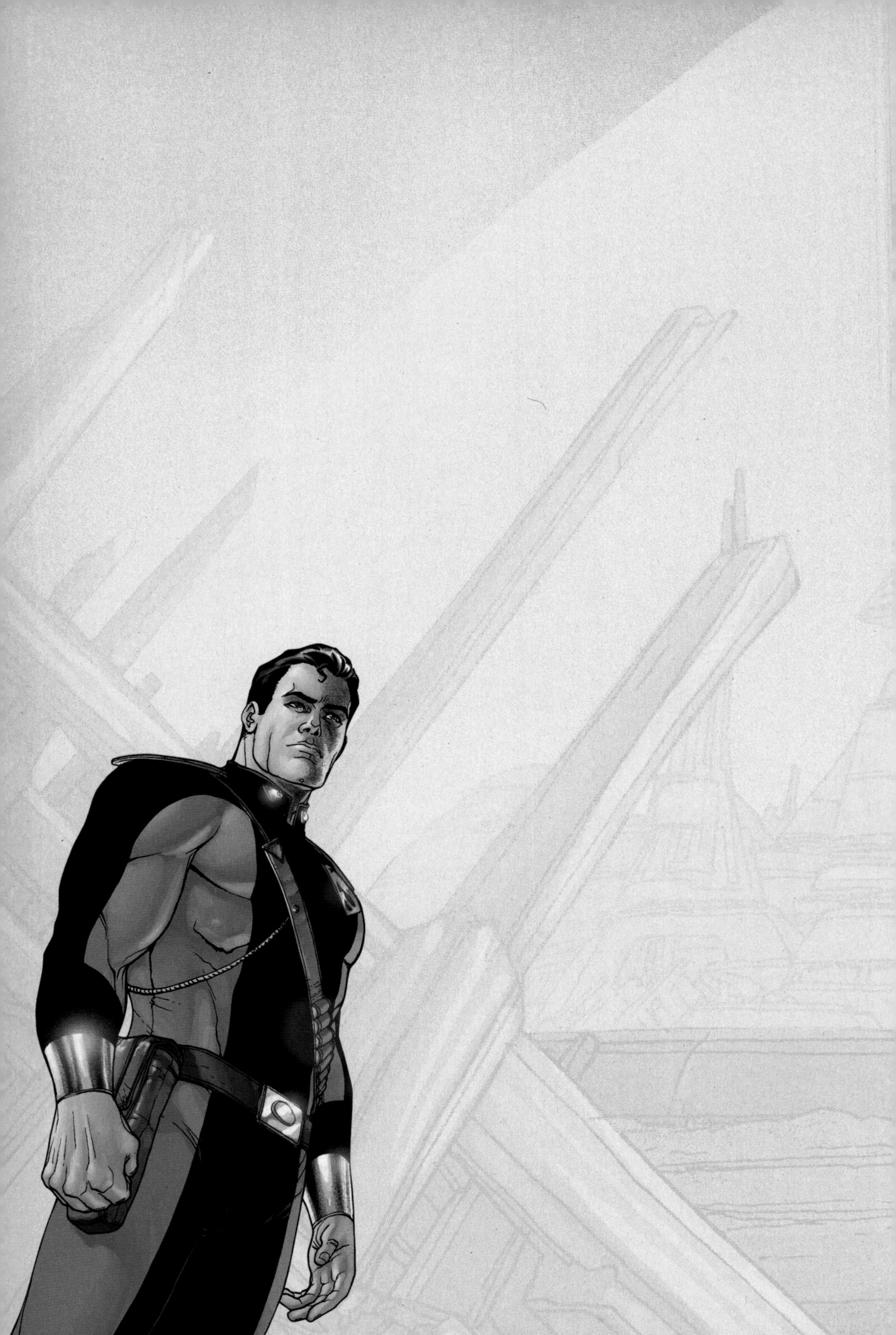

WORLD OF NEW KRYPTON <PART FIVE>
COVER BY **GARY FRANK** WITH **BRAD ANDERSON**

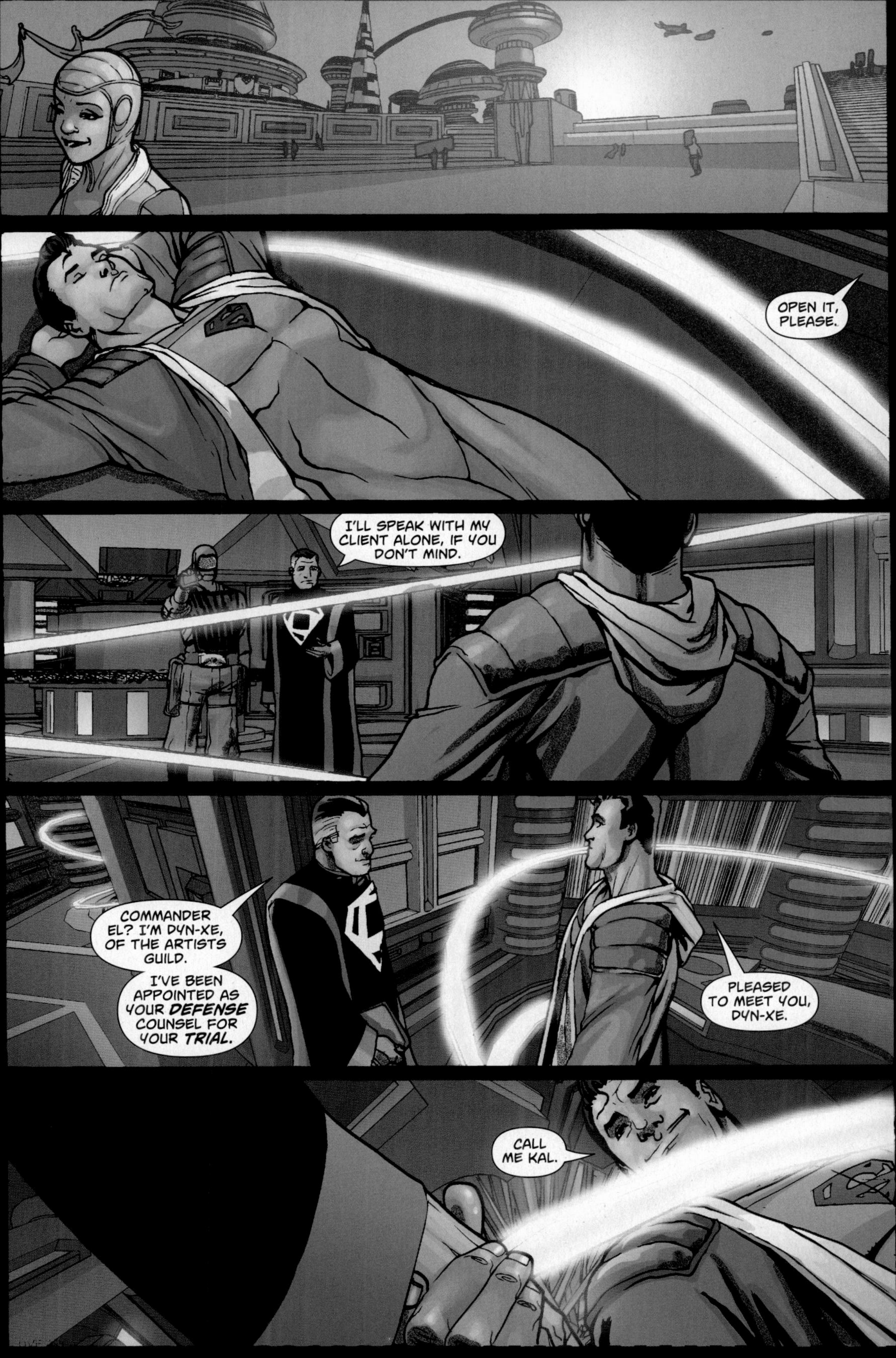

OPEN IT, PLEASE.
I'LL SPEAK WITH MY CLIENT ALONE, IF YOU DON'T MIND.
COMMANDER EL? I'M DYN-XE, OF THE ARTISTS GUILD.
I'VE BEEN APPOINTED AS YOUR *DEFENSE* COUNSEL FOR YOUR *TRIAL.*
PLEASED TO MEET YOU, DYN-XE.
CALL ME KAL.

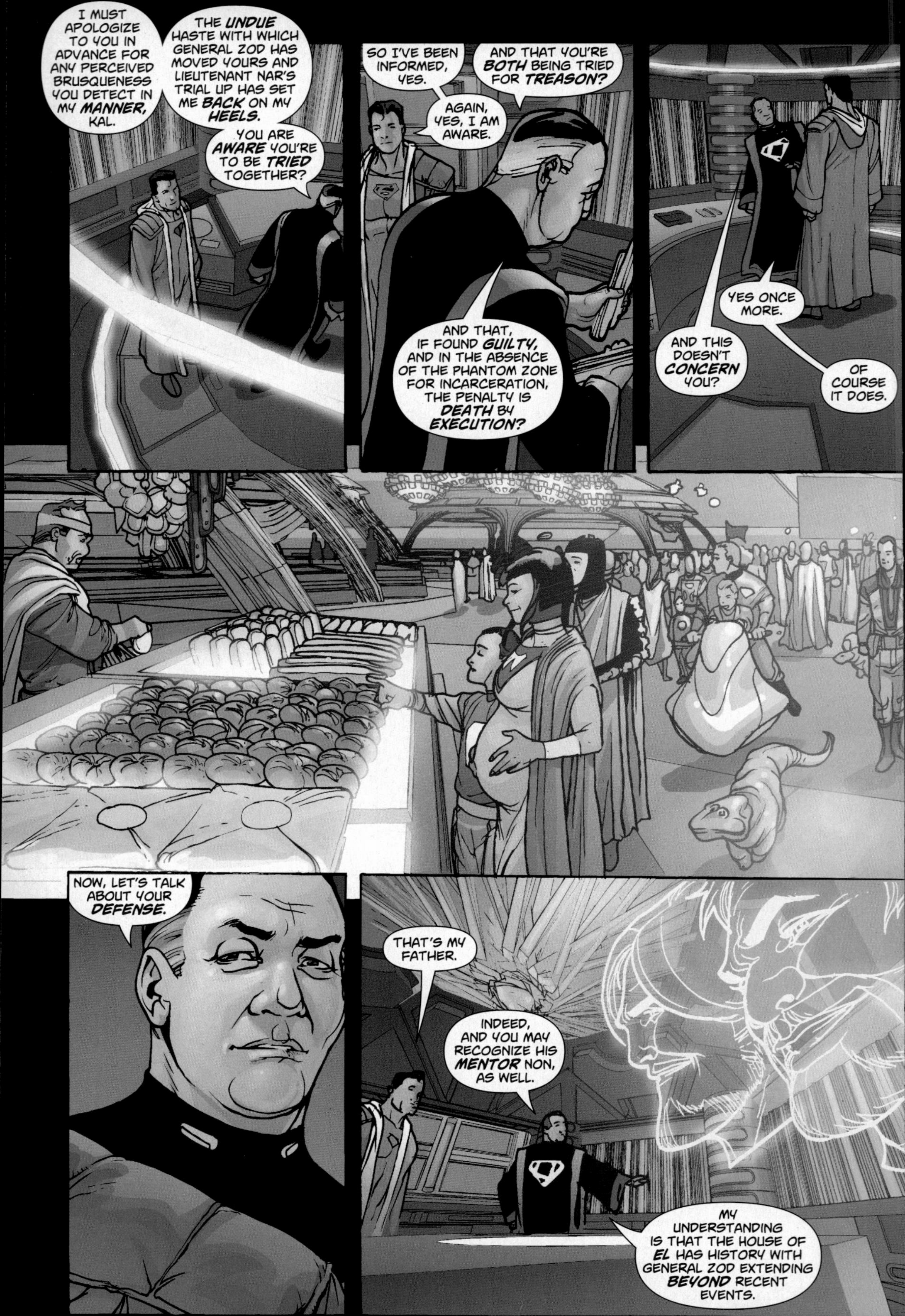

I MUST APOLOGIZE TO YOU IN ADVANCE FOR ANY PERCEIVED BRUSQUENESS YOU DETECT IN MY MANNER, KAL.
THE UNDUE HASTE WITH WHICH GENERAL ZOD HAS MOVED YOURS AND LIEUTENANT NAR'S TRIAL UP HAS SET ME BACK ON MY HEELS.
YOU ARE AWARE YOU'RE TO BE TRIED TOGETHER?
SO I'VE BEEN INFORMED, YES.
AND THAT YOU'RE BOTH BEING TRIED FOR TREASON?
AGAIN, YES, I AM AWARE.
AND THAT, IF FOUND GUILTY, AND IN THE ABSENCE OF THE PHANTOM ZONE FOR INCARCERATION, THE PENALTY IS DEATH BY EXECUTION?
YES ONCE MORE.
AND THIS DOESN'T CONCERN YOU?
OF COURSE IT DOES.
NOW, LET'S TALK ABOUT YOUR DEFENSE.
THAT'S MY FATHER.
INDEED, AND YOU MAY RECOGNIZE HIS MENTOR NON, AS WELL.
MY UNDERSTANDING IS THAT THE HOUSE OF EL HAS HISTORY WITH GENERAL ZOD EXTENDING BEYOND RECENT EVENTS.

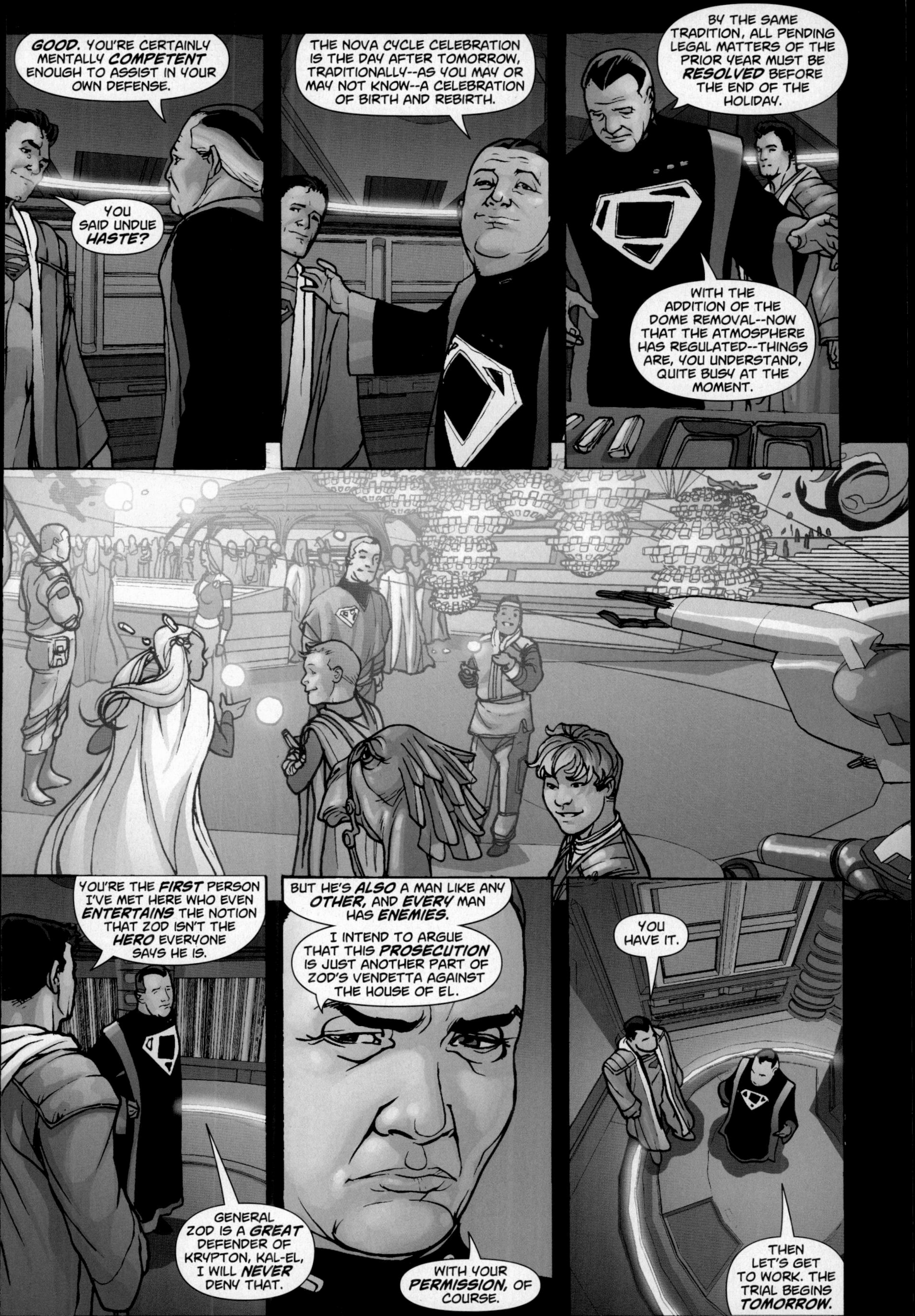
GOOD. YOU'RE CERTAINLY MENTALLY COMPETENT ENOUGH TO ASSIST IN YOUR OWN DEFENSE.
YOU SAID UNDUE HASTE?
THE NOVA CYCLE CELEBRATION IS THE DAY AFTER TOMORROW, TRADITIONALLY--AS YOU MAY OR MAY NOT KNOW--A CELEBRATION OF BIRTH AND REBIRTH.
BY THE SAME TRADITION, ALL PENDING LEGAL MATTERS OF THE PRIOR YEAR MUST BE RESOLVED BEFORE THE END OF THE HOLIDAY.
WITH THE ADDITION OF THE DOME REMOVAL--NOW THAT THE ATMOSPHERE HAS REGULATED--THINGS ARE, YOU UNDERSTAND, QUITE BUSY AT THE MOMENT.
YOU'RE THE FIRST PERSON I'VE MET HERE WHO EVEN ENTERTAINS THE NOTION THAT ZOD ISN'T THE HERO EVERYONE SAYS HE IS.
GENERAL ZOD IS A GREAT DEFENDER OF KRYPTON, KAL-EL, I WILL NEVER DENY THAT.
BUT HE'S ALSO A MAN LIKE ANY OTHER, AND EVERY MAN HAS ENEMIES.
I INTEND TO ARGUE THAT THIS PROSECUTION IS JUST ANOTHER PART OF ZOD'S VENDETTA AGAINST THE HOUSE OF EL.
WITH YOUR PERMISSION, OF COURSE.
YOU HAVE IT.
THEN LET'S GET TO WORK. THE TRIAL BEGINS TOMORROW.

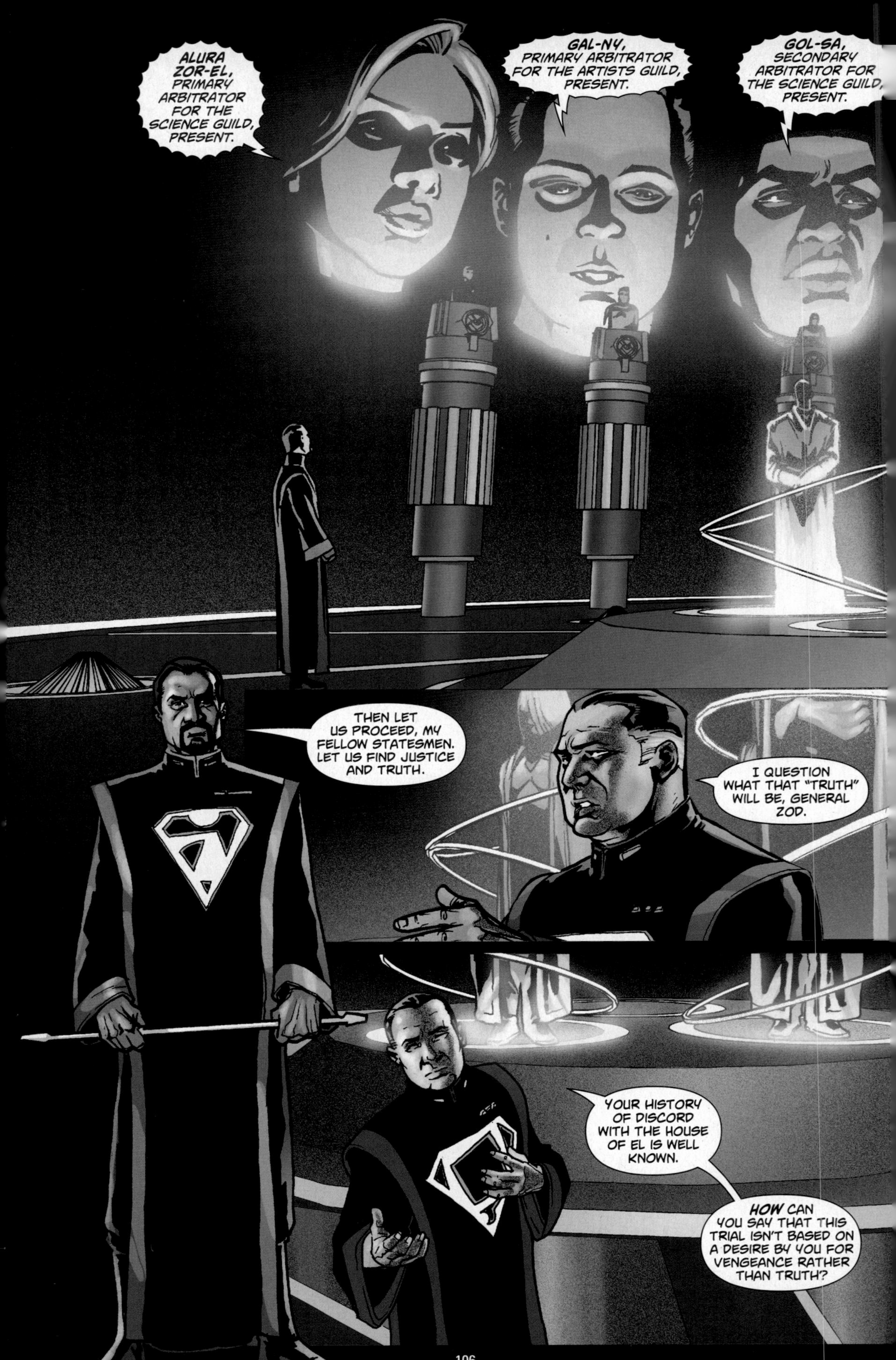
ALURA ZOR-EL, PRIMARY ARBITRATOR FOR THE SCIENCE GUILD, PRESENT.
GAL-NY, PRIMARY ARBITRATOR FOR THE ARTISTS GUILD, PRESENT.
GOL-SA, SECONDARY ARBITRATOR FOR THE SCIENCE GUILD, PRESENT.
THEN LET US PROCEED, MY FELLOW STATESMEN. LET US FIND JUSTICE AND TRUTH.
I QUESTION WHAT THAT "TRUTH" WILL BE, GENERAL ZOD.
YOUR HISTORY OF DISCORD WITH THE HOUSE OF EL IS WELL KNOWN.
HOW CAN YOU SAY THAT THIS TRIAL ISN'T BASED ON A DESIRE BY YOU FOR VENGEANCE RATHER THAN TRUTH?

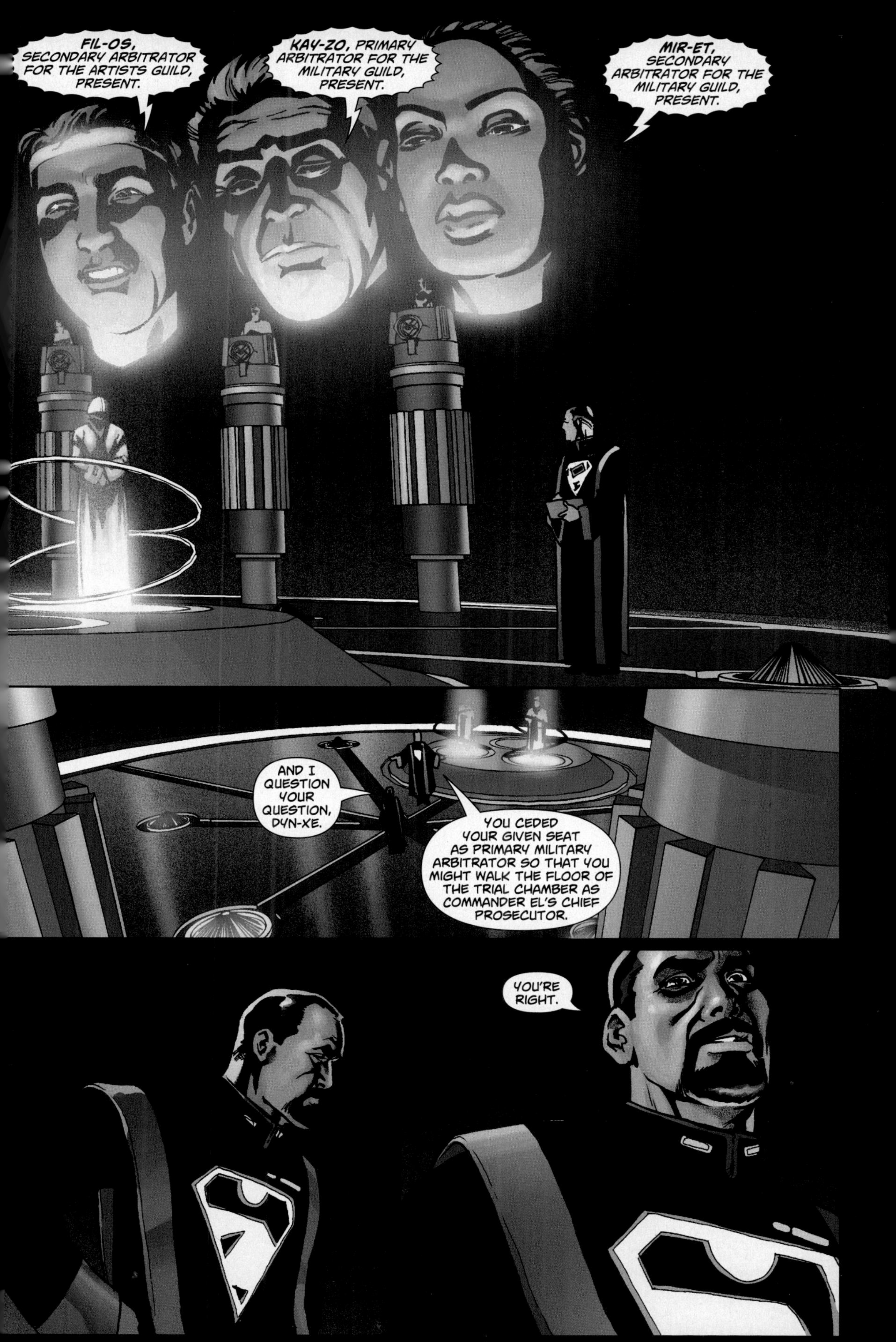
FIL-OS, SECONDARY ARBITRATOR FOR THE ARTISTS GUILD, PRESENT.
KAY-ZO, PRIMARY ARBITRATOR FOR THE MILITARY GUILD, PRESENT.
MIR-ET, SECONDARY ARBITRATOR FOR THE MILITARY GUILD, PRESENT.
AND I QUESTION YOUR QUESTION, DYN-XE.
YOU CEDED YOUR GIVEN SEAT AS PRIMARY MILITARY ARBITRATOR SO THAT YOU MIGHT WALK THE FLOOR OF THE TRIAL CHAMBER AS COMMANDER EL'S CHIEF PROSECUTOR.
YOU'RE RIGHT.

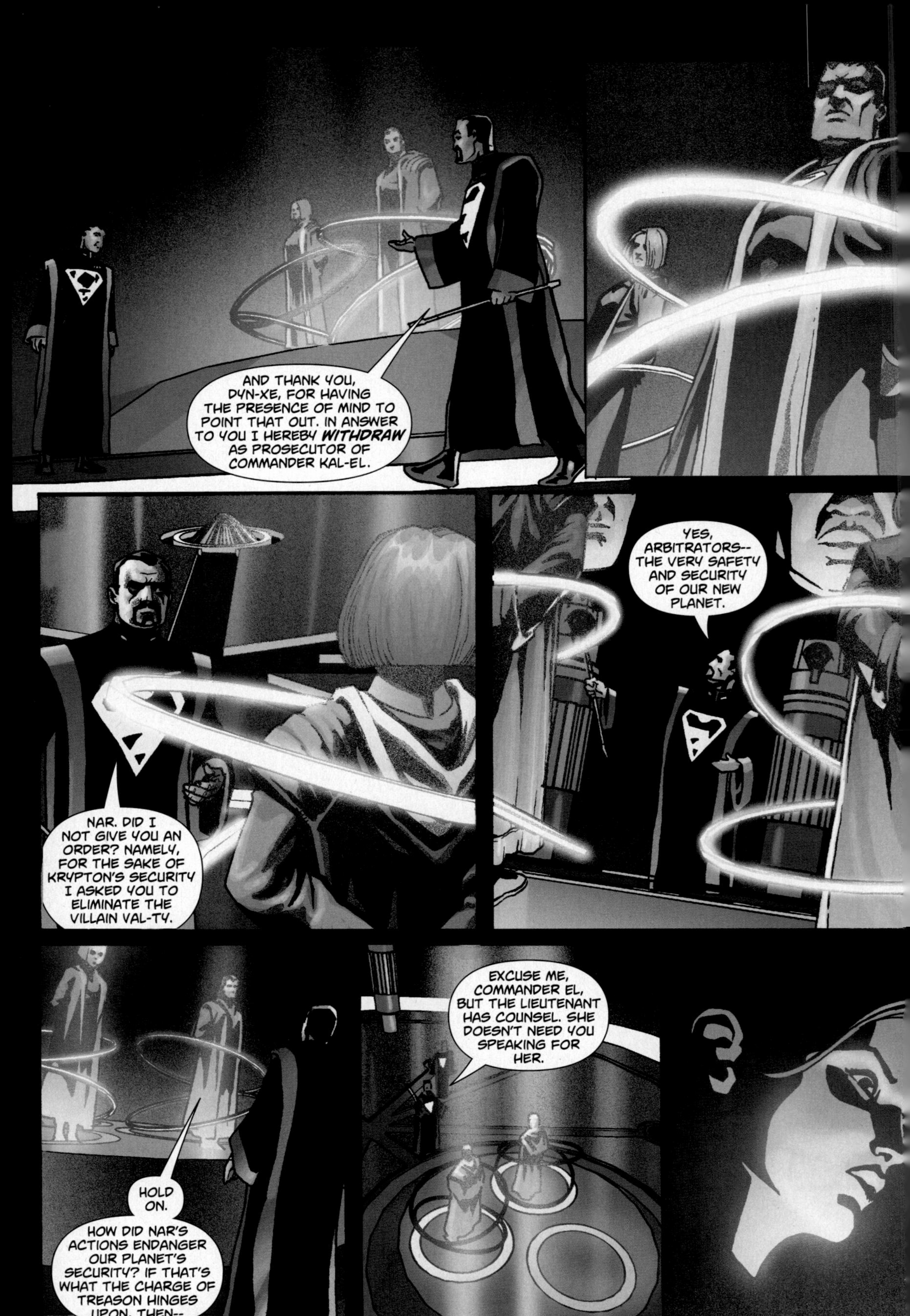
AND THANK YOU, DYN-XE, FOR HAVING THE PRESENCE OF MIND TO POINT THAT OUT. IN ANSWER TO YOU I HEREBY WITHDRAW AS PROSECUTOR OF COMMANDER KAL-EL.
NAR. DID I NOT GIVE YOU AN ORDER? NAMELY, FOR THE SAKE OF KRYPTON'S SECURITY I ASKED YOU TO ELIMINATE THE VILLAIN VAL-TY.
YES, ARBITRATORS-- THE VERY SAFETY AND SECURITY OF OUR NEW PLANET.
HOLD ON.
HOW DID NAR'S ACTIONS ENDANGER OUR PLANET'S SECURITY? IF THAT'S WHAT THE CHARGE OF TREASON HINGES UPON, THEN--
EXCUSE ME, COMMANDER EL, BUT THE LIEUTENANT HAS COUNSEL. SHE DOESN'T NEED YOU SPEAKING FOR HER.

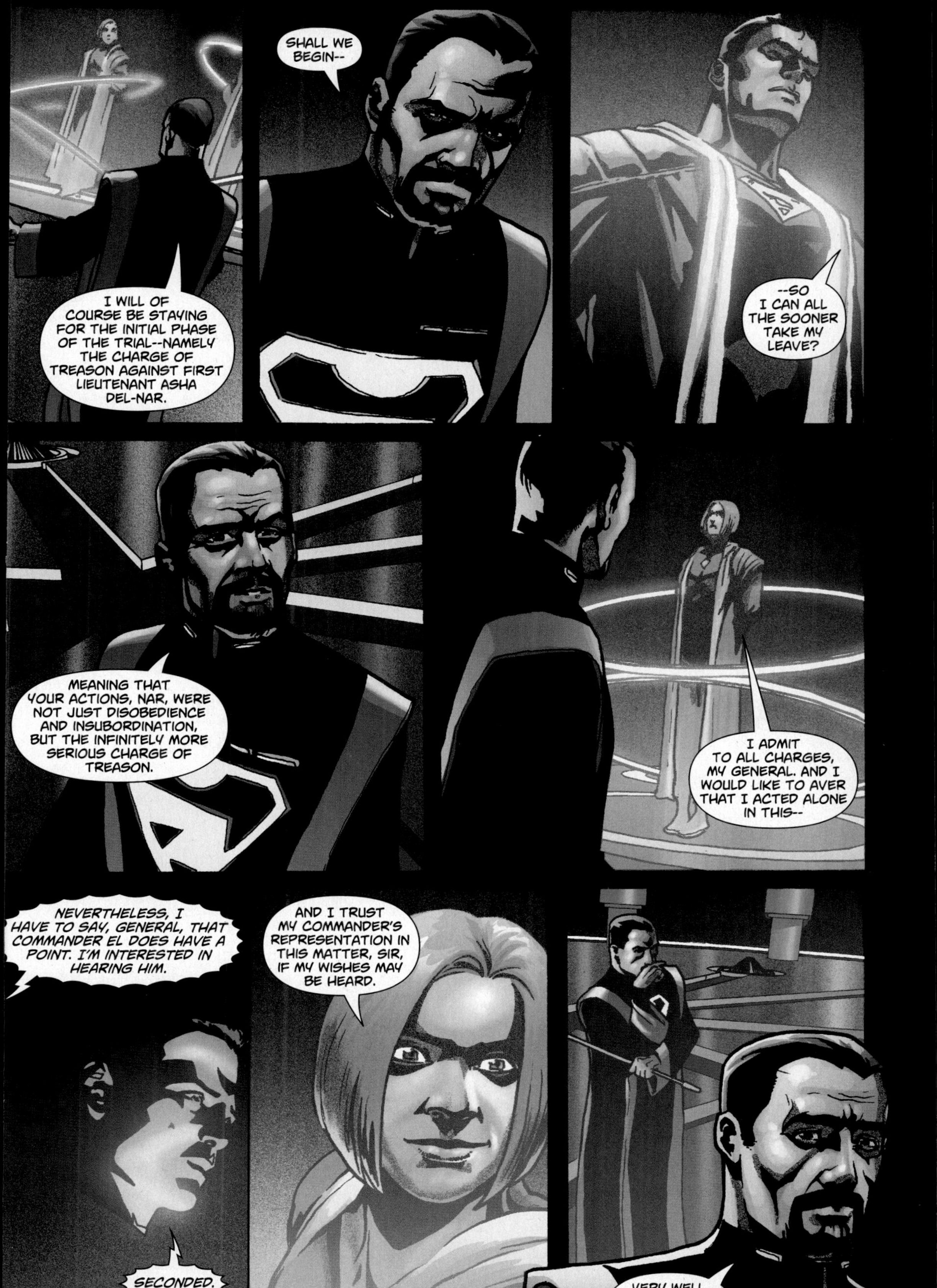
SHALL WE BEGIN--
I WILL OF COURSE BE STAYING FOR THE INITIAL PHASE OF THE TRIAL--NAMELY THE CHARGE OF TREASON AGAINST FIRST LIEUTENANT ASHA DEL-NAR.
--SO I CAN ALL THE SOONER TAKE MY LEAVE?
MEANING THAT YOUR ACTIONS, NAR, WERE NOT JUST DISOBEDIENCE AND INSUBORDINATION, BUT THE INFINITELY MORE SERIOUS CHARGE OF TREASON.
I ADMIT TO ALL CHARGES, MY GENERAL. AND I WOULD LIKE TO AVER THAT I ACTED ALONE IN THIS--
NEVERTHELESS, I HAVE TO SAY, GENERAL, THAT COMMANDER EL DOES HAVE A POINT. I'M INTERESTED IN HEARING HIM.
SECONDED.
AND I TRUST MY COMMANDER'S REPRESENTATION IN THIS MATTER, SIR, IF MY WISHES MAY BE HEARD.
VERY WELL, COMMANDER EL. AS NAR AND THE ARBITRATORS WISH.

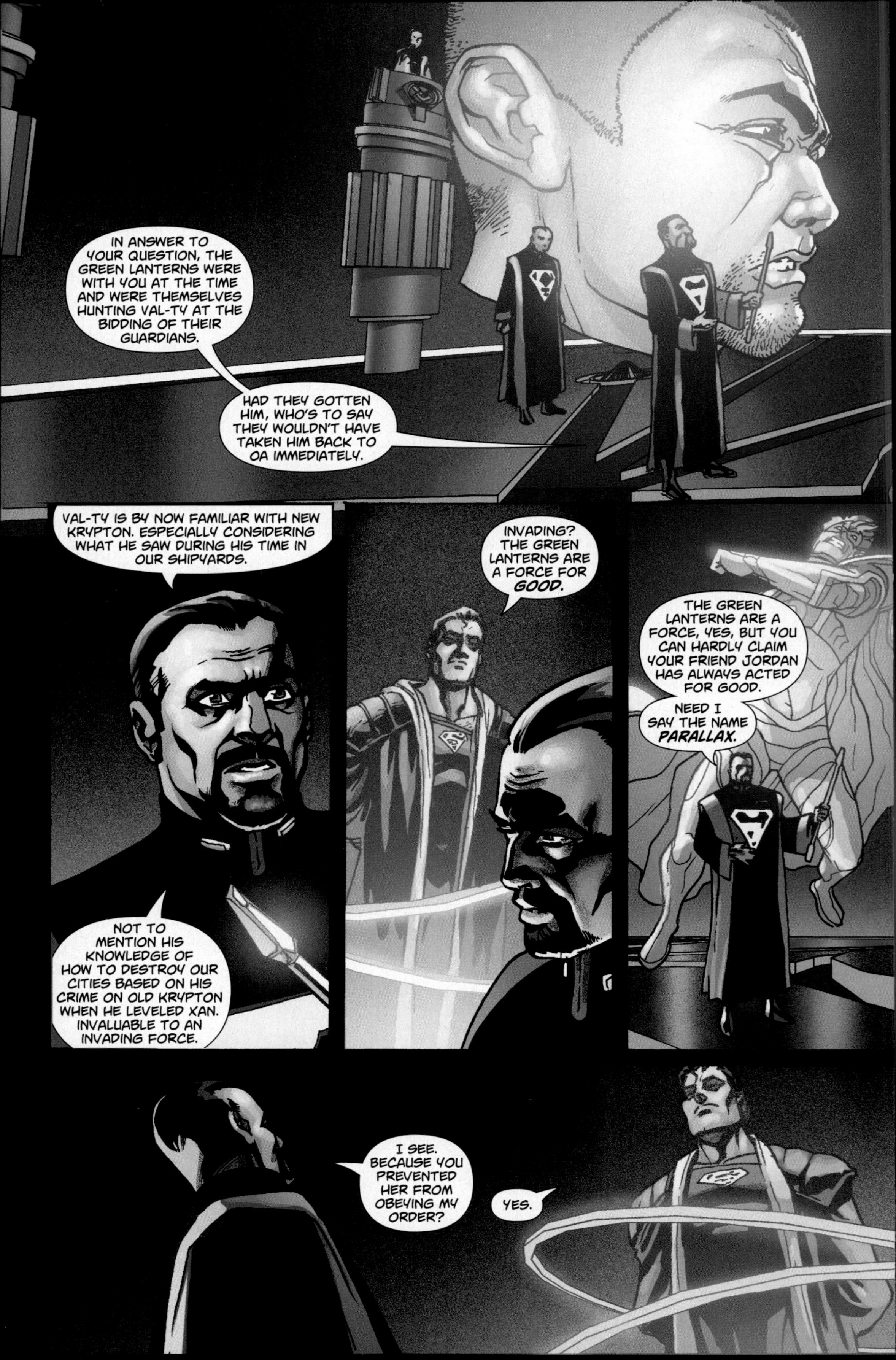
IN ANSWER TO YOUR QUESTION, THE GREEN LANTERNS WERE WITH YOU AT THE TIME AND WERE THEMSELVES HUNTING VAL-TY AT THE BIDDING OF THEIR GUARDIANS.
HAD THEY GOTTEN HIM, WHO'S TO SAY THEY WOULDN'T HAVE TAKEN HIM BACK TO OA IMMEDIATELY.
VAL-TY IS BY NOW FAMILIAR WITH NEW KRYPTON. ESPECIALLY CONSIDERING WHAT HE SAW DURING HIS TIME IN OUR SHIPYARDS.
NOT TO MENTION HIS KNOWLEDGE OF HOW TO DESTROY OUR CITIES BASED ON HIS CRIME ON OLD KRYPTON WHEN HE LEVELED XAN. INVALUABLE TO AN INVADING FORCE.
INVADING? THE GREEN LANTERNS ARE A FORCE FOR **GOOD**.
THE GREEN LANTERNS ARE A FORCE, YES, BUT YOU CAN HARDLY CLAIM YOUR FRIEND JORDAN HAS ALWAYS ACTED FOR GOOD.
NEED I SAY THE NAME **PARALLAX**.
I SEE. BECAUSE YOU PREVENTED HER FROM OBEYING MY ORDER?
YES.

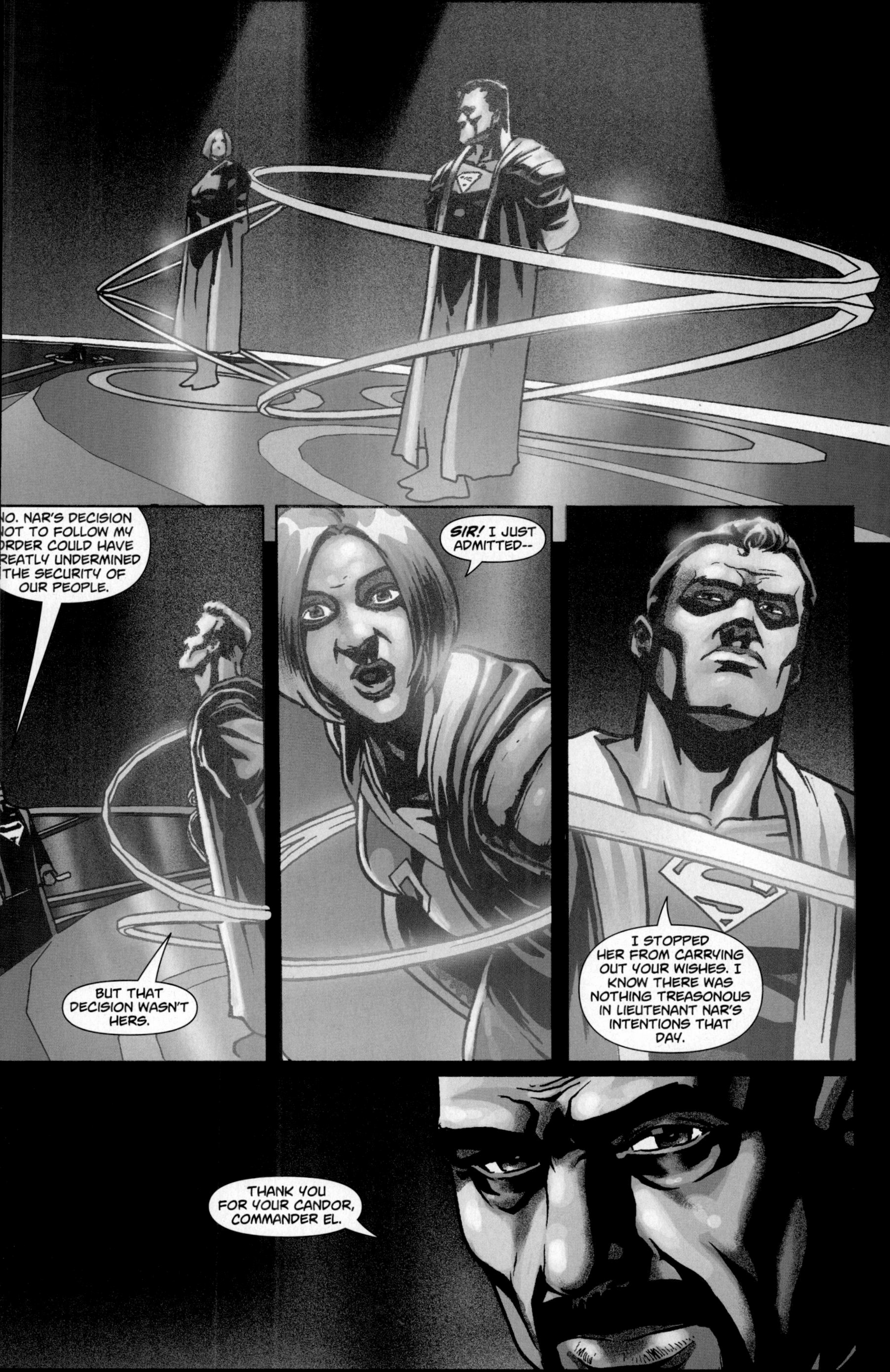
NO. NAR'S DECISION NOT TO FOLLOW MY ORDER COULD HAVE GREATLY UNDERMINED THE SECURITY OF OUR PEOPLE.
BUT THAT DECISION WASN'T HERS.
SIR! I JUST ADMITTED--
I STOPPED HER FROM CARRYING OUT YOUR WISHES. I KNOW THERE WAS NOTHING TREASONOUS IN LIEUTENANT NAR'S INTENTIONS THAT DAY.
THANK YOU FOR YOUR CANDOR, COMMANDER EL.

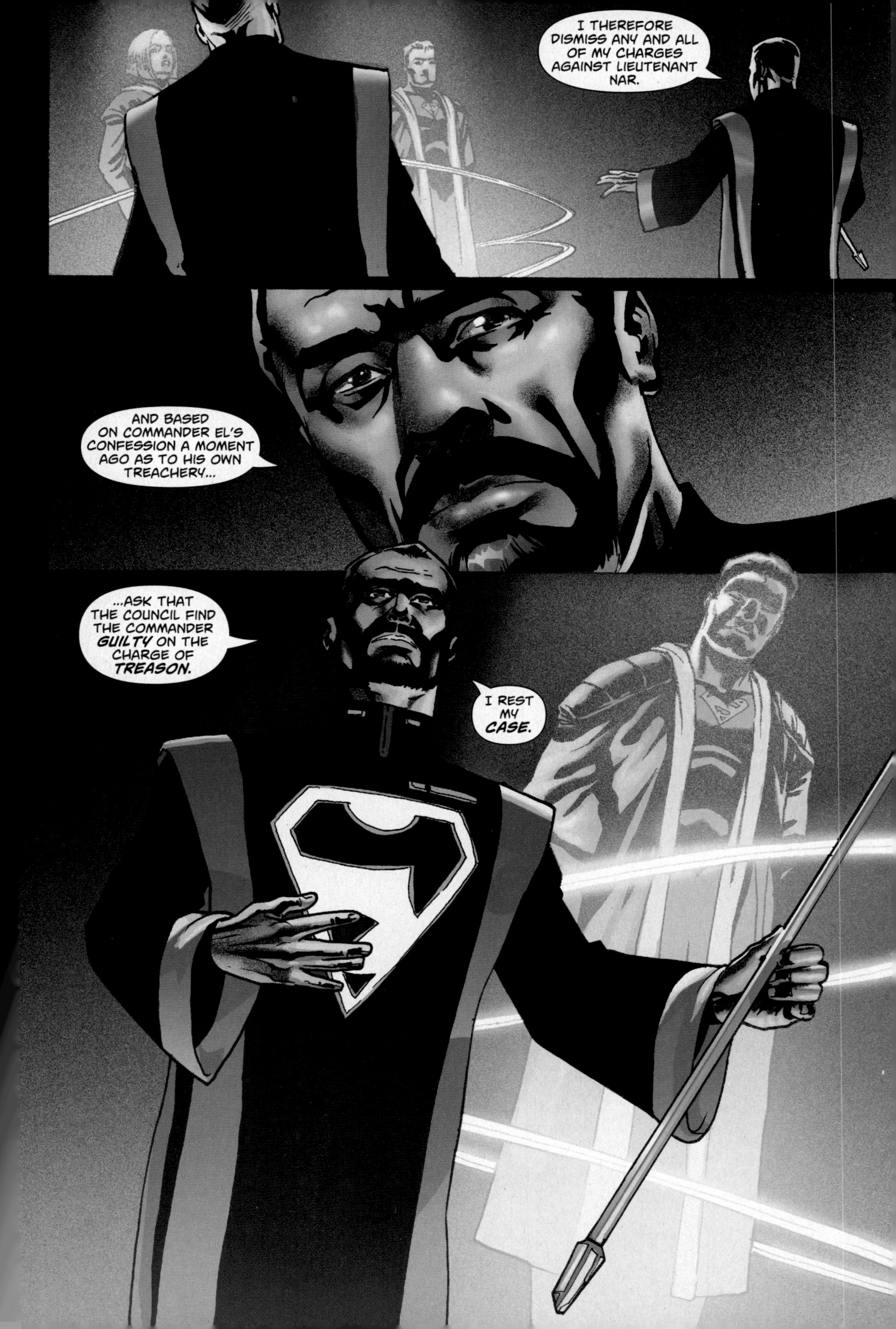
I THEREFORE DISMISS ANY AND ALL OF MY CHARGES AGAINST LIEUTENANT NAR.
AND BASED ON COMMANDER EL'S CONFESSION A MOMENT AGO AS TO HIS OWN TREACHERY...
...ASK THAT THE COUNCIL FIND THE COMMANDER GUILTY ON THE CHARGE OF TREASON.
I REST MY CASE.

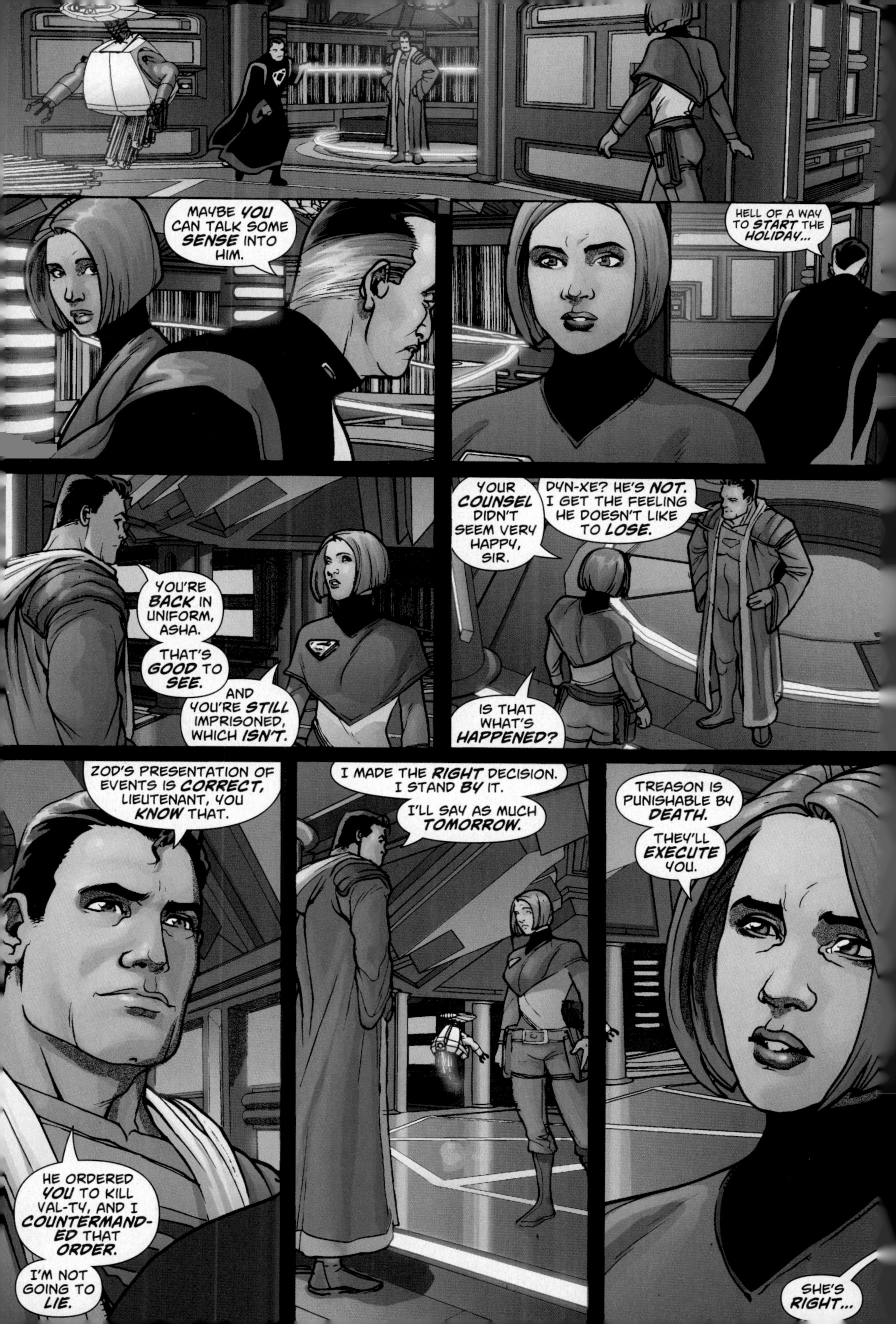
MAYBE YOU CAN TALK SOME SENSE INTO HIM.
HELL OF A WAY TO START THE HOLIDAY...
YOU'RE BACK IN UNIFORM, ASHA.
THAT'S GOOD TO SEE.
AND YOU'RE STILL IMPRISONED, WHICH ISN'T.
YOUR COUNSEL DIDN'T SEEM VERY HAPPY, SIR.
DYN-XE? HE'S NOT. I GET THE FEELING HE DOESN'T LIKE TO LOSE.
IS THAT WHAT'S HAPPENED?
ZOD'S PRESENTATION OF EVENTS IS CORRECT, LIEUTENANT, YOU KNOW THAT.
HE ORDERED YOU TO KILL VAL-TY, AND I COUNTERMANDED THAT ORDER.
I'M NOT GOING TO LIE.
I MADE THE RIGHT DECISION. I STAND BY IT.
I'LL SAY AS MUCH TOMORROW.
TREASON IS PUNISHABLE BY DEATH.
THEY'LL EXECUTE YOU.
SHE'S RIGHT...

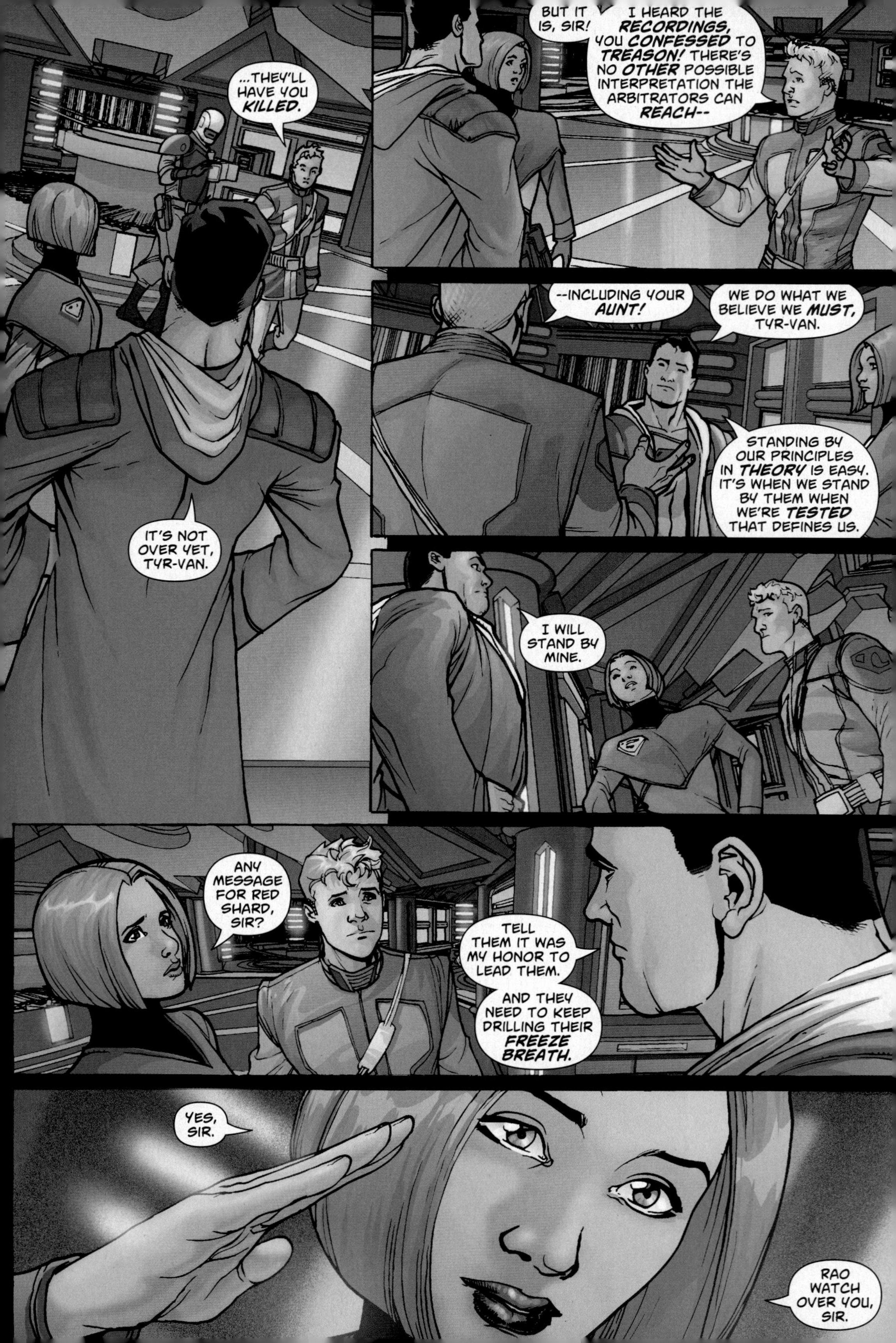
...THEY'LL HAVE YOU KILLED.
IT'S NOT OVER YET, TYR-VAN.
BUT IT IS, SIR!
I HEARD THE RECORDINGS, YOU CONFESSED TO TREASON! THERE'S NO OTHER POSSIBLE INTERPRETATION THE ARBITRATORS CAN REACH--
--INCLUDING YOUR AUNT!
WE DO WHAT WE BELIEVE WE MUST, TYR-VAN.
STANDING BY OUR PRINCIPLES IN THEORY IS EASY. IT'S WHEN WE STAND BY THEM WHEN WE'RE TESTED THAT DEFINES US.
I WILL STAND BY MINE.
ANY MESSAGE FOR RED SHARD, SIR?
TELL THEM IT WAS MY HONOR TO LEAD THEM.
AND THEY NEED TO KEEP DRILLING THEIR FREEZE BREATH.
YES, SIR.
RAO WATCH OVER YOU, SIR.

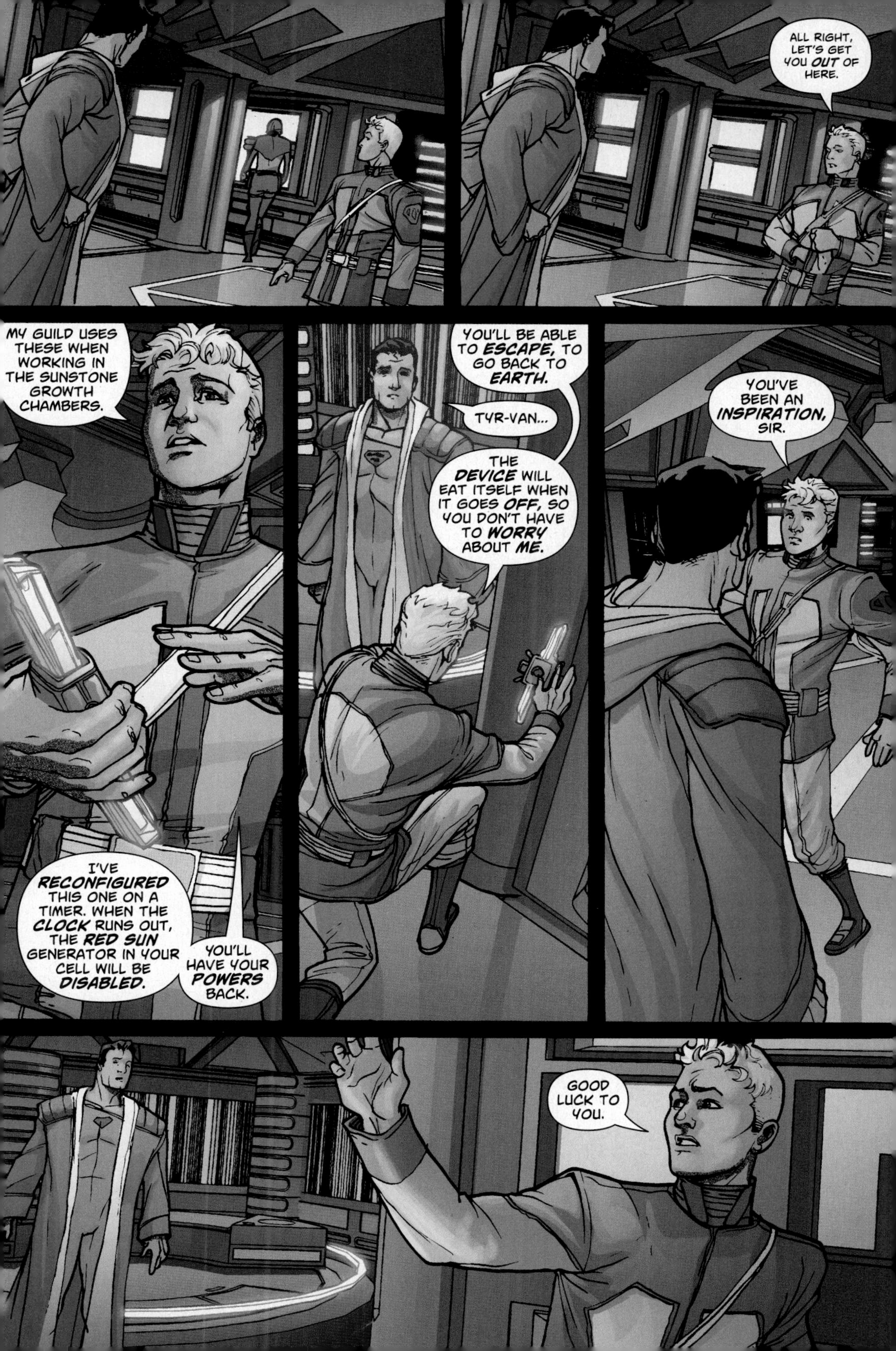
ALL RIGHT, LET'S GET YOU *OUT* OF HERE.
MY GUILD USES THESE WHEN WORKING IN THE SUNSTONE GROWTH CHAMBERS.
I'VE *RECONFIGURED* THIS ONE ON A TIMER. WHEN THE *CLOCK* RUNS OUT, THE *RED SUN* GENERATOR IN YOUR CELL WILL BE *DISABLED.*
YOU'LL HAVE YOUR *POWERS* BACK.
YOU'LL BE ABLE TO *ESCAPE,* TO GO BACK TO *EARTH.*
TYR-VAN...
THE *DEVICE* WILL EAT ITSELF WHEN IT GOES *OFF,* SO YOU DON'T HAVE TO *WORRY* ABOUT *ME.*
YOU'VE BEEN AN *INSPIRATION,* SIR.
GOOD LUCK TO YOU.

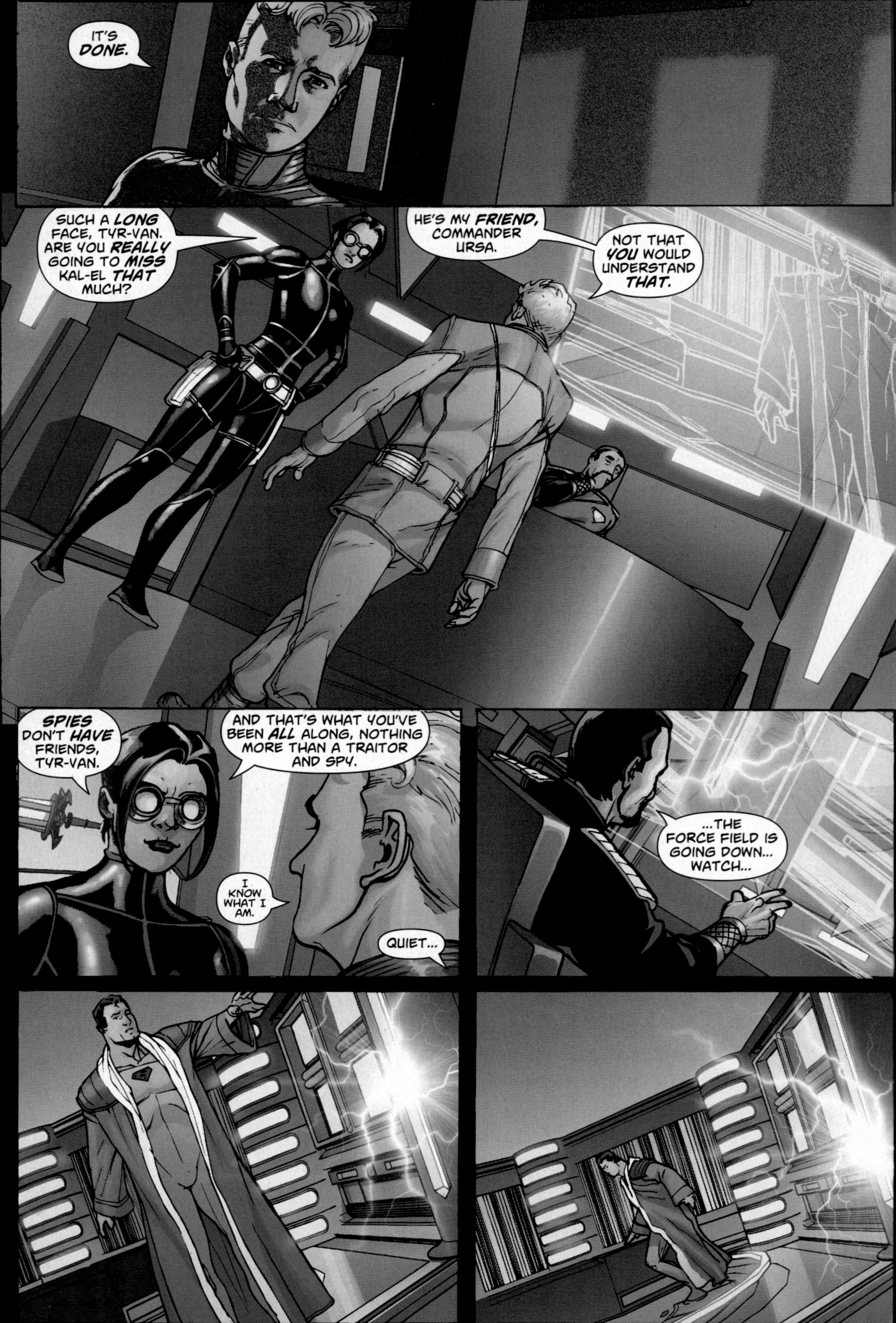
IT'S DONE.
SUCH A LONG FACE, TYR-VAN. ARE YOU REALLY GOING TO MISS KAL-EL THAT MUCH?
HE'S MY FRIEND, COMMANDER URSA.
NOT THAT YOU WOULD UNDERSTAND THAT.
SPIES DON'T HAVE FRIENDS, TYR-VAN.
AND THAT'S WHAT YOU'VE BEEN ALL ALONG, NOTHING MORE THAN A TRAITOR AND SPY.
I KNOW WHAT I AM.
QUIET...
...THE FORCE FIELD IS GOING DOWN... WATCH...

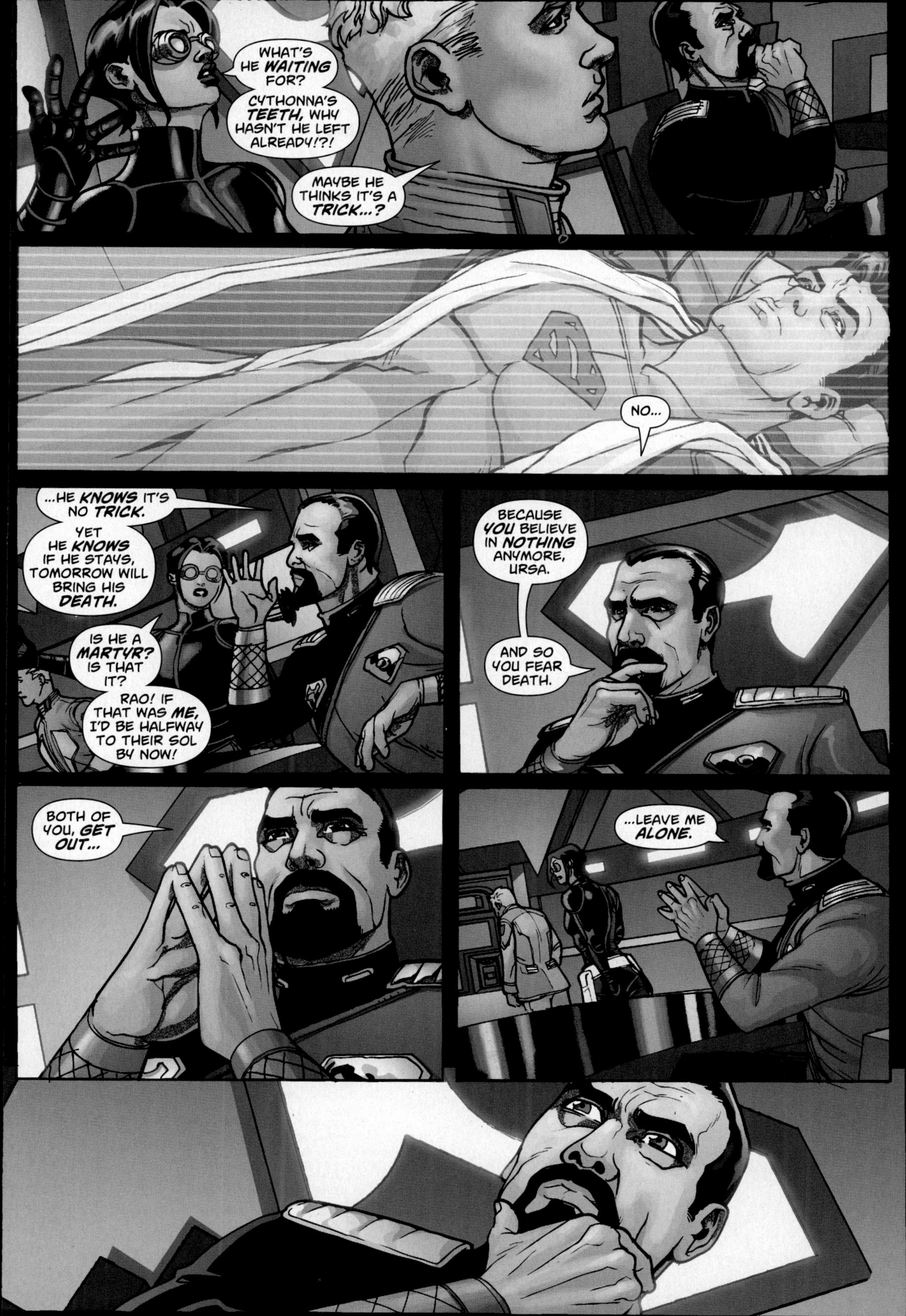
WHAT'S HE *WAITING* FOR?
CYTHONNA'S *TEETH,* WHY HASN'T HE LEFT ALREADY!?!
MAYBE HE THINKS IT'S A *TRICK...?*
NO...
...HE *KNOWS* IT'S NO *TRICK.*
YET HE *KNOWS* IF HE STAYS, TOMORROW WILL BRING HIS *DEATH.*
IS HE A *MARTYR?* IS THAT IT?
RAO! IF THAT WAS *ME,* I'D BE HALFWAY TO THEIR SOL BY NOW!
BECAUSE *YOU* BELIEVE IN *NOTHING* ANYMORE, URSA.
AND SO YOU FEAR DEATH.
BOTH OF YOU, *GET OUT...*
...LEAVE ME *ALONE.*

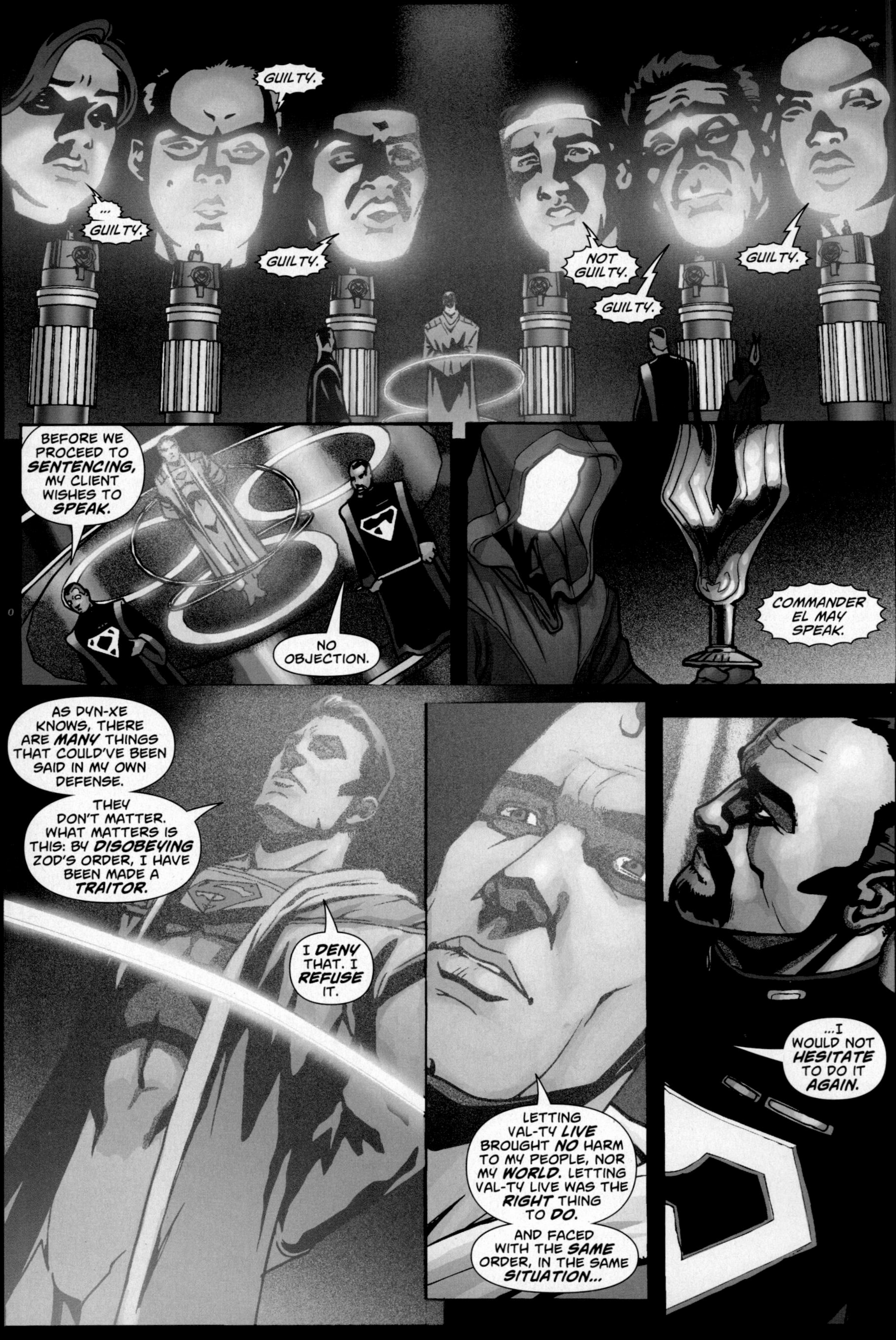
GUILTY.
... GUILTY.
GUILTY.
NOT GUILTY.
GUILTY.
GUILTY.
BEFORE WE PROCEED TO SENTENCING, MY CLIENT WISHES TO SPEAK.
NO OBJECTION.
COMMANDER EL MAY SPEAK.
AS DYN-XE KNOWS, THERE ARE MANY THINGS THAT COULD'VE BEEN SAID IN MY OWN DEFENSE.
THEY DON'T MATTER. WHAT MATTERS IS THIS: BY DISOBEYING ZOD'S ORDER, I HAVE BEEN MADE A TRAITOR.
I DENY THAT. I REFUSE IT.
LETTING VAL-TY LIVE BROUGHT NO HARM TO MY PEOPLE, NOR MY WORLD. LETTING VAL-TY LIVE WAS THE RIGHT THING TO DO.
AND FACED WITH THE SAME ORDER, IN THE SAME SITUATION...
...I WOULD NOT HESITATE TO DO IT AGAIN.

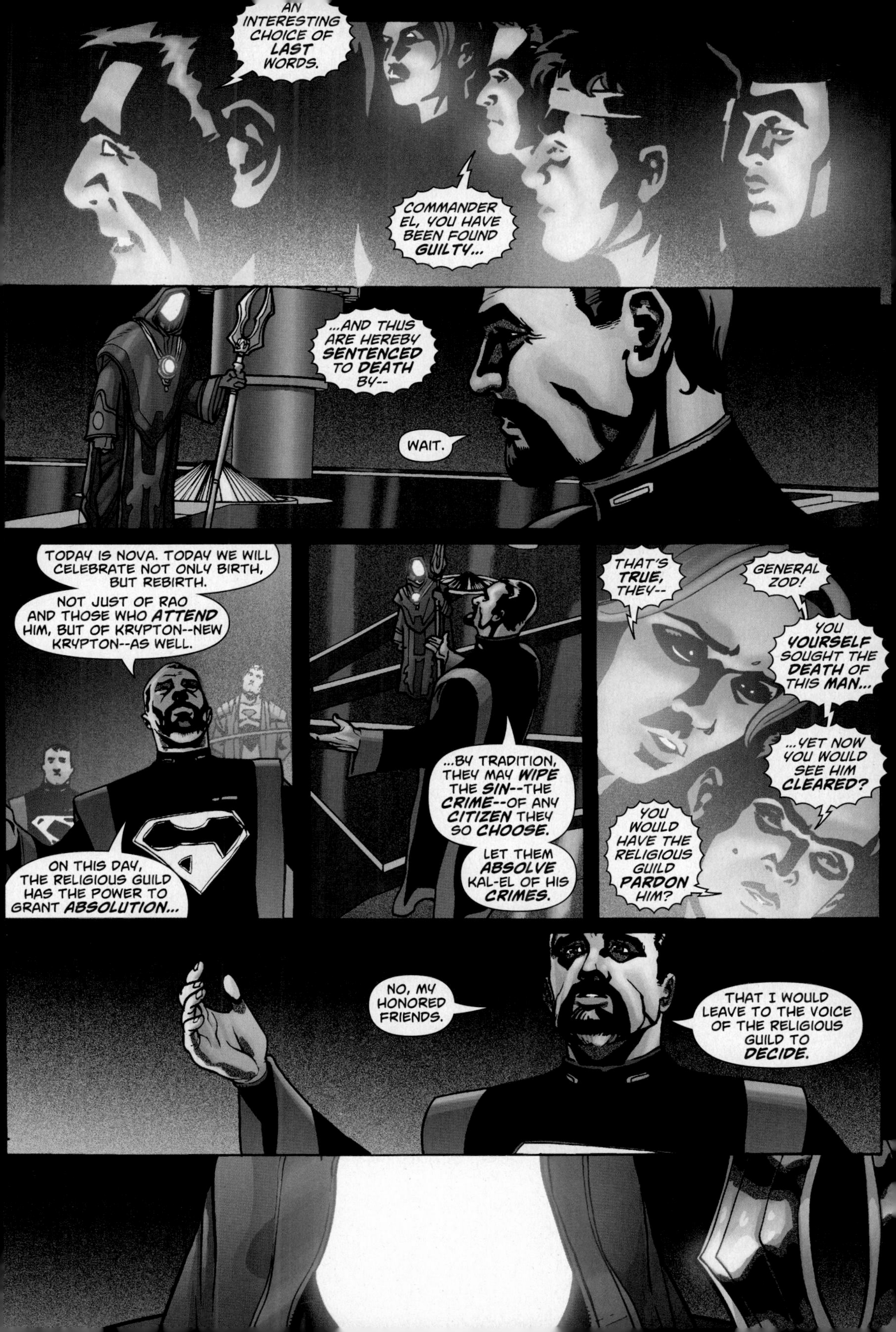
AN INTERESTING CHOICE OF LAST WORDS.
COMMANDER EL, YOU HAVE BEEN FOUND GUILTY...
...AND THUS ARE HEREBY SENTENCED TO DEATH BY--
WAIT.
TODAY IS NOVA. TODAY WE WILL CELEBRATE NOT ONLY BIRTH, BUT REBIRTH.
NOT JUST OF RAO AND THOSE WHO ATTEND HIM, BUT OF KRYPTON--NEW KRYPTON--AS WELL.
ON THIS DAY, THE RELIGIOUS GUILD HAS THE POWER TO GRANT ABSOLUTION...
...BY TRADITION, THEY MAY WIPE THE SIN--THE CRIME--OF ANY CITIZEN THEY SO CHOOSE.
LET THEM ABSOLVE KAL-EL OF HIS CRIMES.
THAT'S TRUE, THEY--
GENERAL ZOD!
YOU YOURSELF SOUGHT THE DEATH OF THIS MAN...
...YET NOW YOU WOULD SEE HIM CLEARED?
YOU WOULD HAVE THE RELIGIOUS GUILD PARDON HIM?
NO, MY HONORED FRIENDS.
THAT I WOULD LEAVE TO THE VOICE OF THE RELIGIOUS GUILD TO DECIDE.

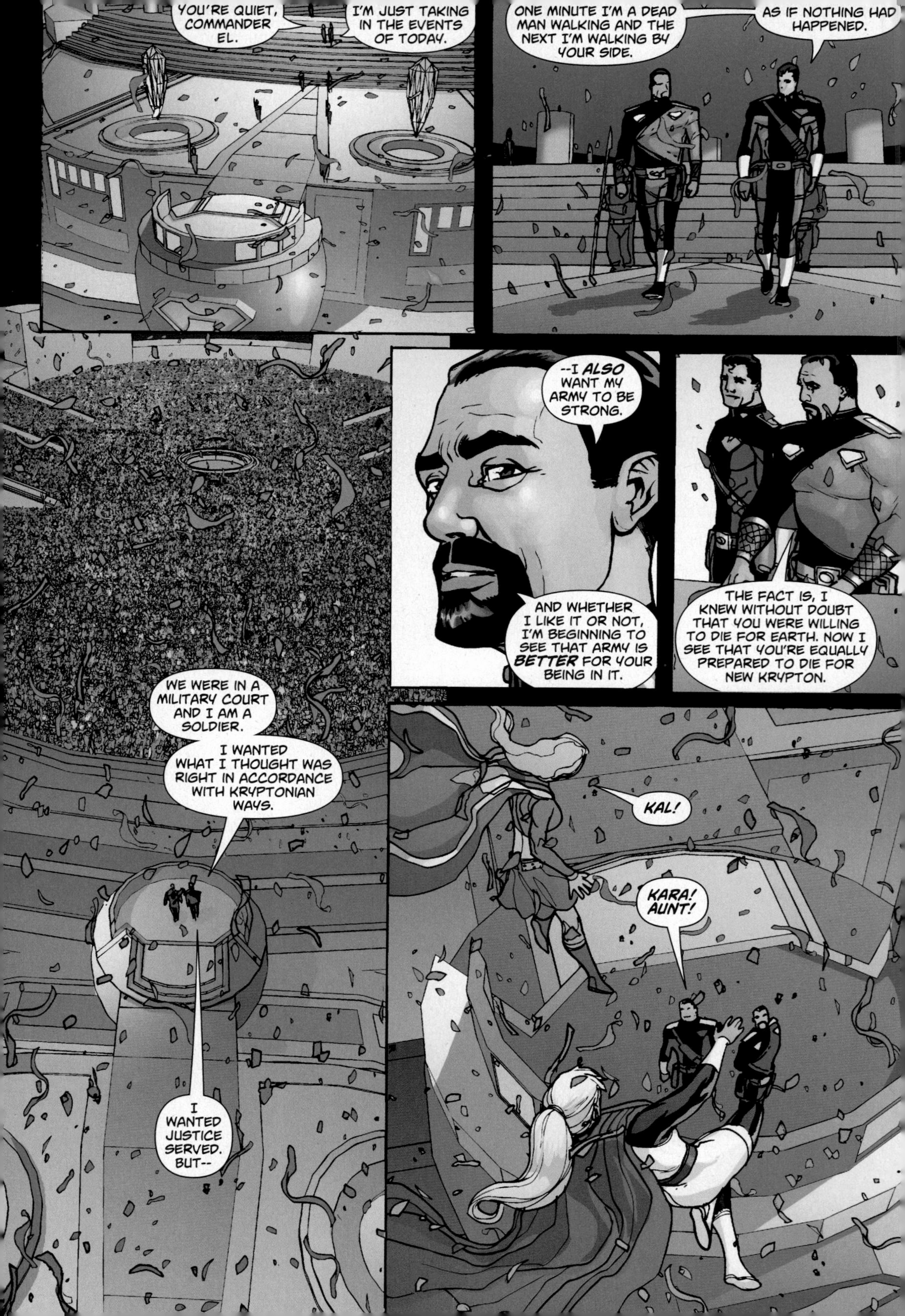
YOU'RE QUIET, COMMANDER EL.
I'M JUST TAKING IN THE EVENTS OF TODAY.
ONE MINUTE I'M A DEAD MAN WALKING AND THE NEXT I'M WALKING BY YOUR SIDE.
AS IF NOTHING HAD HAPPENED.
WE WERE IN A MILITARY COURT AND I AM A SOLDIER.
I WANTED WHAT I THOUGHT WAS RIGHT IN ACCORDANCE WITH KRYPTONIAN WAYS.
I WANTED JUSTICE SERVED. BUT--
--I ALSO WANT MY ARMY TO BE STRONG.
AND WHETHER I LIKE IT OR NOT, I'M BEGINNING TO SEE THAT ARMY IS BETTER FOR YOUR BEING IN IT.
THE FACT IS, I KNEW WITHOUT DOUBT THAT YOU WERE WILLING TO DIE FOR EARTH. NOW I SEE THAT YOU'RE EQUALLY PREPARED TO DIE FOR NEW KRYPTON.
KAL!
KARA! AUNT!

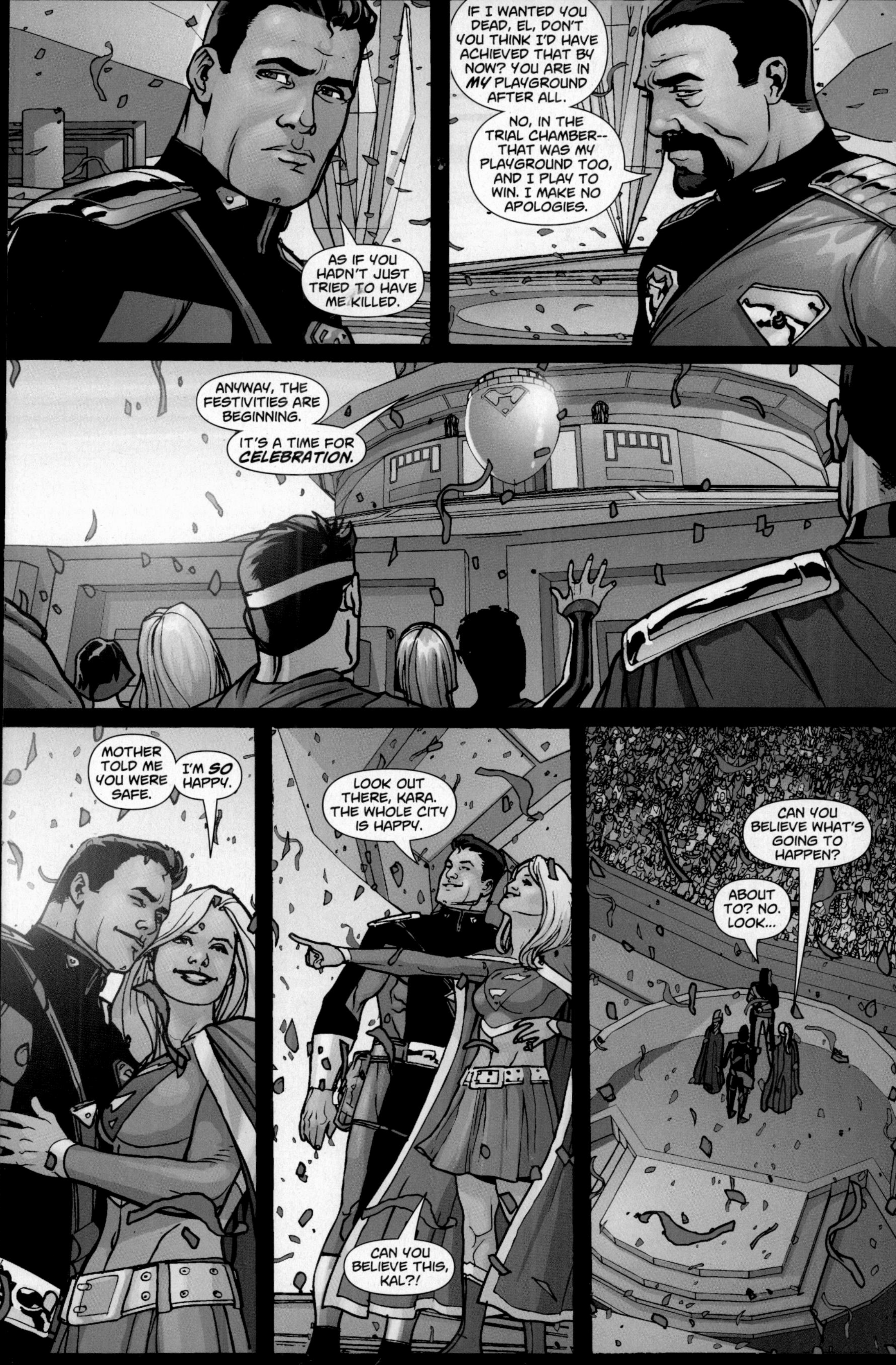
AS IF YOU HADN'T JUST TRIED TO HAVE ME KILLED.
IF I WANTED YOU DEAD, EL, DON'T YOU THINK I'D HAVE ACHIEVED THAT BY NOW? YOU ARE IN *MY* PLAYGROUND AFTER ALL.
NO, IN THE TRIAL CHAMBER--THAT WAS MY PLAYGROUND TOO, AND I PLAY TO WIN. I MAKE NO APOLOGIES.
ANYWAY, THE FESTIVITIES ARE BEGINNING.
IT'S A TIME FOR *CELEBRATION*.
MOTHER TOLD ME YOU WERE SAFE.
I'M *SO* HAPPY.
LOOK OUT THERE, KARA. THE WHOLE CITY IS HAPPY.
CAN YOU BELIEVE THIS, KAL?!
CAN YOU BELIEVE WHAT'S GOING TO HAPPEN?
ABOUT TO? NO. LOOK...

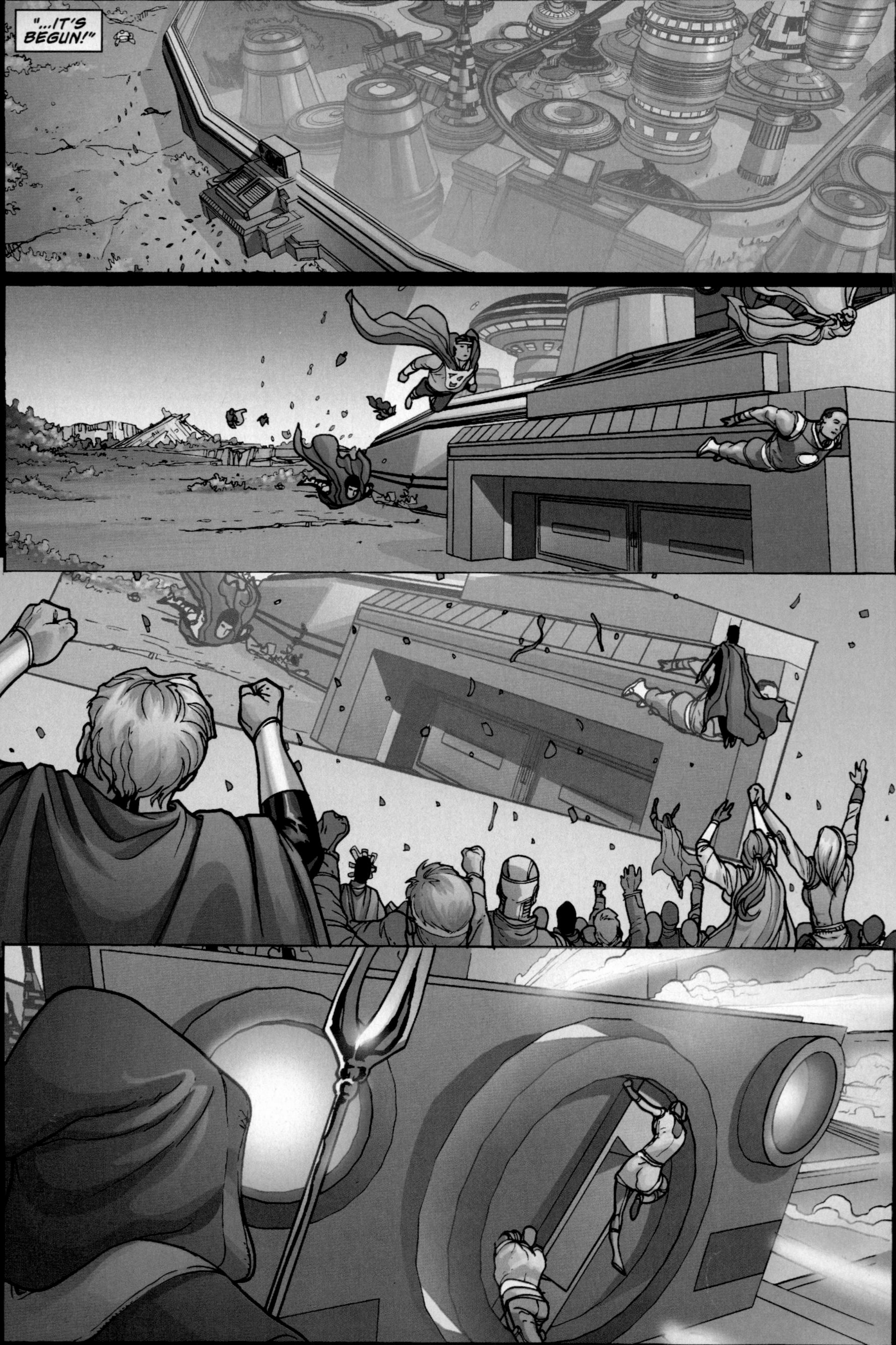
"...IT'S BEGUN!"

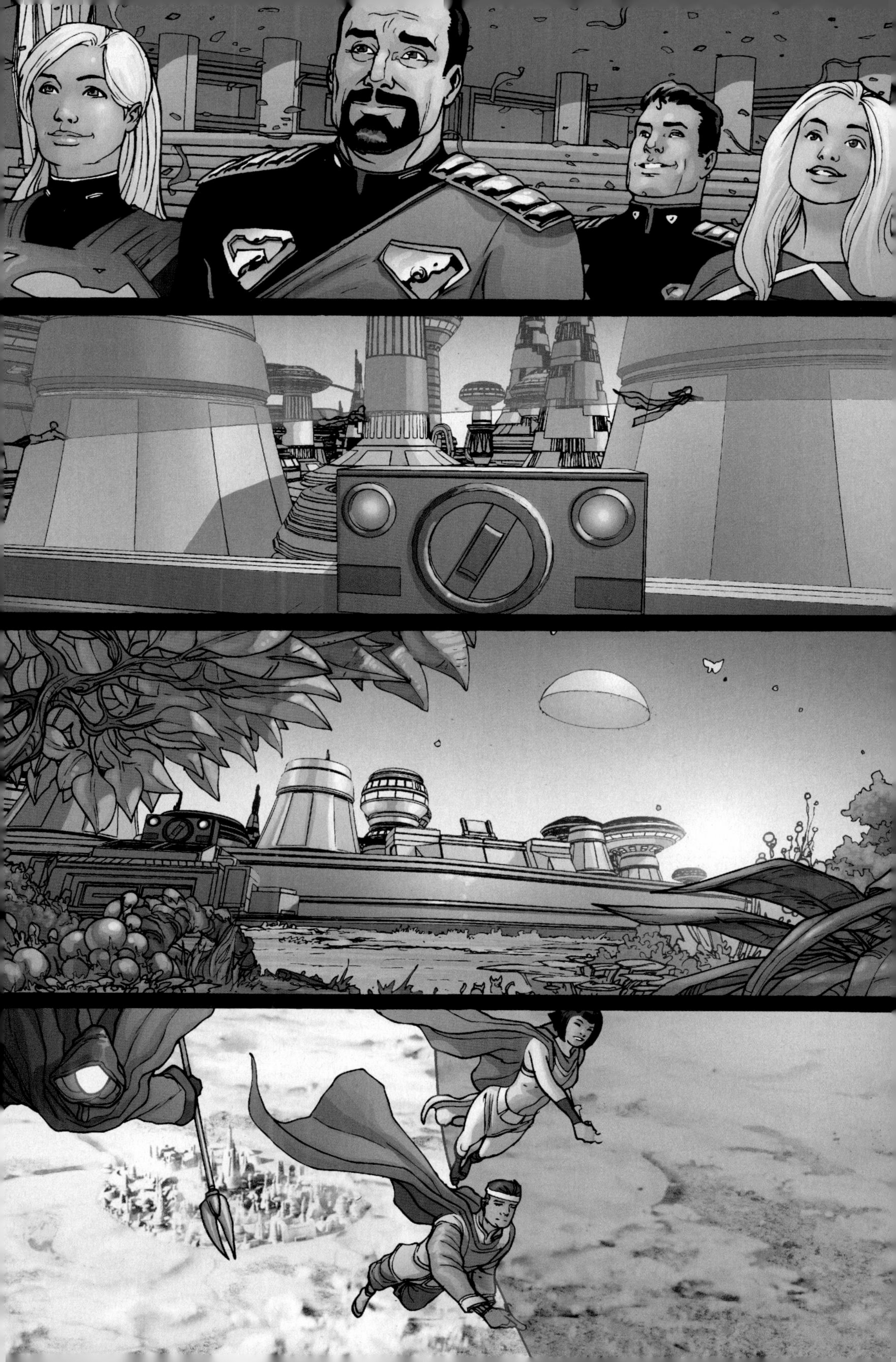

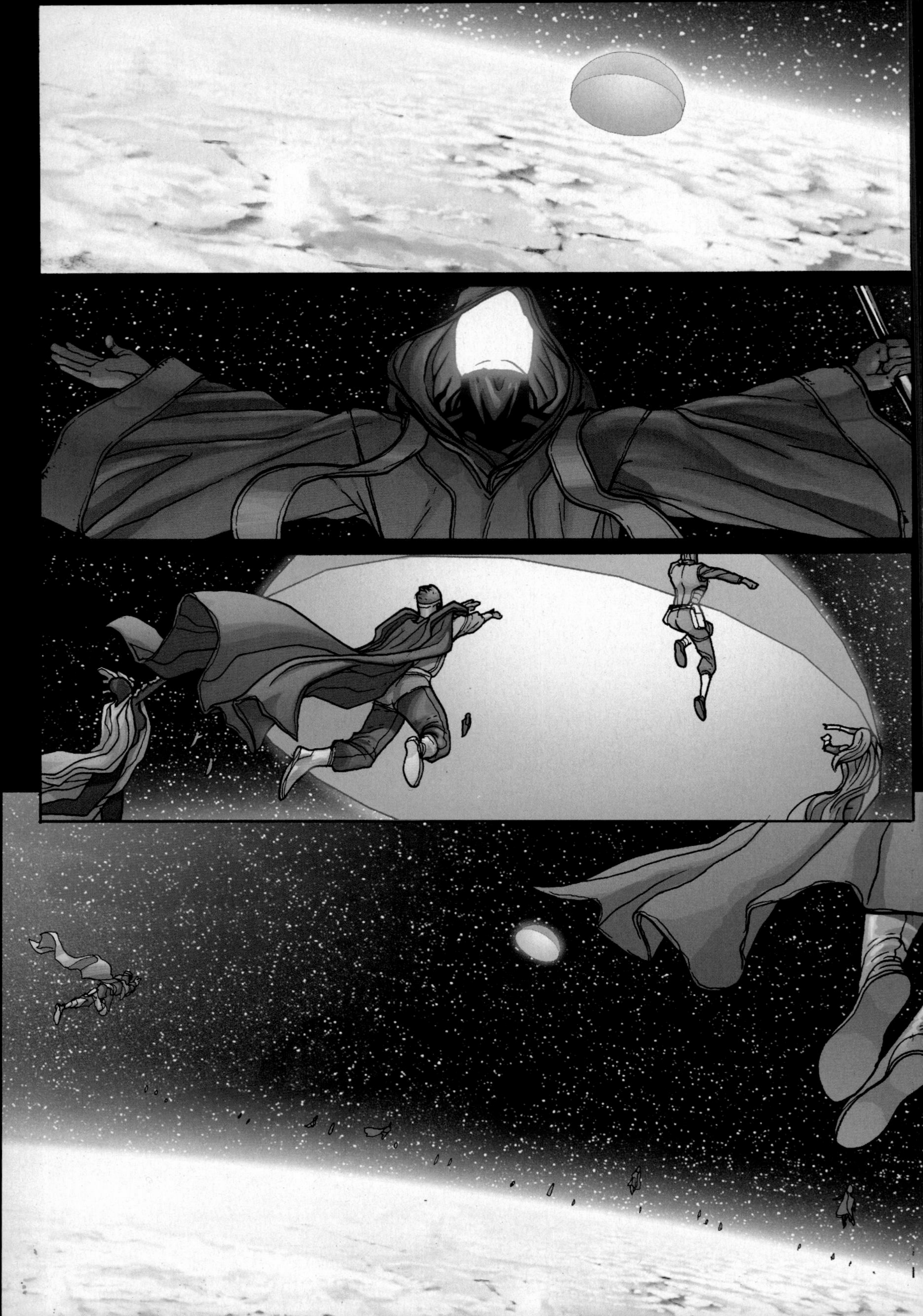

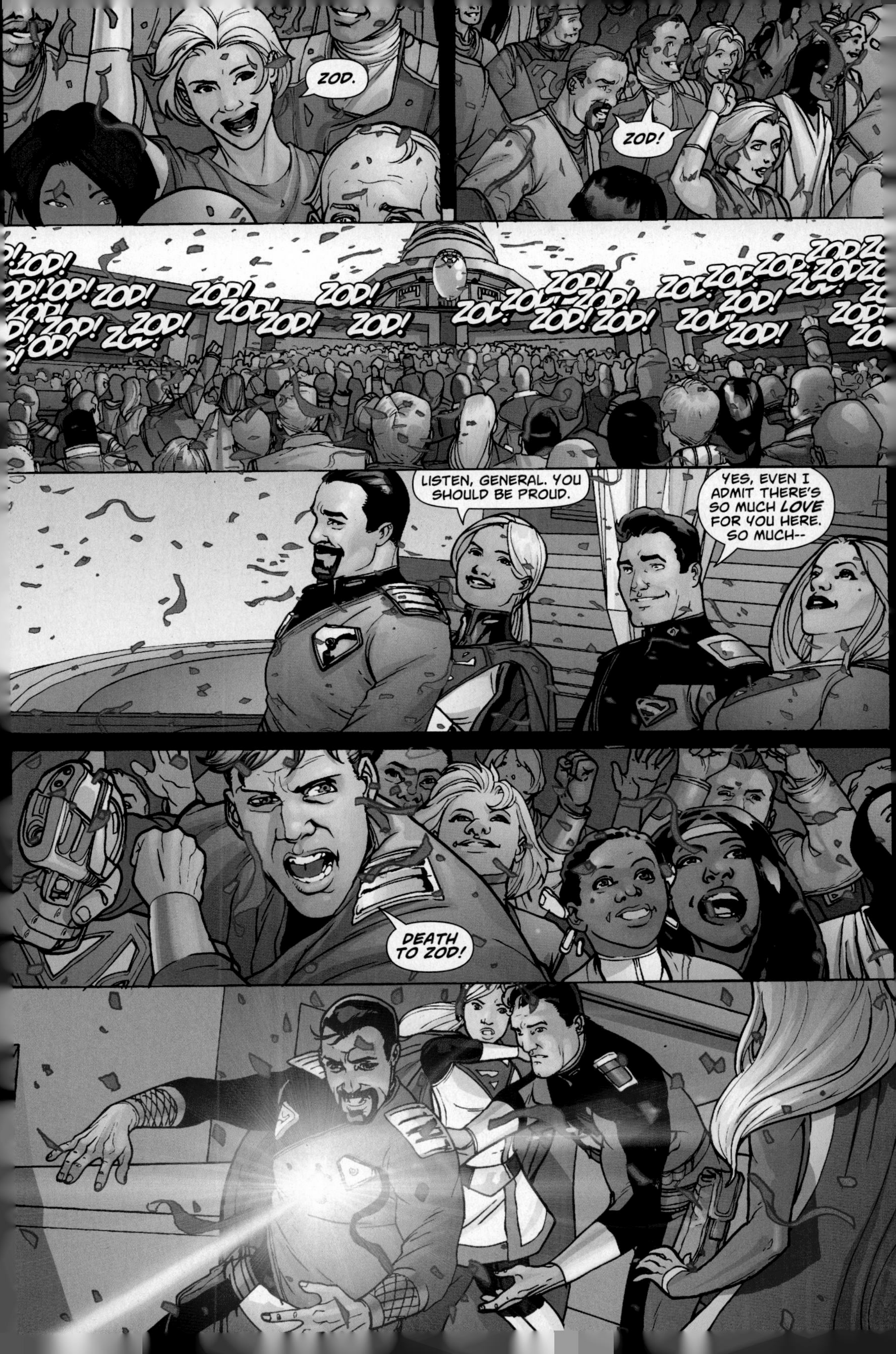
ZOD.
ZOD!
ZOD! ZOD! ZOD! ZOD! ZOD! ZOD! ZOD! ZOD! ZOD! ZOD! ZOD! ZOD! ZOD! ZOD! ZOD! ZOD! ZOD! ZOD!
LISTEN, GENERAL. YOU SHOULD BE PROUD.
YES, EVEN I ADMIT THERE'S SO MUCH *LOVE* FOR YOU HERE. SO MUCH--
DEATH TO ZOD!

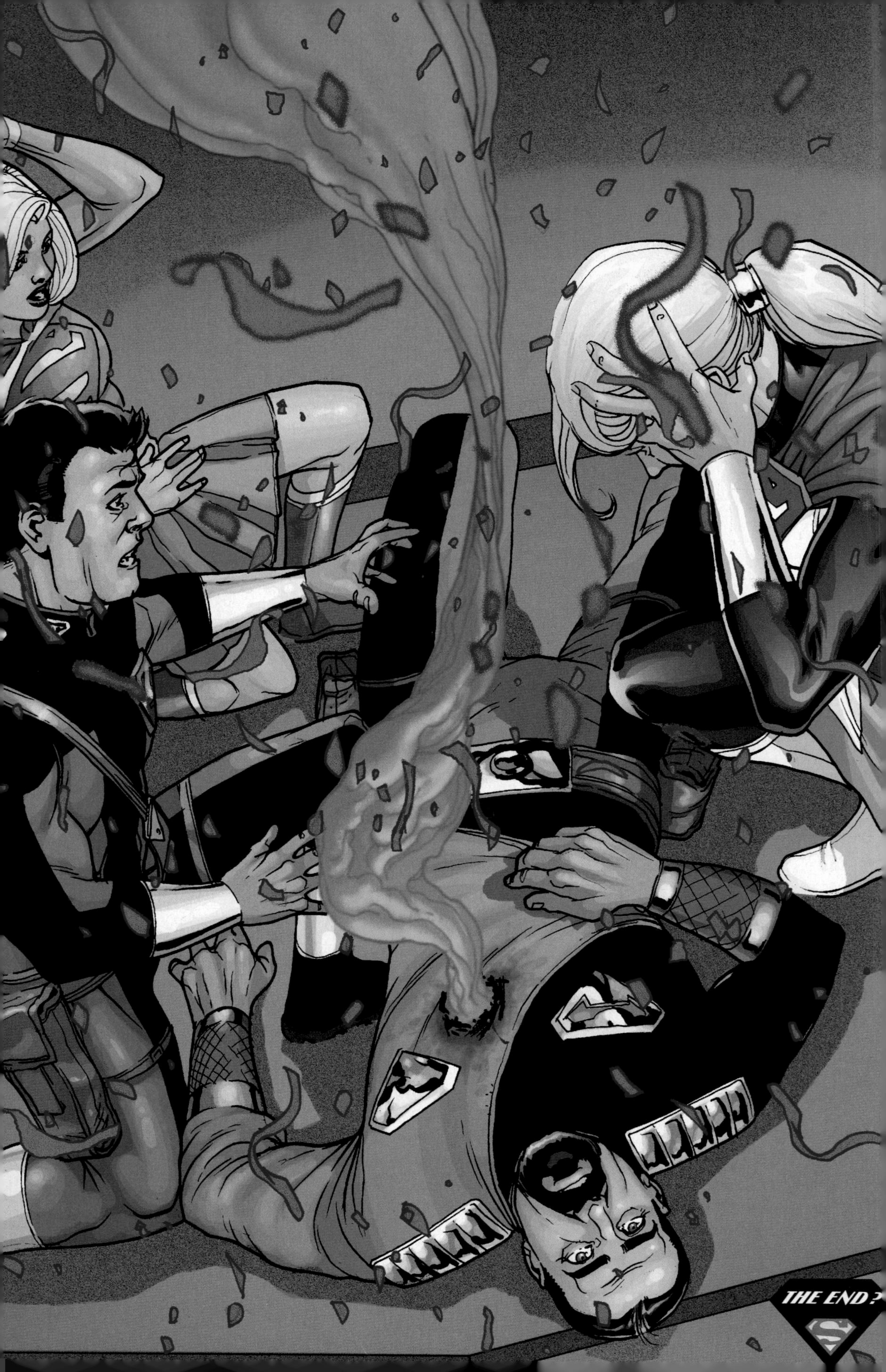
THE END?

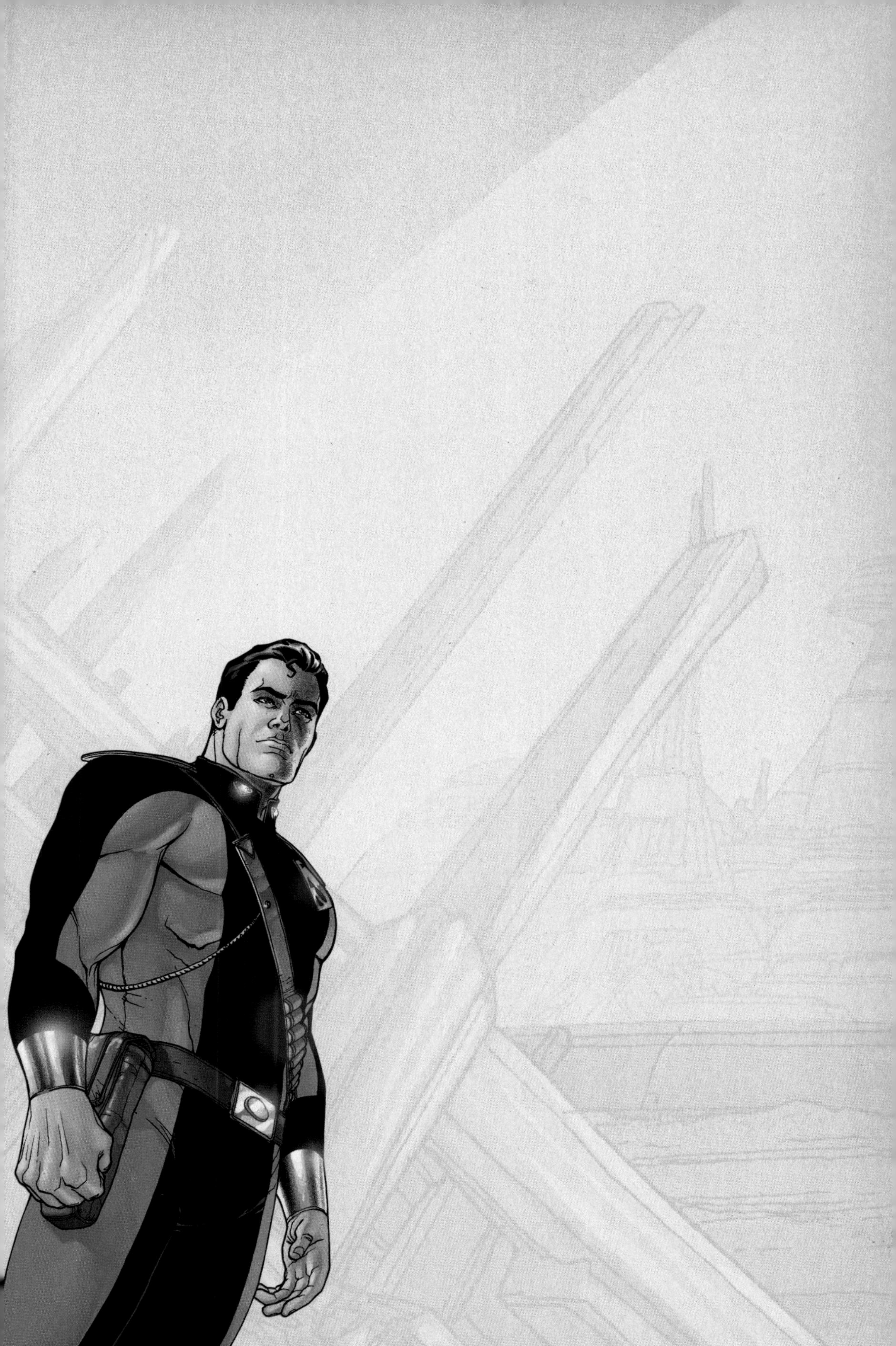

THE CRIMINALS OF KRYPTON

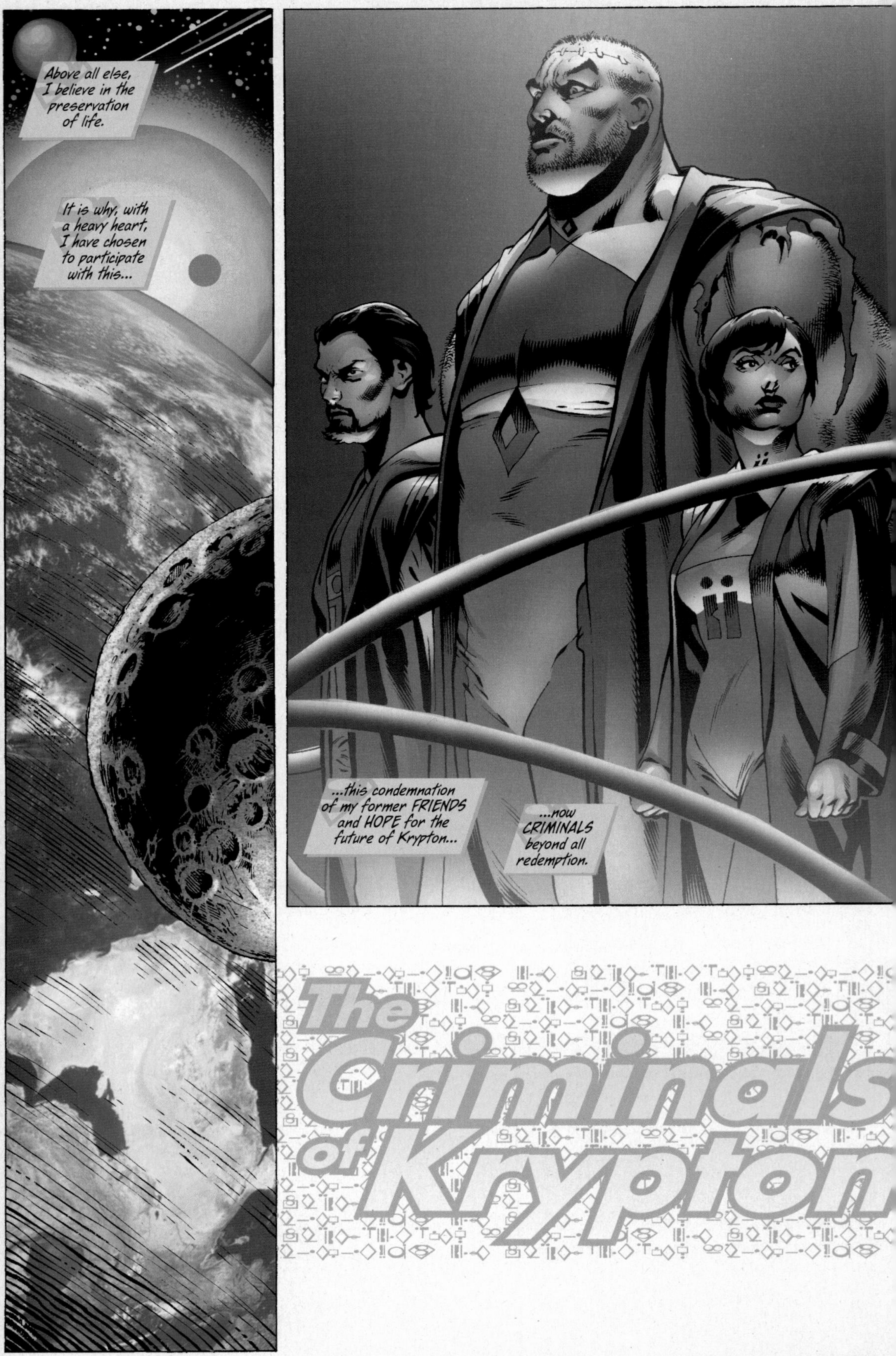
Above all else, I believe in the preservation of life.
It is why, with a heavy heart, I have chosen to participate with this...
...this condemnation of my former FRIENDS and HOPE for the future of Krypton...
...now CRIMINALS beyond all redemption.
The Criminals of Krypton

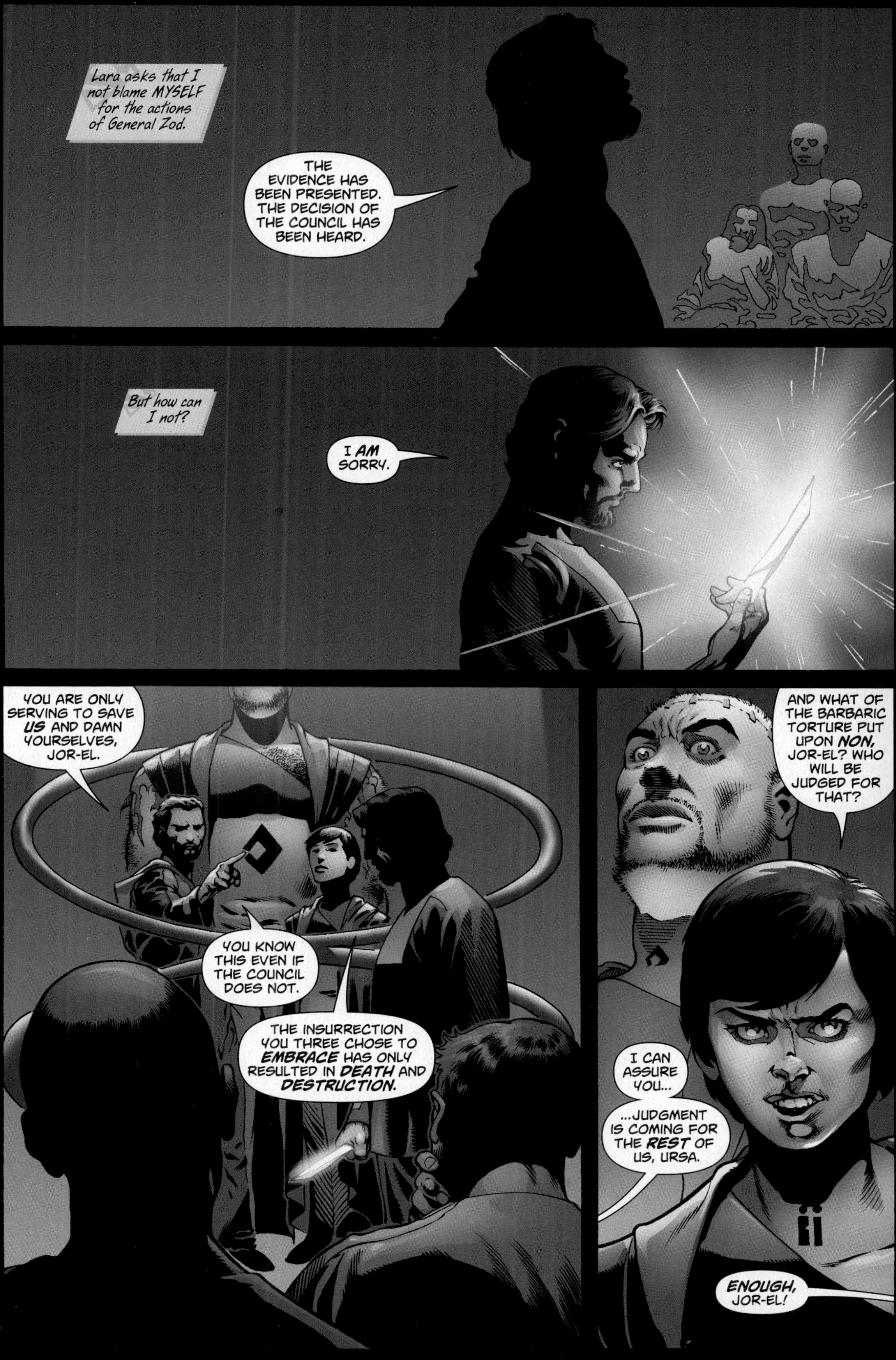
Lara asks that I not blame MYSELF for the actions of General Zod.
THE EVIDENCE HAS BEEN PRESENTED. THE DECISION OF THE COUNCIL HAS BEEN HEARD.
But how can I not?
I AM SORRY.
YOU ARE ONLY SERVING TO SAVE US AND DAMN YOURSELVES, JOR-EL.
YOU KNOW THIS EVEN IF THE COUNCIL DOES NOT.
THE INSURRECTION YOU THREE CHOSE TO EMBRACE HAS ONLY RESULTED IN DEATH AND DESTRUCTION.
AND WHAT OF THE BARBARIC TORTURE PUT UPON NON, JOR-EL? WHO WILL BE JUDGED FOR THAT?
I CAN ASSURE YOU...
...JUDGMENT IS COMING FOR THE REST OF US, URSA.
ENOUGH, JOR-EL!

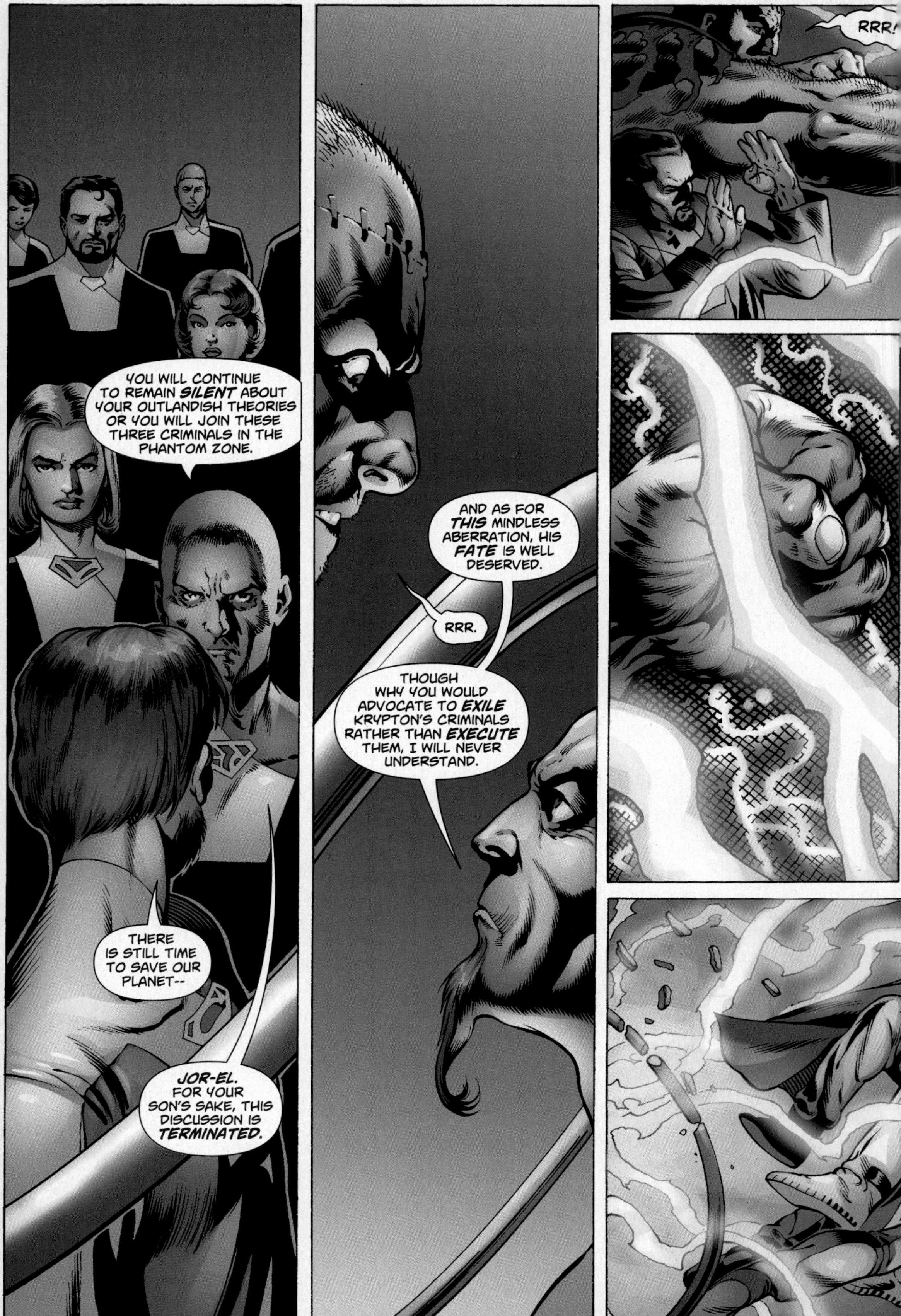
YOU WILL CONTINUE TO REMAIN SILENT ABOUT YOUR OUTLANDISH THEORIES OR YOU WILL JOIN THESE THREE CRIMINALS IN THE PHANTOM ZONE.
THERE IS STILL TIME TO SAVE OUR PLANET--
JOR-EL. FOR YOUR SON'S SAKE, THIS DISCUSSION IS TERMINATED.
AND AS FOR THIS MINDLESS ABERRATION, HIS FATE IS WELL DESERVED.
RRR.
THOUGH WHY YOU WOULD ADVOCATE TO EXILE KRYPTON'S CRIMINALS RATHER THAN EXECUTE THEM, I WILL NEVER UNDERSTAND.
RRR!

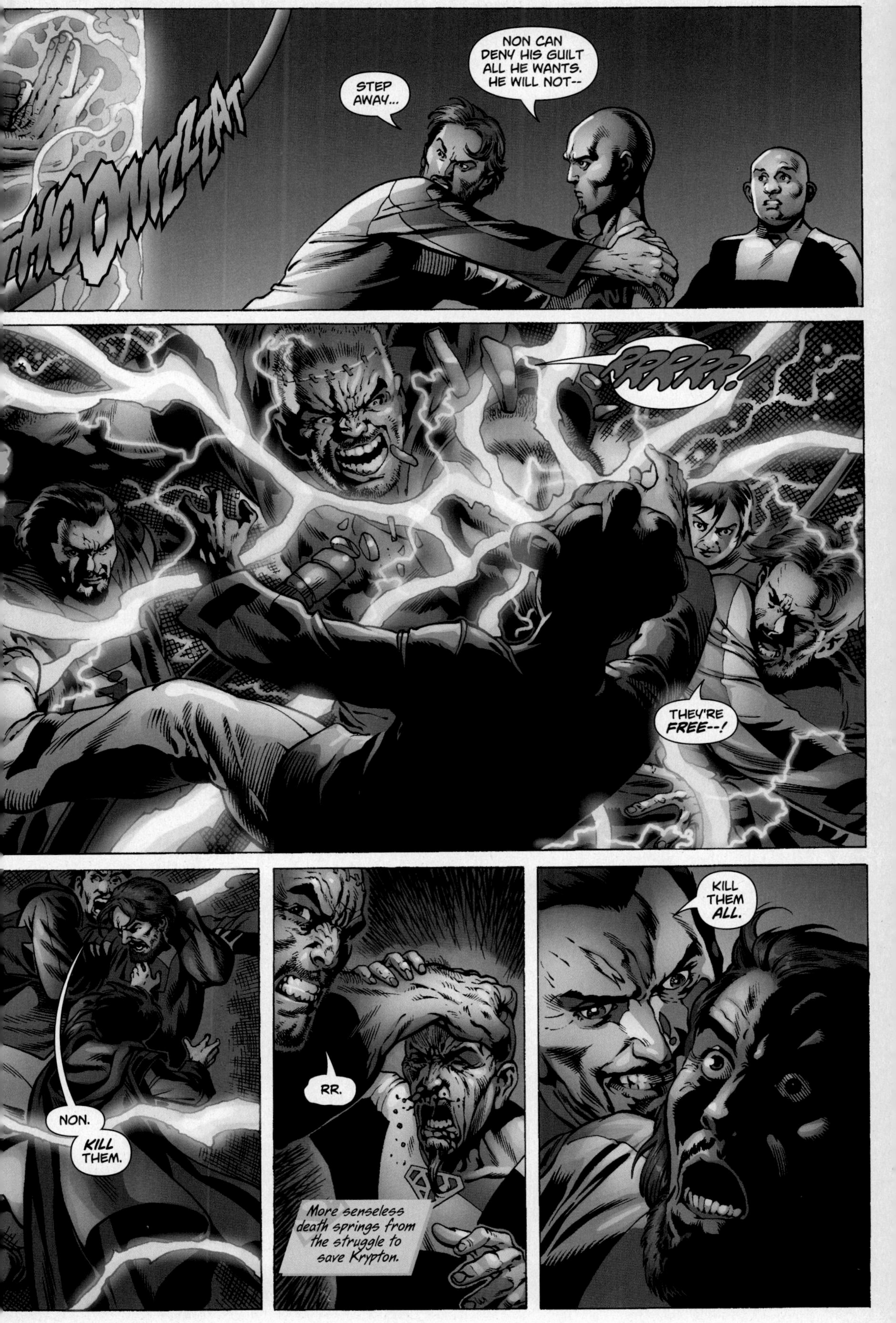
THOOMZZZAT
STEP AWAY...
NON CAN DENY HIS GUILT ALL HE WANTS. HE WILL NOT--
RRRRRR!
THEY'RE FREE--!
NON. KILL THEM.
RR.
More senseless death springs from the struggle to save Krypton.
KILL THEM ALL.

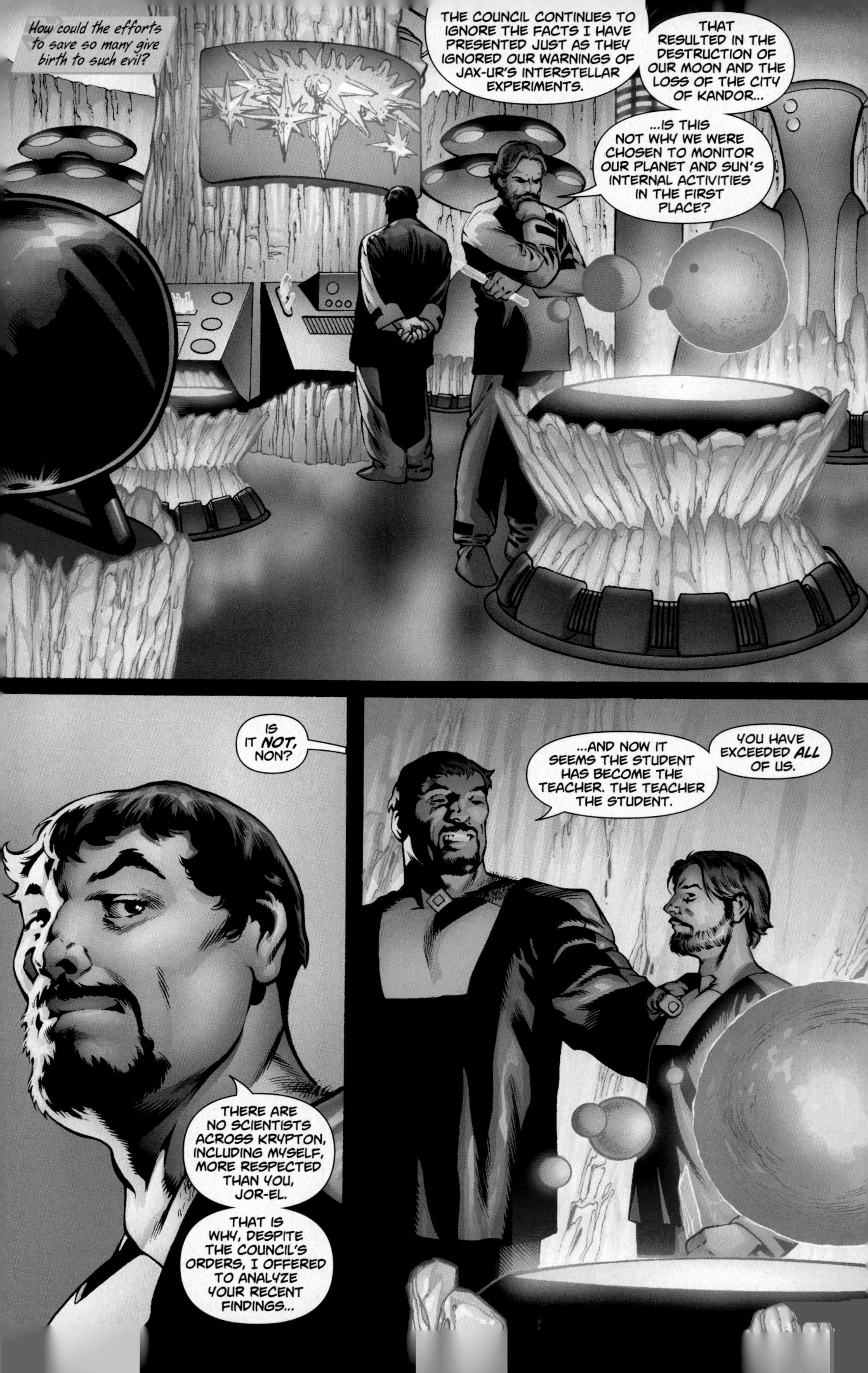
How could the efforts to save so many give birth to such evil?
THE COUNCIL CONTINUES TO IGNORE THE FACTS I HAVE PRESENTED JUST AS THEY IGNORED OUR WARNINGS OF JAX-UR'S INTERSTELLAR EXPERIMENTS.
THAT RESULTED IN THE DESTRUCTION OF OUR MOON AND THE LOSS OF THE CITY OF KANDOR...
...IS THIS NOT WHY WE WERE CHOSEN TO MONITOR OUR PLANET AND SUN'S INTERNAL ACTIVITIES IN THE FIRST PLACE?
IS IT NOT, NON?
THERE ARE NO SCIENTISTS ACROSS KRYPTON, INCLUDING MYSELF, MORE RESPECTED THAN YOU, JOR-EL.
THAT IS WHY, DESPITE THE COUNCIL'S ORDERS, I OFFERED TO ANALYZE YOUR RECENT FINDINGS...
...AND NOW IT SEEMS THE STUDENT HAS BECOME THE TEACHER. THE TEACHER THE STUDENT.
YOU HAVE EXCEEDED ALL OF US.

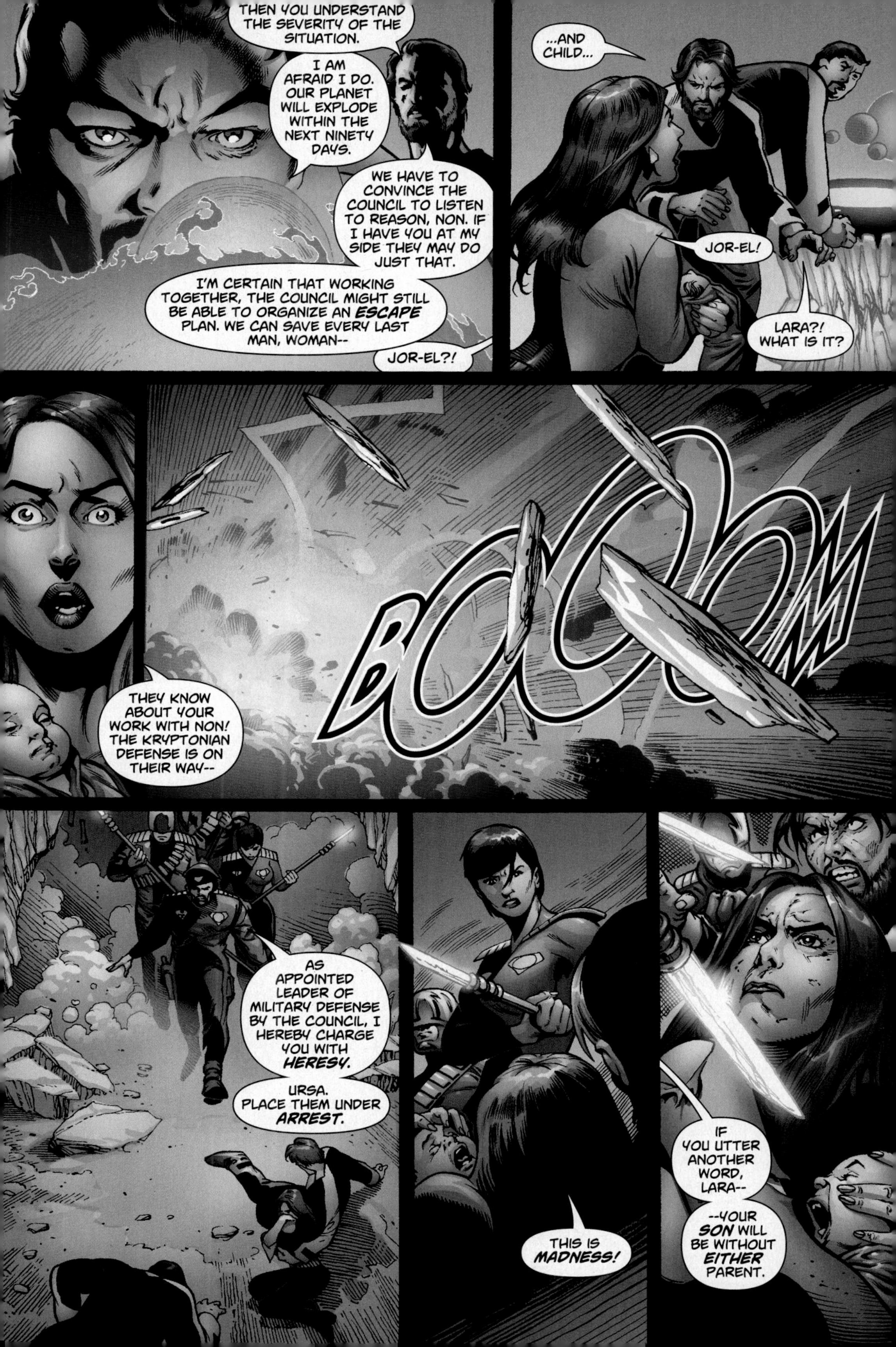

THEN YOU UNDERSTAND THE SEVERITY OF THE SITUATION.
I AM AFRAID I DO. OUR PLANET WILL EXPLODE WITHIN THE NEXT NINETY DAYS.
WE HAVE TO CONVINCE THE COUNCIL TO LISTEN TO REASON, NON. IF I HAVE YOU AT MY SIDE THEY MAY DO JUST THAT.
I'M CERTAIN THAT WORKING TOGETHER, THE COUNCIL MIGHT STILL BE ABLE TO ORGANIZE AN *ESCAPE* PLAN. WE CAN SAVE EVERY LAST MAN, WOMAN--
JOR-EL?!
...AND CHILD...
JOR-EL!
LARA?! WHAT IS IT?
THEY KNOW ABOUT YOUR WORK WITH NON! THE KRYPTONIAN DEFENSE IS ON THEIR WAY--
BOOOM
AS APPOINTED LEADER OF MILITARY DEFENSE BY THE COUNCIL, I HEREBY CHARGE YOU WITH ***HERESY.***
URSA. PLACE THEM UNDER ***ARREST.***
THIS IS ***MADNESS!***
IF YOU UTTER ANOTHER WORD, LARA--
--YOUR ***SON*** WILL BE WITHOUT ***EITHER*** PARENT.

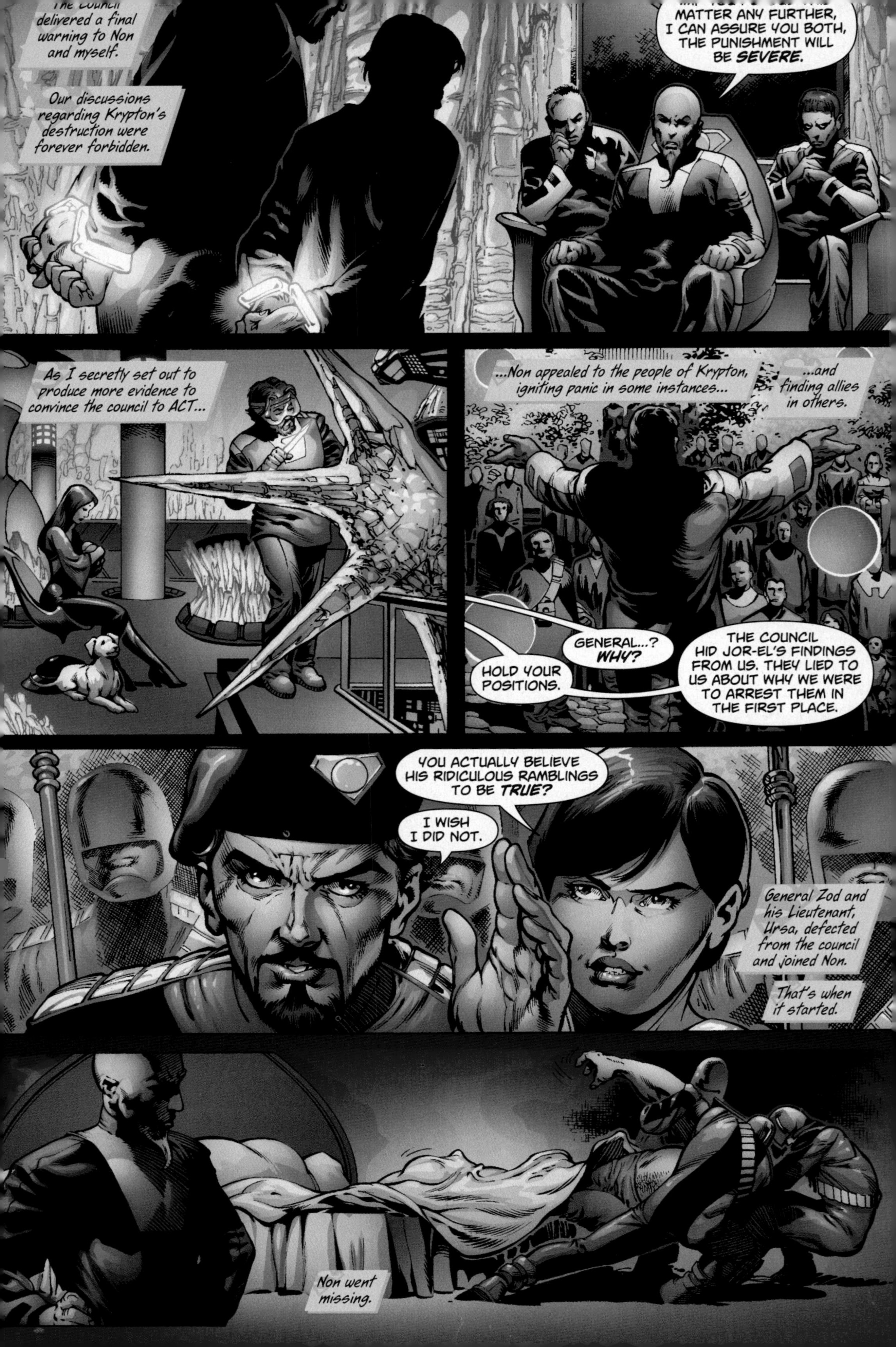

delivered a final warning to Non and myself.
Our discussions regarding Krypton's destruction were forever forbidden.
MATTER ANY FURTHER, I CAN ASSURE YOU BOTH, THE PUNISHMENT WILL BE SEVERE.
As I secretly set out to produce more evidence to convince the council to ACT...
...Non appealed to the people of Krypton, igniting panic in some instances...
...and finding allies in others.
GENERAL...? WHY?
HOLD YOUR POSITIONS.
THE COUNCIL HID JOR-EL'S FINDINGS FROM US. THEY LIED TO US ABOUT WHY WE WERE TO ARREST THEM IN THE FIRST PLACE.
YOU ACTUALLY BELIEVE HIS RIDICULOUS RAMBLINGS TO BE TRUE?
I WISH I DID NOT.
General Zod and his Lieutenant, Ursa, defected from the council and joined Non.
That's when it started.
Non went missing.

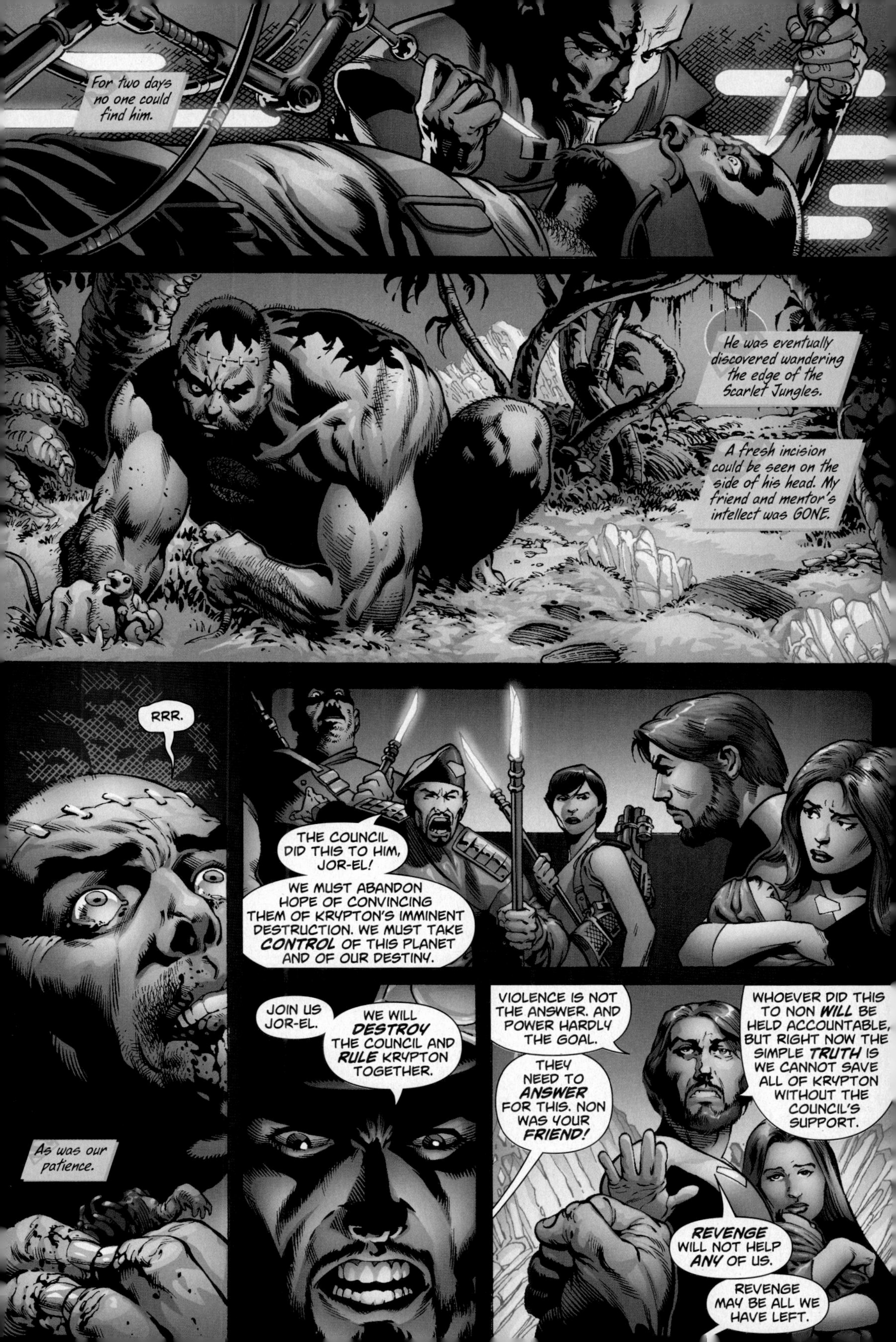
For two days no one could find him.
He was eventually discovered wandering the edge of the Scarlet Jungles.
A fresh incision could be seen on the side of his head. My friend and mentor's intellect was GONE.
RRR.
As was our patience.
THE COUNCIL DID THIS TO HIM, JOR-EL!
WE MUST ABANDON HOPE OF CONVINCING THEM OF KRYPTON'S IMMINENT DESTRUCTION. WE MUST TAKE CONTROL OF THIS PLANET AND OF OUR DESTINY.
JOIN US JOR-EL.
WE WILL DESTROY THE COUNCIL AND RULE KRYPTON TOGETHER.
VIOLENCE IS NOT THE ANSWER. AND POWER HARDLY THE GOAL.
THEY NEED TO ANSWER FOR THIS. NON WAS YOUR FRIEND!
WHOEVER DID THIS TO NON WILL BE HELD ACCOUNTABLE, BUT RIGHT NOW THE SIMPLE TRUTH IS WE CANNOT SAVE ALL OF KRYPTON WITHOUT THE COUNCIL'S SUPPORT.
REVENGE WILL NOT HELP ANY OF US.
REVENGE MAY BE ALL WE HAVE LEFT.

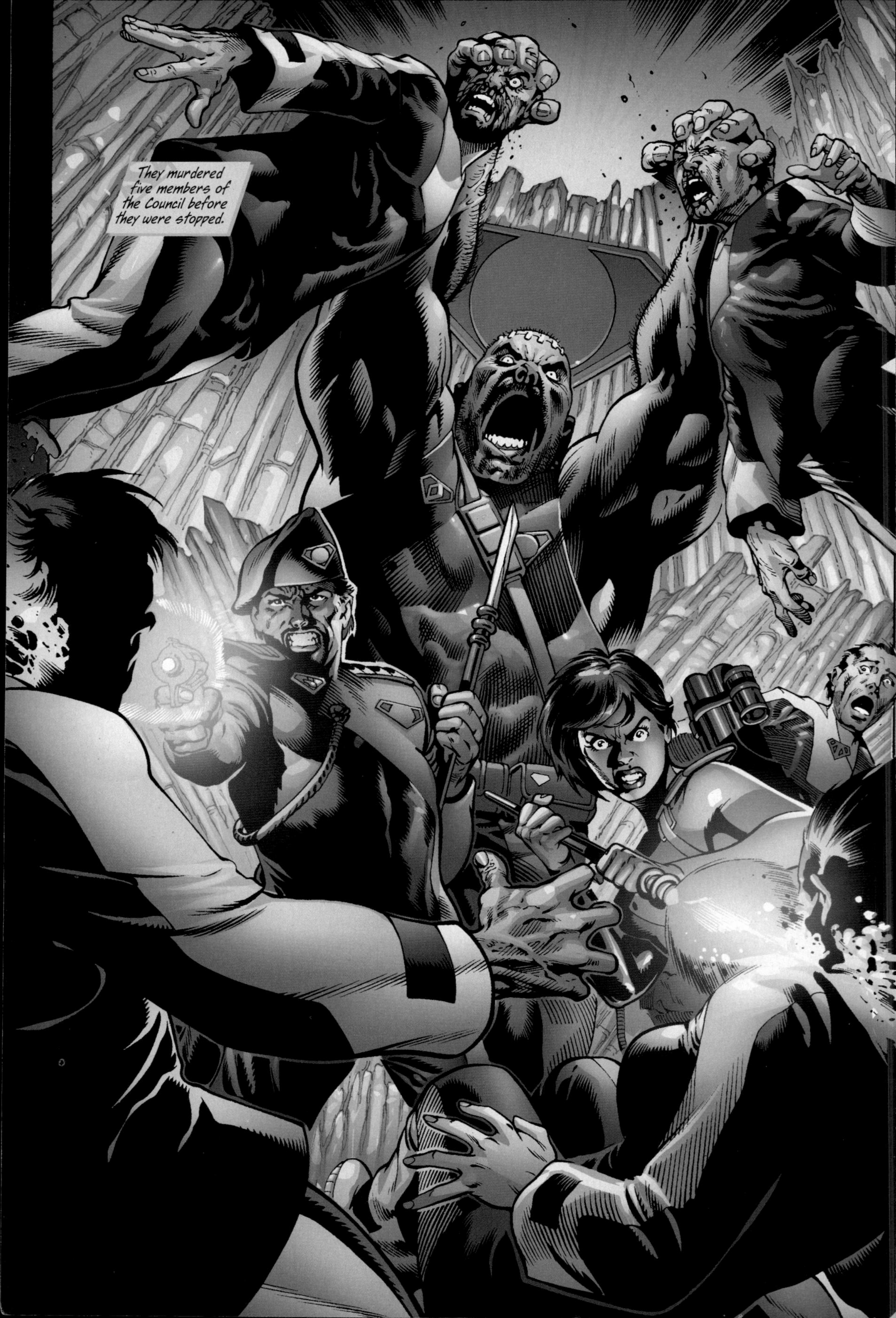
They murdered five members of the Council before they were stopped.

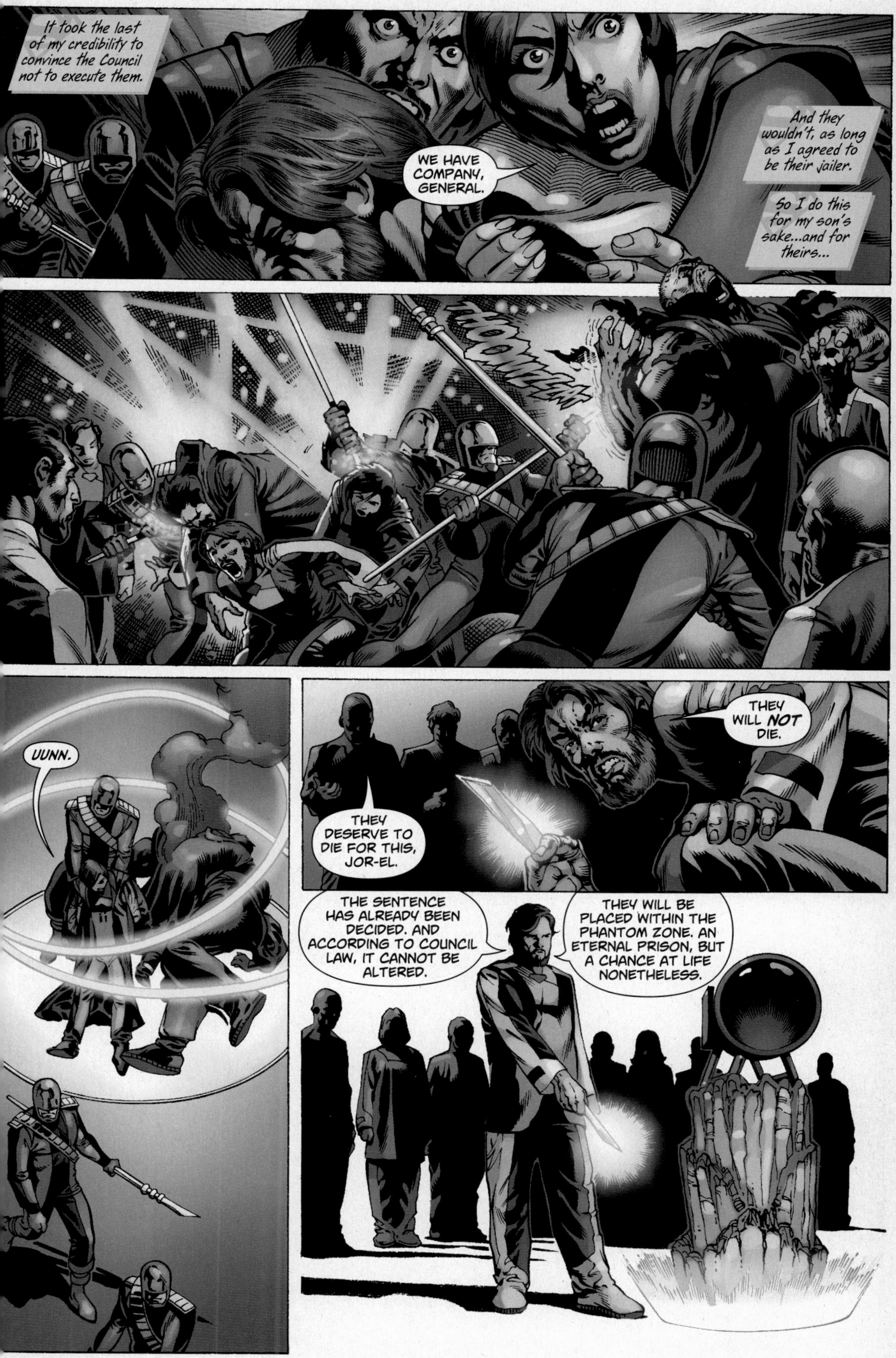

It took the last of my credibility to convince the Council not to execute them.
WE HAVE COMPANY, GENERAL.
And they wouldn't, as long as I agreed to be their jailer.
So I do this for my son's sake...and for theirs...
THOOMMM
UUNN.
THEY WILL NOT DIE.
THEY DESERVE TO DIE FOR THIS, JOR-EL.
THE SENTENCE HAS ALREADY BEEN DECIDED. AND ACCORDING TO COUNCIL LAW, IT CANNOT BE ALTERED.
THEY WILL BE PLACED WITHIN THE PHANTOM ZONE. AN ETERNAL PRISON, BUT A CHANCE AT LIFE NONETHELESS.

YOU WILL NOT DENY ME MY *REVENGE*, JOR-EL.

YOU WILL USE YOUR SCIENCE TO SAVE THE PLANET KRYPTON AND ONE DAY WE WILL *RETURN*, AND WHEN WE DO *I*, WILL BE KRYPTON'S RULER.

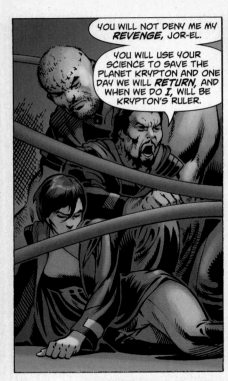

AND THEN...I WILL MAKE YOU THE *SLAVE* TO ME THAT YOU ARE TO THE COUNCIL. YOU WILL KNEEL BEFORE ME.

BOTH *YOU* AND ONE DAY...

...YOUR SON!

NO, GENERAL.

I WILL NOT.

AND NEITHER WILL KAL-EL.

AAAIEEE?!

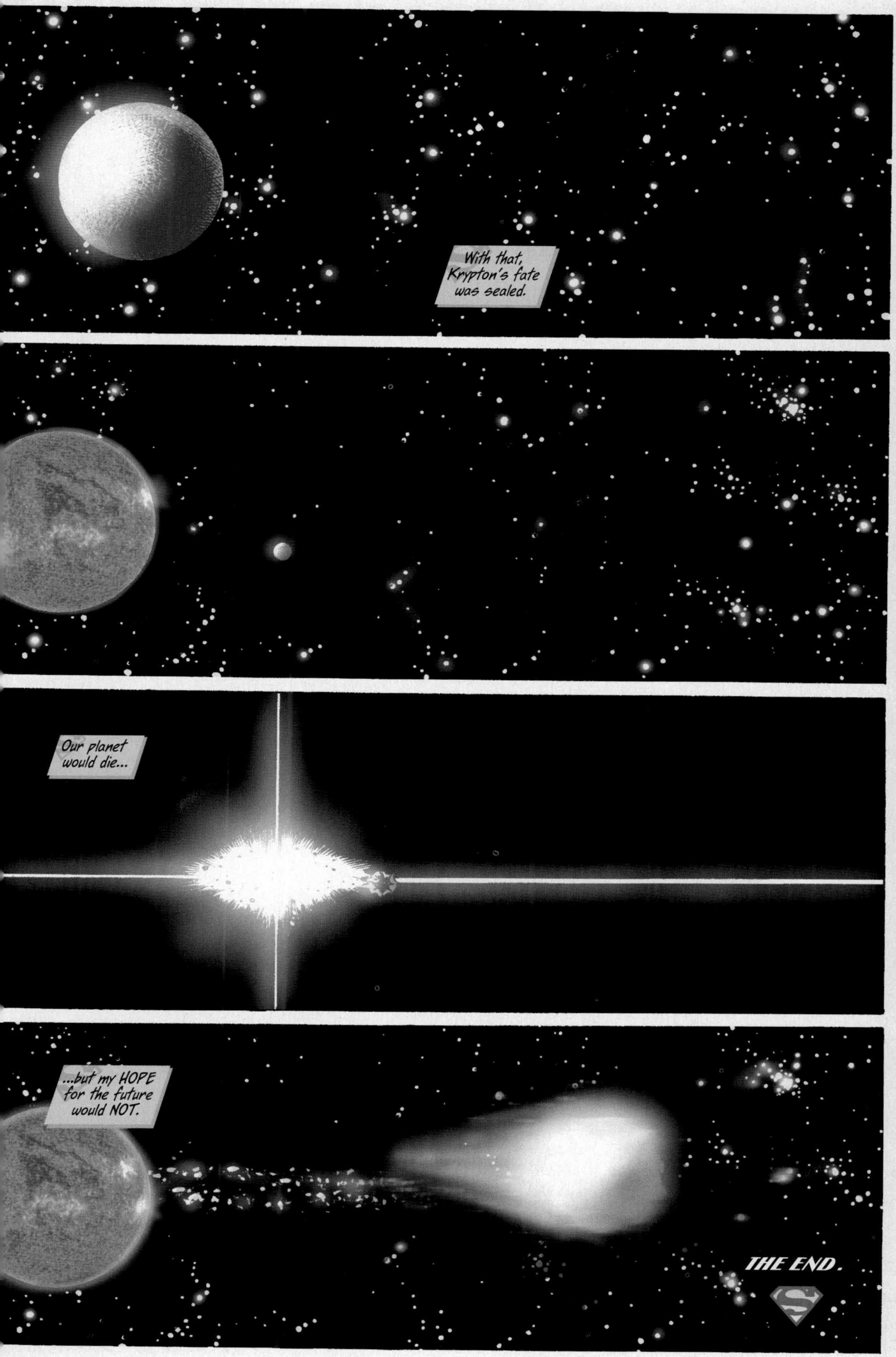
With that, Krypton's fate was sealed.
Our planet would die...
...but my HOPE for the future would NOT.
THE END.

SUPERMAN: WORLD OF NEW KRYPTON #1 <VARIANT BY LADRÖNN>

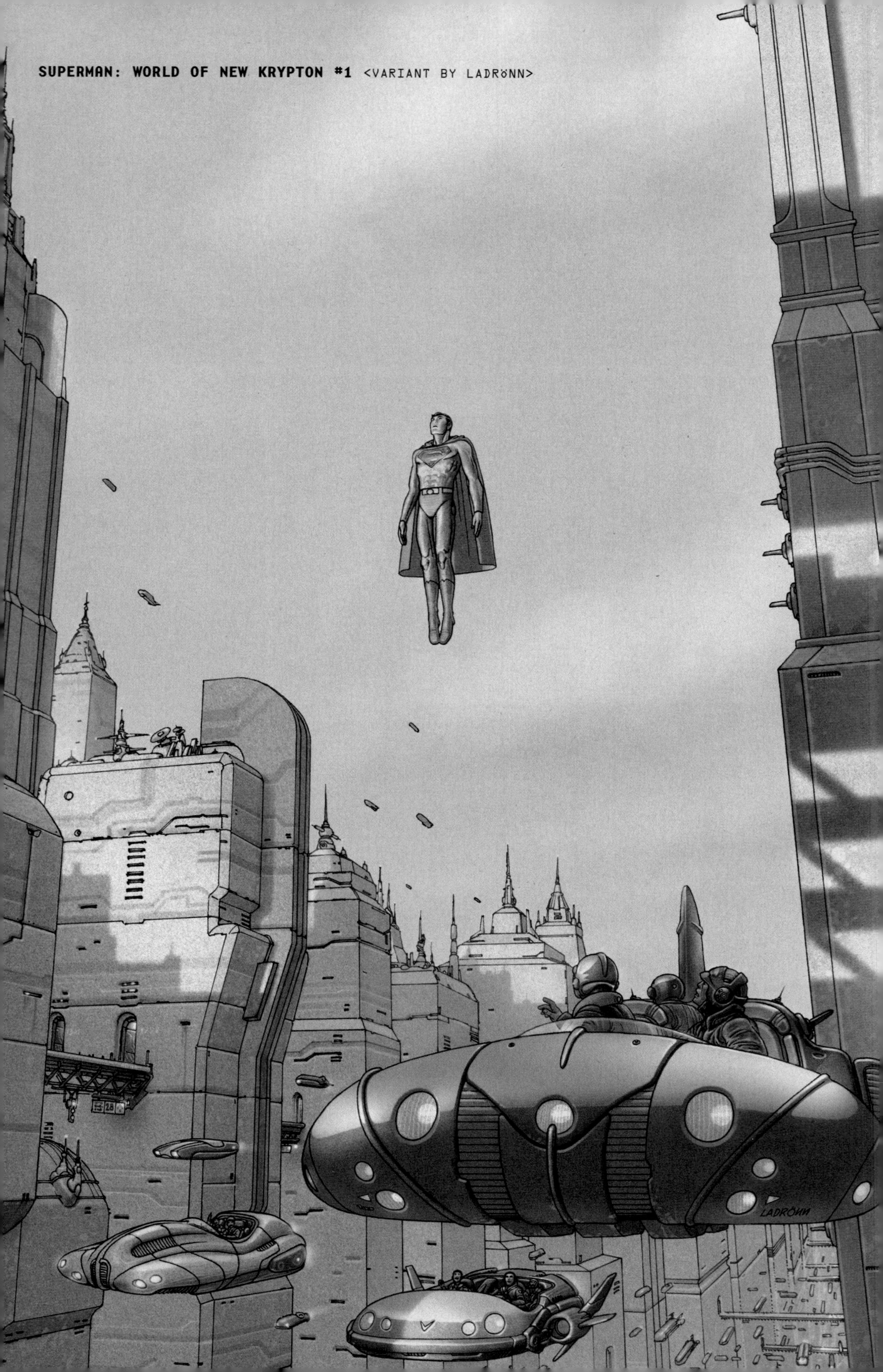
LADRÖNN

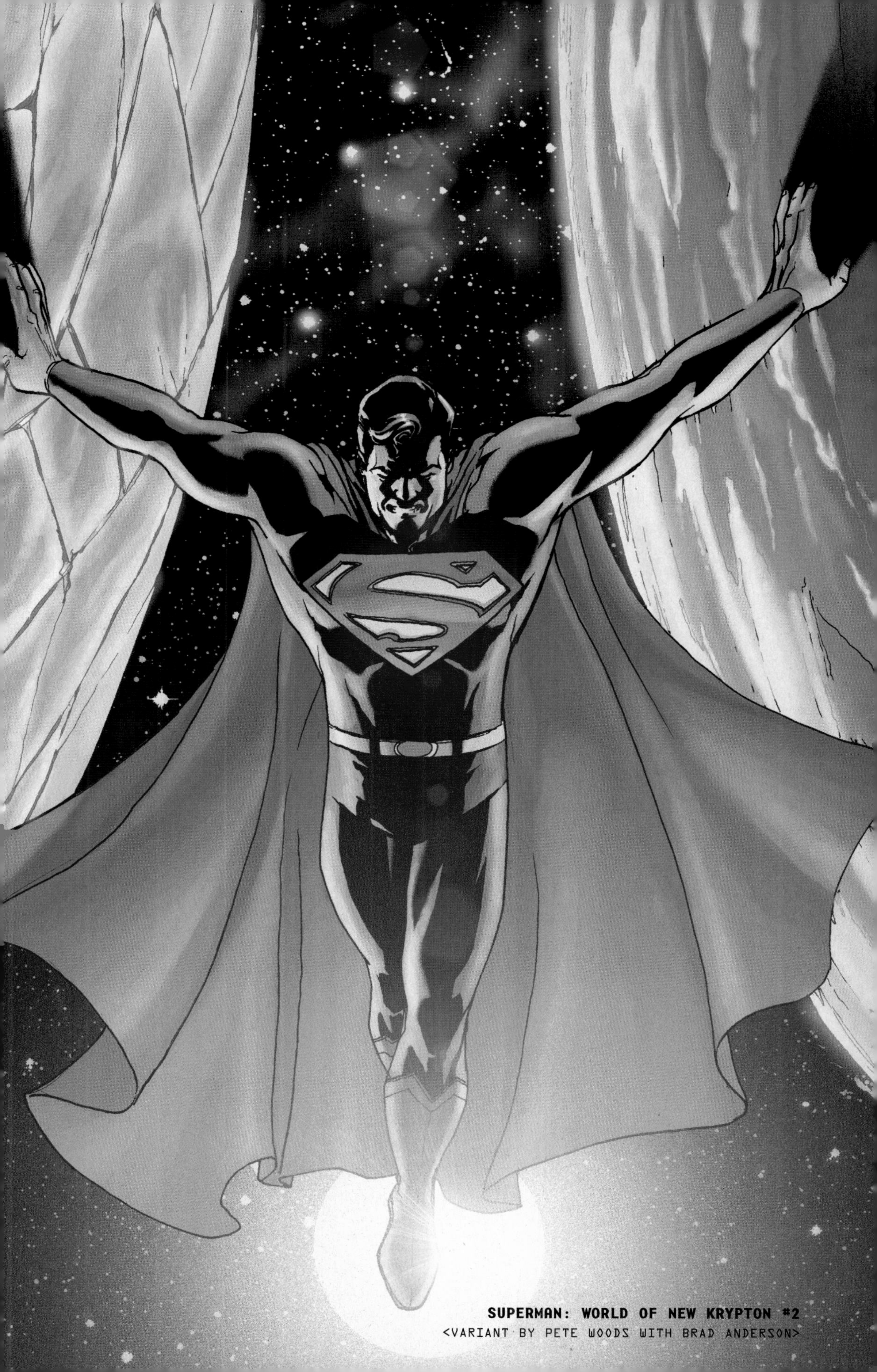

SUPERMAN: WORLD OF NEW KRYPTON #2
<VARIANT BY PETE WOODS WITH BRAD ANDERSON>

SUPERMAN: WORLD OF NEW KRYPTON #3
<VARIANT BY HOWARD CHAYKIN WITH EDGAR DELGADO>

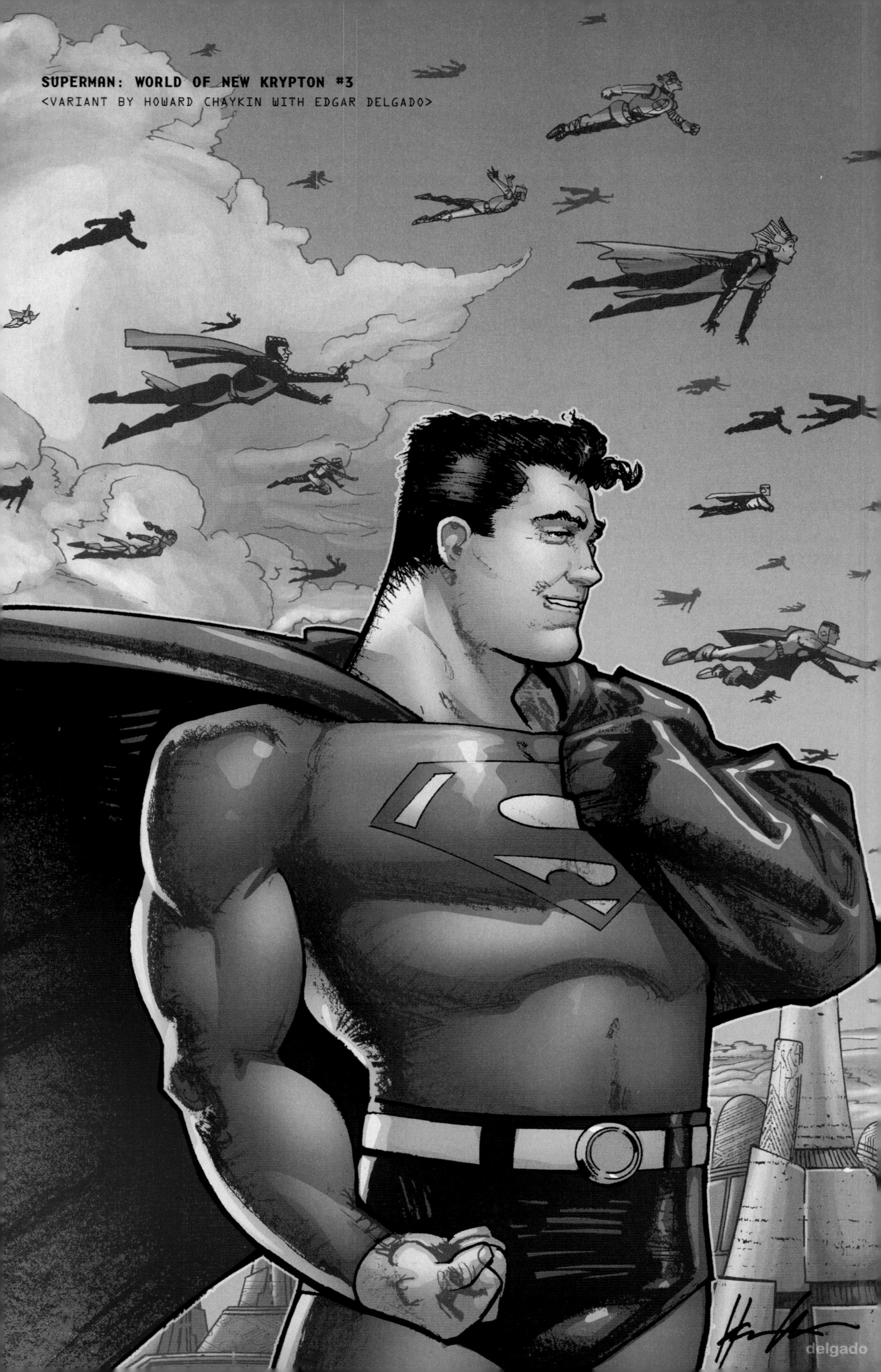
delgado